enhancing graduate employability in

business and management hospitality leisure sport tourism

EDITED BY NINA BECKET AND PATSY KEMP

First published 2006 by
Threshold Press Ltd
Norfolk House
75 Bartholomew Street
Newbury Berks RG14 5DU
Phone 01635-230272 and fax 01635-44804
email: publish@threshold-press.co.uk
www.threshold-press.co.uk

Reprinted 2008, 2010

ISBN-10 1-903152-15-1
ISBN-13 978-1-903152-15-7

Cover design Jim Weaver Design
Typeset by Threshold Press

Printed in Wales by MWL Digital Solutions Ltd, New Inn, Pontypool.

The editors

Nina Becket is Assistant Director of the Hospitality, Leisure, Sport and Tourism Subject Centre, responsible for leading the network's academic development work. Prior to taking on this role, Nina was Undergraduate Programme Director in the Department of Hotel and Restaurant Management at Oxford Brookes.

Patsy Kemp has work experience within the public and private sectors, in business training, language teaching, project management and management consultancy. As Academic Developer for the Hospitality, Leisure, Sport and Tourism Subject Centre, she works to support practitioners in their roles within Higher Education.

Acknowledgements

The editors would like to acknowledge the contribution of the former Business, Management and Accountancy Subject Centre (BEST), and especially that of David Hawkridge, Emeritus Professor of Applied Educational Sciences at the Open University.

Enhancing Graduate Employability
in
Business and Management
Hospitality
Leisure
Sport
Tourism

ALSO PUBLISHED WITH THE HOSPITALITY, LEISURE, SPORT AND TOURISM AND
BUSINESS MANAGEMENT ACCOUNTANCY AND FINANCE SUBJECT CENTRES:

*Enhancing the International Learning Experience in Business
and Management, Hospitality, Leisure, Sport, Tourism*
edited by Richard Atfield & Patsy Kemp (2008)

*Enhancing Student-centred Learning in Business and Management,
Hospitality, Leisure, Sport, Tourism*
edited by John Buswell and Nina Becket (2009)

*Enhancing Learning through Assessment in Business
and Management, Hospitality, Leisure, Sport, Tourism*
edited by Patsy Kemp, Richard Atfield & Richard Tong (2010)

*Enhancing Graduate Impact in Business
and Management, Hospitality, Leisure, Sport, Tourism*
edited by Patsy Kemp and Richard Atfield (2011)

Contents

Introduction
Employability in context
Rob Ward

Employability is by no means a new issue for higher education (HE); the need for graduates to make an effective contribution to the labour market was highlighted in the Robbins Report (Committee on Higher Education, 1963). Subsequently, the report of the National Committee of Inquiry into Higher Education, the Dearing Report (1997), made explicit the importance of education for employability and highlighted the value of key skills development and work experience in developing students' potential for employment.*

These, and later developments, should be seen within the context of the increasingly strong governmental emphasis on linking higher-level learning to economic outcomes, both for enhancing incomes for individual graduates over a working lifespan † and for the UK economy as a whole (see CVCP/DFEE, (1998): 97ff; Elias and Purcell, 2004). Research has been undertaken by a variety of organisations on changes in the workplace and the corresponding need for HE to support the development of 'critical, reflective and potentially transformative students' as well as graduates to 'fit into organisational culture and add value through working effectively with others' (Harvey, Moon and Geall, 1997).

The term 'employability' itself has spawned a wide range of definitions. Watts (2006: 7) suggests these can be considered in terms of those focusing on:
❑ immediate employment
❑ immediate employability (in terms of work readiness and the ability to obtain 'a graduate job')
❑ sustainable employability, the ability not only to obtain that first position, but to remain employable throughout life.

The essence of this has been captured in the Enhancing Student Employability Co-ordination Team (ESECT) definition of employability:

a set of skills,‡ knowledge and personal attributes that make an individual more likely to secure and to be successful in their chosen occupation(s) to the benefits of themselves, the workforce, the community and the economy. (Yorke and Knight, 2006: 3)

---

* To avoid repetition, this introduction draws directly upon material provided in the case studies, and this is gratefully acknowledged.

† The figures cited for the 'graduate premium' compare the incomes of graduates and non-graduates over a lifetime. Recent work at the University of Wales Swansea suggests that the much-vaunted £400k in a lifetime is now something of an overestimate. (O'Leary and Sloane, 2006)

‡ The term 'skills' is used partly at least in the recognition that academic staff themselves generally talk the language of skills. In doing so, the concern of ESECT to try to talk of 'skilful practice' is also valued, not least to get away from the simplistic connotations of skills.

ESECT further proposed:

> *a considerable degree of alignment between 'education for employability' and good student learning (and the teaching, learning and curricula that go with it).* (Yorke and Knight, 2006: 3)

as well as emphasising employability as a process rather than a state. Yorke and Knight describe employability as a blend of understanding, skilful practices, efficacy beliefs (or legitimate self confidence) and reflectiveness (or meta-cognition).[¶] This perspective reinforces the view of employability as a complex and multi-dimensional concept which goes beyond the 'key skills' agenda.[§] It connects well with the term 'sustainable employability' (Watts, 2006) and with the necessary requisites for Personal Development Planning (PDP).

The work of ESECT has been paralleled and followed by a range of funding and other initiatives. These include the Employability Enhancement theme (2004–06) and the strategic project funding for Employability (2007–09) in Scotland, while in Wales since 2003 the focus on employability has been within institutional learning, teaching and assessment strategies. In England the Measuring and Recording Student Achievement Scoping Group,[*] while not directly connected to employability, noted the importance of:

> *engaging students in representing their own learning, in creating customised information about their learning and achievements and communicating this information to different audiences with different needs and interests.* (2004: 22)

Today there is increased emphasis on progression within vocational learning contexts in higher level learning programmes.[†] This can be seen in developments such as:

□ foundation degrees
□ Lifelong Learning Networks, facilitating approaches to support vocational learners' progression into and through HE, and thus to widen participation in higher-level learning
□ the HEFCE initiative on 'engaging employers'.

In order to support implementation, the Quality Assurance Agency (QAA) have offered guidance to universities on how to embed employability within their institutional strategies and how this might translate into provision for student courses. This includes, for example, the National Qualifications Framework (QAA, 2001a) and the Code of Practice on Career Education, Information and Guidance (CEIG) (QAA, 2001b). The Level H descriptors (honours degree level) in the qualifications framework clearly outline the qualities and skills necessary for graduate employment. While the CEIG more explicitly aims to help institutions ensure:

> *both that they are meeting students' expectations in respect of their preparedness for their future career, and that they are producing graduates equipped to meet the demands of the employment market of today and tomorrow.'* (QAA, 2001b: 4)

As identified above, Personal Development Planning (PDP) is a key contributor to student career development skills. The original guidelines on HE progress files (QAA 2001c) defined PDP as:

> *a structured and supported process to develop the capacity of individuals to reflect upon their own learning and achievement and to plan for their own personal educational and career development.*

The QAA Code of Practice for CEIG reinforces this by emphasising the need for students and graduates to:

> *develop the skills to manage their own career including the abilities to reflect and review, to plan and make decisions to use information resources effectively, to create and to take opportunities, and to make provision for lifelong learning.* (QAA, 2001b: 4)

Both highlight the importance of supporting and connecting PDP and career development work . As documented by Ward et al (2006), it is expected that the process of PDP, when implemented effectively, will:

□ Support effective learning.
□ Provide a context within which graduates may

¶ Also known as the USEM model.

§ We do not seek to generate more lists of 'skills' that employers claim to seek. Some further discussion of these can be found in 'Pedagogy for Employability' (HE Academy, 2006).

* The Burgess Group – see: http://bookshop.universitiesuk.ac.uk/ – set up following the Future of Higher Education White Paper (http://www.dfes.gov.uk/)

† See http://www.foundationdegree.org.uk/ and http://www.hefce.ac.uk/

recognise, record and from which they may later provide evidence of their possession of the skills, qualities and capabilities that employers claim to seek.

❏ Inculcate the processes of self-management that will support 'sustainable employability'. (Watts, 2006)

The case studies

This collection of case studies is drawn from a broad range of HE provision covering the areas of business, management, accountancy and finance and hospitality, leisure, sport and tourism. While many of the programmes are vocationally oriented, many may not have the tightly defined career progression routes that often follow from specialist qualifications in areas such as law or education.‡ As the case studies demonstrate, institutions and programmes are addressing the issue of employability in a broad and rich range of ways. However, they are all heavily influenced by the perspectives on employability of the ESECT team, and closely aligned to 'sustainable employability'.

The QAA Codes of Practice for both CEIG and Postgraduate Research Programmes (QAA, 2004) confirm that there are a variety of responses to the question of 'how' to deliver employability. Yorke and Knight (2006) suggest five ways in which employability is located in, or could be developed through, the curriculum:

1 employability through the whole curriculum
2 employability in the core curriculum
3 work-based or work-related learning incorporated as one or more components within the curriculum
4 employability-related module(s) within the curriculum
5 work-based or work-related learning in parallel with the curriculum.

These approaches are often found in combination in courses and Yorke (2004) is keen to point out that a variety of approaches are likely to work very effectively in tandem. Many of the case studies illustrate this point, notably those from Worcester, Sheffield Hallam,

Oxford Brookes, Ulster and Leeds Metropolitan universities.

The range of approaches identified in the case studies can also be defined as including:

❏ Structured and well-founded whole institutional (Bournemouth) or whole subject-area initiatives (Tourism at Leeds Metropolitan and Bedfordshire, Business Studies at Ulster). The Bournemouth case study also provides a clear acknowledgement of the challenges that might be faced in such approaches, for example: concerns about bureaucracy; pressure on resources; innovation fatigue; and a failure to acknowledge existing good practice.

❏ The development of new and innovative approaches to employability learning. These include: a demand-led approach for purely work-based learners at Sunderland; Nottingham Business School's sponsored two-year in-company work placements; Aston Business School's in-depth preparation of students for their placements and the sustained encouragement of reflection on such experience; 'co-operative education' at Auckland University of Technology and Unitec; 'virtual group working' at the University of Abertay, Dundee, and involvement of the local community shown by the coaching and sports academies development work at UWIC. Some of these have important implications for curriculum design. Sunderland in particular emphasises the

> an emphasis on unlocking the learner's tacit knowledge, personal development, and on effective relationship building between staff and students

necessity of taking very different approaches to curriculum design, student support (including peer support) and assessment, with an emphasis on unlocking the learner's tacit knowledge, personal development, and on effective relationship building between staff and students.

❏ Delivery through existing or new modules:
  → Where employability features explicitly in single dedicated modules: career planning for hospitality and tourism at Oxford Brookes; in

---

‡ Accountancy is an important exception here.

tourism and management at Bath Spa – where innovative assessment techniques and employer involvement also feature. Or in a combination of modules with clear and progressive links, as an 'employability strand' within a programme: for example, in the evolution of employability at London South Bank; work-based learning at Ulster; and in the tourism curriculum at Leeds Metropolitan and the University of Bedfordshire.

→ Via an opportunity (or opportunities) to bring together and reflect upon a range of experience seen for example: in the languages department at Sheffield Hallam; the integrated approach of Auckland University of Technology and Unitec; and the post- placement experience at Aston.

→ By infusing employability into existing programme provision (integrated embedding in business and technology at Sheffield Hallam and the framework modules at London South Bank).

Showing creative use of ICT, there are good examples of providing online support and information for students such as: the placement-planning scheme at Ulster; the provision of industry specific careers information and guidance at Northumbria; online discussion facilities at Abertay; and the promotion of discussion on professionalism as a stimulus for student reflection and planning at Gloucestershire.

Many of the case study examples emphasise the importance of 'real-world' challenges, whether through off-campus learning or by importing such experiences into the curriculum via 'real-world'

activities or consultancy. For example, there is an emphasis on making more in terms of student learning from what might be termed conventional workplace learning opportunities, such as: the more structured and extended preparation for, and reflection on, placement experience at Aston Business School and Brighton; and for study and work abroad in languages at Sheffield Hallam.

Related to this, and to the integration of employability, PDP-inspired approaches to enable students to derive most benefit from their experiences also feature strongly with examples at Gloucestershire; Worcester; in business and technology at Sheffield Hallam; and in tourism at the University of Bedfordshire. Though recognised as a continuing challenge, in a number of the illustrations this provides a central strategy for helping students to make the most of their experience in a holistic way.

The broad range of perspectives on employability, and the ways in which it has been be effectively incorporated within HE curricula, will become clear on closer reading of the case studies. The earlier chapters provide examples of institution-wide and whole course developments and the later chapters cover implementation within individual modules and the provision of learning relating to the 'real world' within the curriculum. Nevertheless innovation and imaginative development are common to all. It is hoped that this collection will inform and stimulate further creativity in this fundamental aspect of student learning.

References and URLS

Dearing Report, 1977. National Committee of Inquiry into Higher Education, 1997. *Higher Education in the Learning Society/The National Committee of Enquiry into Higher Education* (the Dearing Report) London, NCIHE. Available at http://www.ncl.ac.uk/

CVCP/DFEE, 1998. *Skills Development in Higher Education: full report.* London: CVCP

Elias, P. and Purcell, K. 2004. SOC (HE) *A classification of occupations for studying the graduate labour market.* Research Report 6. Available at www.warwick.ac.uk/

Harvey, L., Moon, S. and Geall, V. 1997. *Graduates Work: Organisational change and students' attributes.* Birmingham: Centre for Research into Quality, University of Central England

HE Academy, 2006. *Pedagogy for Employability.* Oxford: Higher Education Academy

Knight, P and Yorke, M. 2003. Employability and Good Learning in Higher Education. *Teaching in Higher Education* **8** (1) January 2003

O'Leary, N. C. and Sloane, P. J. The changing wage return to an undergraduate education. At http://cee.lse.ac.uk/.

QAA, 2001a. *Framework for Higher Education Qualifications.* Gloucester: QAA

QAA, 2001b. *Code of Practice for the Assurance of Academic Quality and Standards in Higher Education: Career Education, Information and Guidance.* QAA

QAA, 2001c. *Guidelines for HE Progress Files.* QAA

QAA, 2004. *Code of Practice Postgraduate Research Programmes.* Gloucester: QAA

Committee on Higher Education, 1963. *Higher Education: Report of the Committee of Lord Robbins, 1961–63.* (the Robbins report) Cmnd. 2154, and five appendices. London: HMSO

Watts, A. G. 2006. *Career Development Learning and Employability.* Learning and Employability Series Two. York: Higher Education Academy

Ward, R. (Ed.) 2006. *PDP and Employability.* Learning and Employability Series Two. York: Higher Education Academy

Yorke, M and Knight, P. 2006. *Embedding Employability into the Curriculum.* Learning and Employability Series One. York: Higher Education Academy

ROB WARD is the Director of the Centre for Recording Achievement (CRA), a national network organisation, registered educational charity, and associate centre of the Higher Education Academy. With over fifty HE members, the CRA provides a unique national cross-sectoral network committed to maximising the benefits of personal development planning and related processes for individuals and the organisations to which they belong. Through its work with the Academy, it supports the implementation of PDP and e-portfolio throughout UK HE.

Implementing Bournemouth University's employability strategy

1

Jacqui Gush

This case study describes Bournemouth University's approach to designing and implementing a strategy for enhancing student employability, outlining how we developed a list of employability attributes and directly implemented them in an employability resource zone. It highlights experience of implementation within the Hospitality, Leisure, Sport and Tourism (HLST) subject area and how this can enhance teaching, learning and assessment practice that directly impacts on 'education for employability' (Knight and Yorke, 2000).

This section outlines the position of employability in Bournemouth University's teaching and learning strategy and the university's objectives for employability. It includes the case study objectives.

Employability is an explicit part of the current Learning and Teaching (L&T) strategy at Bournemouth University which aims to:

- integrate employability skills and their assessment
- link this with personal development planning (PDP) and progress files (and Bologna diploma supplements).

The introduction of PDP is already an established strand of the institutional L&T strategy. Although it remains a separate initiative, supported by its own facilities, PDP is now an integral part of the university's work in employability. Indeed, at Bournemouth, employability has become an overarching concept which embraces a raft of strategic initiatives on the teaching and learning agenda, namely:

- enhancing the first-year experience
- internationalisation of the curriculum
- developing entrepreneurial skills in students
- embedding global perspectives into all curricula
- PDP.

The Employability Strategy (developed in 2004) included the following points:

1. Develop skills, attributes and qualities in our students based on those developed by Knight and Yorke, through: the use of the curriculum; teaching, learning and assessment approaches; tutoring and support services.

2. Support the Bournemouth L&T Strategy in the introduction of the following topics into the undergraduate curricula throughout the university and to contextualise/embed these in the subject teaching where they do not already exist:
   - international awareness/global perspectives
   - career-management skills
   - accreditation of work-based learning
   - Personal Development Planning/portfolio compilation
   - entrepreneurship and creativity.

The objective of this case study is to outline the institutional approach to enhancing the employability of our students and graduates, to explain how this has been achieved across the university and to outline the findings from initial implementation across the HLST subject area within the School of Services Management.

Context and rationale

This section places the development of the Bournemouth initiative in the context of the changing environment of higher education (HE) and explains the institutional approach taken.

In response to the publication of the White Paper (DfES, 2003), Bournemouth established a Curriculum Think Tank (CTT) in 2004 to formulate a response to the issues it raised for the future of the university. The goal of the group was to articulate a vision for learning at Bournemouth in the post-2006 higher education landscape in the context of top-up fees, which increased competition and raised expectations from students and other stakeholders.

In this context it was seen that the concept of employability brought together many of the key issues in a changing environment. By focusing on continually enhancing the employability of students through building on our strengths and established success, we could develop distinctiveness for the 21st century.

Bournemouth's intention was to use this concept as a fundamental strategic principle around which most of its student-centred activities would be focused in the future. It thus became an umbrella concept for other initiatives which formed part of the government's agenda for the future of HE.

> by focusing on continually enhancing the employability of students through building on our strengths and established success, we could develop distinctiveness for the 21st century

Strategic task groups were established for five key areas, with employability acting as the hub for these interdependent working groups, namely:
- PDP
- global perspectives
- internationalisation
- first-year experience
- entrepreneurship.

Each reflects different aspects of the skills, knowledge and characteristics contained in the definition of the Bournemouth graduate developed by the CTT.

Characteristics of a Bournemouth graduate

By 2010, all graduates from Bournemouth University will be highly valued by local, national and international employers. They will be:
- independent, reflective and ambitious learners
- secure and confident in their subject knowledge and understanding

- effective team players
- adaptable to change
- good communicators
- confident in using, analysing and manipulating quantitative information
- clear thinkers who can translate ideas into appropriate actions
- competent IT users
- informed and responsible global citizens
- positive contributors to a variety of work environments and locations.

Defining what we mean by employability

For implementation, we planned four main headings which covered all aspects of the student experience. These are reflected in the statement by the Enhancement Themes initiative, which asserts that practical implementation and good practice fall under these same headings:
- Curriculum design which promotes active, independent learning that is relevant to the world of work, thus embedding employability explicitly in the curriculum.
- The use of PDP processes which encourage students to reflect on and monitor their learning and development at each stage.
- The provision of suitable and meaningful work-related experiences and learning.
- Student support initiatives which are co-curricular in nature and led by the appropriate services, e.g. Careers, Learner Support and the Students' Union.

(Enhancement Themes 2005, See Figure 1)

To produce a workable agenda for implementation, we needed to spell out what we meant by the attributes of employability. We drew on the extensive research and well standardised findings of Knight and Yorke (2001) as part of the Skills *Plus* project (op cit). Using the USEM (Understanding of subject matter, Skilful practices, Efficacy beliefs and Meta-cognition) model, their research produced a list of 39 attributes which could serve as a workable checklist for the auditing of current practice and (re)design of curriculum content, teaching, learning and assessment approaches.

However, it was felt that this list could be further

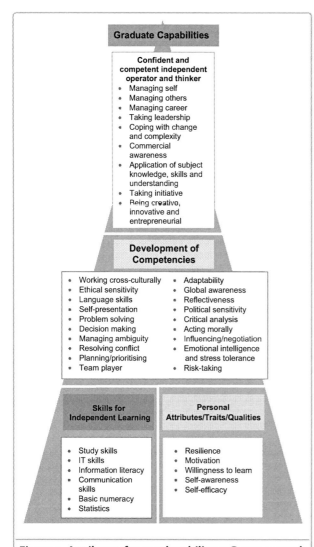

Figure 1 Attributes for employability at Bournemouth University: a hierarchy of development

refined to enable it to be more workable and meaningful in terms of an individual's development and progression. Thus the attributes were reformulated into a hierarchical structure, suggestive of educational stages, which sought to eliminate repetition and demonstrated progression and development. This cumulated in capstone graduate employability attributes which subsumed the skills and competencies which underpinned them.

Using this approach, a template for auditing purposes was developed. This asked all undergraduate programme teams to audit their current practice against a summary of these attributes

and determine where in their programme, by level, these attributes were taught, developed and/or assessed. The matrix template offered a simple 'tick box' approach in order to make the exercise easy for staff to complete. This was further developed by one staff member who converted the matrix into an Excel spreadsheet, so that a summary of teaching, development and assessments (T, D & AS) was automatically calculated. The function of the form was to encourage the initiation of debate among programme teams based on the findings that emerged (See Figure 2, Audit of employability attributes by programme).

Description

This section describes the approach to implementation taken and details the development of the employability resource zone (ERZ). The employability task group led this initiative.

Once agreement was gained on proposals, they had to be promulgated to each of the academic schools. Communication to ensure awareness and understanding was achieved through presentations to and discussion with senior management. This was cascaded down through the schools to programme leaders and their teams. These formal communication channels were supported by a programme of staff development workshops.

By the end of the academic year 2004/05, all programme teams, with the emphasis on undergraduate level, were asked to undertake the following:
❏ An audit of employability attributes by unit and level within each programme, using the template provided: to reflect on the findings, to identify gaps and where enhancements could be made to teaching and learning practice.

> a comprehensive employability resource zone (ERZ) was instigated in order to support staff in the development and enhancement of employability in their professional practice

❏ To commit these to an action plan for the coming year, which would be formally recorded in the Annual Report on Programme Monitoring

Figure 2 Audit of employability attributes by programme

Programme... School..

Employability attribute	Level C	T,D,A	Level I	T,D,A	Placement	Level H	T,D,A
Skills for independent learning							
Study skills Study techniques, note-taking, understanding learning styles, exam techniques, IT skills.							
Information literacy including skills for electronic searching.							
Communication skills Verbal, written, listening, understanding body language.							
Basic numeracy including appropriate IT skills, e.g. spreadsheets.							
Statistics including use of appropriate IT skills, e.g. Excel and SPSS.							
Self-awareness Self-assessment of personality, values, motivations, interests, abilities.							
Reflection and goal-setting Use of reflective skills and ability to plan and take action.							
Self-assessment/self-efficacy Assessment of strengths and weaknesses, confidence and disposition towards learning.							
Development of competences							
Global awareness includes: assessing own values, acting morally, cultural awareness, ethical sensitivity, international perspectives in subject, working with diversity, language skills, debating.							
Group working includes: resolving conflict, interpersonal skills, planning, political sensitivity, negotiation/influencing, leadership, resilience, motivation, problem-solving, decision-making.							
Adaptability includes: coping with change and complexity, analytical skills, managing ambiguity, emotional intelligence, willingness to learn.							
Self-presentation and career management includes: building a CV, understanding organisational needs, making effective applications, handling the selection process, learning from feedback.							
Creativity/innovation includes: taking risks, problem-solving, being entrepreneurial, generating ideas, adopting a positive, can-do attitude.							

Teams are asked to:
- ❏ Indicate the units within which these attributes are **T**aught, **D**eveloped and/or **A**ssessed.
- ❏ Check if this educational approach is reflected accurately in the unit descriptor – is it **E**xplicit?
- ❏ Reflect on where gaps occur and plan what they could do about this in the a) short and b) longer term.
- ❏ Reflect on where they could enhance/strengthen their practice in these areas with reference to Resource Help Zones
- ❏ Commit to an action plan for Employability in your Annual Report on Programme Monitoring (APRM) for 2005/06.

(ARPM). As progress on action plans is monitored and recorded at each programme committee meeting during the following year, i.e. 2005/06, this would ensure that programme teams worked on the development and enhancement of student employability during the current academic year.

- ❏ The Employability Task Group would audit these reports to achieve an institutional picture which could identify where we have strengths and weaknesses and where further support/action was needed.
- ❏ A new set of institutional academic guidelines was produced as a required reference point for all programmes under development and/or existing programmes coming up for review from 2005 onwards. These guidelines ensured that the full range of employability attributes were designed into their curricula and teaching and learning approaches.

The development of a comprehensive employability resource zone (ERZ) was instigated in order to support staff in the development and enhancement of employability in their professional practice. This is envisioned as eventually having both a physical and web-based presence, a student audience and a separate staff audience.

However, within the first year, it was decided to develop a web-based resource base for staff. The aim was to have this ready at the beginning of the academic year 2005/06 to directly support the action plan resulting from the auditing and planning process they were expected to undertake from the beginning of the academic year.

Figure 3 The structure of the employability resource zone website

General structure:
    Introduction
    Employability at BU
    Curriculum
    Teaching and Learning
    Student Support
    Co-Curricular Services
    Labour Market Information
    Staff Development
    Case Studies
    Reading List
    HEA Subject Centres
    Key Resources.

Curriculum
Curriculum design, content and organisation provide the hub for opportunities to develop employability attributes, skills, knowledge and understandings in our students. The website brings together a wide range of resources and information for ideas, examples, models of best practice, including case studies that relate to employability in the curriculum.

We would welcome more examples of good practice to further enhance and develop the resources on an ongoing basis.
    Global Perspectives
    Internationalisation
    Work-Based Learning
    Personal Development Planning (PDP)
    Entrepreneurship/Business
      Development
    Career Management.

Teaching, Learning & Assessment
Good teaching is all about motivating and inspiring students to learn and the approaches and methods we use to enable and facilitate their learning. This section offers examples of how BU staff have developed different TL&A approaches that enhance students' employability attributes.

We are grateful to all the staff who have been willing to share examples of their practice and have contributed to this growing resource base.

We would welcome more examples. Please contact Jacqui Gush with examples of practice that you have used successfully and/or additional resources you have located or any other helpful comments and inputs.
    Group Work
    Skills Development
    Independent Learning
    Problem-Based Learning
    Peer/Self-Assessment
    Reflection
    Simulations/Business Games
    Creativity
    Real World Projects
    Portfolio Assessment

Please note that access to the Case Studies is restricted to BU staff.

Employability resource zone

In line with the good-practice principles outlined above, the focus of activity was to be on:

- ❏ curriculum content and organisation
- ❏ teaching and learning approaches
- ❏ co-curricular activities
- ❏ student support.

The purpose of the website was visualised as a set of resources to support staff in developing innovative approaches to enhancing the employability attributes of their students and graduates. In addition, it provided a communication channel for important external information from employment organisations, the labour market and related bodies such as the Regional Development Agency (RDA) and Learning and Skills Council (LSC).

This provided an excellent dissemination point for

the other strategic task groups whose outputs/purposes directly contributed to graduate employability.

Populating the website

Staff from across the university were invited to contribute ideas, models and examples from their practice and/or research in the form of case studies, introductions and other resources in areas where they have developed interest, experience and expertise. In addition, selected links to external resources were provided using annotations to help staff easily locate the information required. Thus the website provided a set of resources which offered examples of good practice, new ideas, case studies and models for all Bournemouth staff to draw on. It has consequently become an important vehicle for dissemination of practical ideas.

Evaluation

This section analyses and evaluates findings from the implementation process in the School of Services Management.

The HLST programme teams in the school have audited their current programmes using the template and have reflected on the pattern that emerges in order to identify gaps and discuss opportunities for improvement. Here are some of the key findings.

Programme 1

From the pattern that emerged from the matrix, the team was able to identify the lack of career-management skills development in level C (year one). Through this analysis they were able to explain why it is often difficult to get the second-year (level I) students to start taking placement preparation seriously from the start and to be able to produce an acceptable CV. As a result, immediate plans were put in place for improvements from the start of academic year 2005/06 which involved 'tweaking' the content of an appropriate unit in level C in order to strengthen the development of career management skills in students at an earlier stage. A creative approach was taken to closer monitoring of the CVs produced by the second years, which imposed higher standards and stricter deadlines. A further finding was that there appeared to be more 'T's (teaching) at level H than at level C!

This prompted the team to further review teaching and learning strategies at these levels.

Programme 2

Examples of good practice were identified with group working, where the teaching of group working skills occurred in level C and there was a good balance between development and assessment across the programme as a whole. The programme was able to identify a strength across all their pathways on the development and assessment of creativity and innovation and that teaching aspects were well placed in level C. However, they also identified that opportunities for students to develop adaptability were lacking. One of their subsequent action plans was to 'review opportunities to develop adaptability with particular reference to level C'.

Programme 3

This programme team was able to identify a lack of focus on study skills at level C (year one) and discovered that there appeared to be more teaching and assessment of these skills in the other two levels. They also discovered that, although there were opportunities for skills of reflection to be developed (D) across the programme and that these were assessed (A) in equal measure, they were never really taught to students. However, they were able to demonstrate good practice in the teaching, learning and assessment of communication skills, with the pattern across the levels reflecting a progressive development through the appropriate level of teaching, self-development and assessment.

Indeed, by analysing the summary column on the Excel spreadsheet, the team discovered that there is a tendency to assess (A) employability attributes which are taught (T) or developed (D) disproportionately less. When analysing the summary information across the levels, they discovered, as with Programme 1, that there seems to be more teaching of employability attributes at level I, (the second year) than at level C.

Discussion

Our employability strategy sets out to develop an 'education for employability' (Knight and Yorke, 2000) that is:

- coherent and joined-up
- structured and consistent
- articulated and explicit
- leading-edge and focused.

The purpose of the form was to generate an agenda for discussion of enhancing our practice around these principles through programme content, design and organisation.

With reference to the design of the form, the first issue that was encountered was the interpretation of the descriptors on the first iteration of the audit matrix. For example, did all staff understand global awareness to be the same thing? What attributes or competences are implied from being globally aware? Some staff queried why IT skills were not listed separately, whereas when the form was designed, it had been assumed that staff would see IT skills as inherent in areas such as study skills, communication skills, numeracy and information literacy. It soon became obvious that the main descriptors needed to be teased out and the final form was annotated, as in Figure 2. However, the issue of a common understanding of descriptors and language used when carrying out an audit, in order to minimise interpretation, is an important general point.

The exercise also provides an opportunity for teams to cross-reference the ticks on the form with their unit specifications and clarify the learning intended through each unit or module. Both of these issues address the issues of explicitness and articulation.

If our programmes are typical, one general finding that the exercise has highlighted is the importance of attending to the content and design of the curriculum at level C (year one) and how important well-designed learning opportunities are in the first year for establishing the foundation of good employability education. It was the coherence, structure and consistency of the programmes with reference to the development of employability that was sometimes found wanting from the exercise.

The evidence above demonstrates conclusively the potential benefits to be gained from undertaking this exercise, but there is no assurance that all academics will treat the exercise with the same seriousness. Reasons for this are many, of which time pressures are an obvious one. However, we have tried to tie this into the cycle of accountability for the role of programme leader; and as the ARPMs are audited, the university will be scrutinising the outcomes. Leadership and the ability to manage and co-ordinate the team will be a key requirement for the success of the exercise and for developing employability as a strategic imperative.

Bournemouth takes this concept very seriously and staff are generally extremely interested in helping their students to realise their employability potential. As a result there is a sense that we are already good at developing our students for employment and that there is little need for such bureaucratic exercises or the change/enhancement it implies. Therefore there is evidence of complacency amongst staff about this initiative. This may be a common reaction amongst

> the exercise has highlighted how important well-designed learning opportunities are in the first year for establishing the foundation of good employability education

vocational and professional programme-based institutions such as ours and it is important to acknowledge and celebrate achievements to date. However, in a rapidly changing environment, it is also important that any pockets of complacency are shaken and stirred out of this state! The principle of being focused and 'leading-edge' tries to address this issue. However, there is initiative fatigue and with continuing pressure on resources, the key is always to find ways to work with staff. In the academic environment, as a result, implementing new initiatives and reaching objectives takes longer and requires more effort.

We are confident that the building blocks are in place to ensure a focus on employability in the future. A base-lining exercise providing institutional benchmarks is in place and teams will be accountable for measurable progress and development over time towards the achievement of objectives.

It is early days to report on reaction to the ERZ website. The steering group members were honest enough to say that it was too institutional in appearance and was not inviting enough. Staff asked why it could not look more like the PDP website, which has been specifically designed to appeal directly to students. In comparison, they accuse the employability website of being boring.

Regardless of how we respond to these comments, the general feeling is that when staff need to plan for change, at the time of programme review or development, or in response to feedback relating to the enhancement of employability or teaching and learning generally, this resource base will provide a ready made set of ideas, examples and case studies for them to draw on.

References and URLs

DfES (Department for Education and Skills) 2003. *The Future of Higher Education*. (CM 5753) Norwich: The Stationery Office

Enhancement Themes 2005 http://www.enhancement-themes.ac.uk/

ESECT http://www.heacademy.ac.uk/869.htm

Knight, P. and Yorke, M. 2000. *Skills* plus*: Tuning the Undergraduate Curriculum*. Skills *plus* Project Report

Knight, P. 2001. Employability and Assessment. Skills *plus* – a paper prepared for the fourth colloquium, 3 October 2001

Knight, P. and Yorke, M. 2002. Employability through the Curriculum. *Tertiary Education and Management*, Dec 2002, **8** (4), 261–276

JACQUI GUSH has been a Senior Academic at Bournemouth University for eight years, divided between four years as Head of Quality in the School of Services Management and subsequently four years as Head of Learning & Teaching. She is project leader for the PDP/employability strategic initiative across the university.

Programmes that work for people who work: a process-based model for part-time management studies

2

Gail Sanders

This case study describes an innovative programme designed by the University of Sunderland Business School to attract workers in the North-East of England to part-time study in Business and Management.

This programme is almost entirely work-based, thus time constraints on students are minimised and learning is strengthened by meaningful contextualisation. Other key features include:

- The programme is process-driven. This new approach to course design offers a valuable staff development opportunity as an 'added extra'.
- By making use of the workplace as the main location of learning, students are able to complete their degree in three years instead of the usual four-and-a-half.
- The traditional modular structure adopted by Business School programmes has been abandoned in this case. The BA Applied Management is structured instead around three 'themes' of management, self-development and business. Teaching and assessment is integrative across these themes.
- Introduction of this programme in 2003 resulted in a significant increase in applications for part-time study. The first cohort was subject to a detailed evaluation by an external consultant and feedback was overwhelmingly positive. Student performance exceeded that of any previous cohorts on the more 'traditional' part-time routes.

A key factor in the success of the programme is considered to be the structured use of learning sets and student 'buddying', which allows the sharing of experience. Reflection plays an important role in the learning process, driven by a personal development-planning theme that accounts for one-third of the credits at each level. This paper covers the research that led to this initiative and discusses the structure and delivery of the programme. Findings from the detailed evaluation of the first cohort are presented, and some of the practical issues and problems encountered during the introduction of this programme are discussed.

Objectives

The programme's approach reflects the strong commitment in the university to the concepts of increasing access, widening participation and lifelong learning. The philosophy of the programme is to create an HE opportunity which is considered to be relevant

> Initially we looked at the modules that we already had to see how we could put them together to form this new programme – a false start

and appealing to students and their employers. The priority is to make a strong linkage between learning and development and the workplace.

The teaching and learning approaches adopted aim to create a strong self-managing learning community which provides an interesting and stimulating environment for both students and tutors. The applied nature of the programme assessment aims to improve management behaviour and practice as well as provide a practical and focused education, which can help grow and retain business talent in the region.

Context and rationale

The University of Sunderland is located on the coast of the North-East of England. This was traditionally an area of heavy industry, predominantly shipbuilding and coal mining, but over recent decades there has been a relatively rapid decline in these industries leading to high levels of unemployment. Indeed, the new campus of the university itself is built on the site of the demolished shipyards in Sunderland. Encouraging the local population to 're-skill' and engage in learning is high on the regional agenda and the University of Sunderland has done more than most to bring higher education to people who were previously excluded. More than a quarter of our students are from areas with little track record in HE and around 40% are from the lowest social classes. The university has set up a fund to provide access scholarships and has initiatives for improving take-up of HE. It also maintains close contacts with the community, thus helping to dissipate some of the 'mystery' of universities that can sometimes act as a barrier to participation. This also ensures that students are able to keep in close contact with the 'real world'. However, it is the strong vocational nature of the Sunderland provision that is perhaps the biggest factor in encouraging more people to participate and in gaining the support of local business.

The Business School in particular provides largely work-related programmes with a strong emphasis on employability. Over recent years much effort has been expended on strengthening the provision to make it more valuable to both employers and potential students who may otherwise not consider taking a course in HE. However, one area where the Business School had not been so successful was in attracting those in full-time employment, but without qualifications, to study part-time.

The school had offered part-time courses in business for many years. However, this provision was largely a 'watered down' version of the full-time programme. Part-time students did the same core modules as the full-timers, but for timetabling reasons were offered fewer options. The teaching and assessment approaches were the same as for full-time and did nothing to recognise that, by and large, the part-time students were less of a blank canvas than the full-

The intrinsic reward of academic achievement featured as the strongest positive point

timers and had their own knowledge and experience to contribute to a programme of learning. Retention rates were poor (on one occasion we lost 35% of students in the first semester) and feedback from those who completed was as one might expect from a programme that neglected their specific needs.

Students' opinions of worst things about the programme		
Comment	Score %	Cumulative
Poor lecturing standards	11.8	11.8
Lack of books in library	9.4	21.2
Some lecturers unable to adapt style/manner to suit part-time (PT) students	6.8	28
Inconsistent marking	6.5	34.5
Group assignments	6.5	41
Opening times during holidays	5.3	46.3
The lecturing is not what PT students require – it needs to be more focused	5.3	51.6
Organisation is generally poor	4.7	56.3
Over-assessment	3.5	59.8
Lack of consideration for the constraints of PT students	3.5	83.5
Too much wasted time and breaks	3.5	66.8
Too much generalisation in subjects – not enough specialisation	3.5	70.3
Inconsistent standards expected from lecturers	3.5	73.8
Assignment deadlines not suitable for PT – can't get in from work during the day	2.9	76.7
Reception service not good	2.9	79.6
TCAs organised at inappropriate times	2.9	82.5

Table 1 Nominal group items (negative issues), arranged in descending order of points allocated

Intake to the full range of part-time Business School courses had been around 50 students each year, despite the fact that only 25% of employees in the area were known to have higher-level qualifications (Rowell, 2002). Attracting people to part-time study is one of the key objectives in the university strategy, so clearly this situation had to be improved. To that end, a detailed review of part-time provision was undertaken to identify current students' perceptions of their experience and to try to establish why others were not attracted to the courses.

During the 2000/01 academic year ,feedback was gathered from final-year students to form the basis of a report to management on the state of part-time provision in the school. Feedback was obtained using the nominal group technique. With this technique, students are asked to write down individually what they consider to be the three worst things about the programme and then the three best things. The facilitator then collates the findings from the whole class, eliminating any duplication or ambiguities. Students are then allowed to award ten points to their preferred items on the collated class list in any way they wish (so they may award all ten points to one item, or, at the other extreme, award one point to ten items). Results from the whole group are totalled. In this way, the items most important to the group as a whole can be identified and the scoring gives an indication of how strongly students feel about particular items.

Findings indicated that key concerns were poor lecturing standards, the inability of academic staff to adapt style to suit part-timers, poor organisation and communication and a system that failed to take into

> They are the guys who spent all their years at school looking out of the window because the teachers bored them

sufficient account the requirements of part-time students. The intrinsic reward of academic achievement featured as the strongest positive point. The top 80% of comments obtained from a nominal group session from which this feedback was obtained are shown in Tables 1 and 2.

Overall, the key theme that came out of this review was that part-time students were taught in much the same way as full-timers and they felt that this was not appropriate. It emerged that this was the main source of the perception that lecturing standards were poor. They were keen to have more opportunity to relate their learning to their jobs and indeed to have their existing knowledge and experience valued in the context of their university course.

These findings echo research carried out in other institutions. For example, in a published study by Yorke (1999), 328 part-time students were asked to indicate the influences on their decision to withdraw from their programme. Thirty-nine factors were summarised from the survey results, which were then subjected to principal component analysis. Results of this analysis are shown in Table 3.

Clearly, something needed to be done about the teaching and learning experience offered to part-time students to improve satisfaction levels and improve retention.

The other aspect that we needed to consider was how to further expand

Students' opinions of best things about the programme

Comment	Score %	Cumulative
Gaining a sense of achievement when assignments are complete	13.5	13.5
Lecturers who gear sessions towards helping with assessment	9.5	23
Library staff helpful	8.8	31.8
Help given for assignments and TCAs	8.1	39.9
Some lecturers very good (though in minority)	7.4	47.3
Being with other students	6.8	54.1
Helpful lecture guides and notes	5.4	59.5
Weekend access available	4.7	64.2
Library facilities	4.7	68.9
Awareness that education betters performance in the workplace	4	72.9
New pricing structure	3.4	76.3
Too much generalisation in subjects – not enough specialisation	3.4	79.7
Parking for match days	2.7	82.4
Learning		

Table 2 Nominal group items (positive issues), arranged in descending order of points allocated

Factor number	% variance	Label
1	17.3	Poor quality of the teaching experience
2	8.1	Pressure of work (academic and employment)
3	7.3	Unhappiness with the extra-institutional environment
4	5.6	Problems with relationships and finance
5	4.9	Dissatisfaction with aspects of institutional provision
6	4.6	Wrong choice of programme

Table 3 Reasons for withdrawal of part-time students from programme of study

our part-time numbers – i.e. what needed to be done to attract those who currently chose *not* to come to study with us. Although difficult to establish from the individuals themselves, employers and other agencies provided clues as to what the problem was. Two comments that were made to us perhaps best illustrate the main issue. The first came from the training manager of a major organisation who was interested in developing an in-house staff development programme with us. He described the 'target audience' thus:

These guys are sharp. They can work out a deal in their heads quicker than our trained accountants can. Some of them are on close to £100,000 a year – but none of them have formal qualifications. They are the guys who spent all their years at school looking out of the window because the teachers bored them. If you come in here and just lecture to them and get them to write loads of reports and essays, they'll switch off.

The second quote came from a regional council representative, who had attended an open evening to see what we could offer his local community to encourage them back into education. He said:

The image is wrong. They think of lecturers and university as being snobby, that you'll look down on them. You need to do something sexy to change that.

It seemed clear to us from such comments that if we were really to achieve our aims, we needed to provide quite a different offering to part-timers. So, towards the end of 2002 a small group of us set about developing a course designed specifically for part-time students who were in full-time employment. The result was the BA Applied Management.

Description

Programme structure

During a brainstorming session the ideas for a new part-time in-house course were born, drawing much from the experience we already had with company-based programmes. Initially we looked at the modules that we already had to see how we could put them together to form this new programme – a false start. Having realised that we were simply repeating the same mistakes, we agreed to start with a blank sheet of paper and to decide what we wanted the students to 'look like' when they graduated from the programme, while trying to avoid all the problems of traditional provision. Working backwards from there, the structure of our new course started to emerge.

The new programme is structured around three themes: business, management and self, each contributing 40 credits at each level of study. This is shown diagrammatically in Figure 1.

Management is the key focus of this programme and contributes 80 credits to each level of study, with 'management of self' focused in the 'self' theme and 'management of others' and 'management of resources' contained in the 'management' theme. However, the 'self' theme forms the 'capstone' subject for the programme and integration and reflection on the other themes periodically takes place within 'self'. Self comprises the Personal Development Planning 1,

Table 4 Differentiation by level

Level one	Students focus on their own self-development and self-management and are required to contextualise their learning within their own organisation.
Level two	While continuing their own self-development, students also study the management of others and of resources within a wider business environment, contextualising their learning both within their own organisation and other, contrasting, organisations.
Level three	At this level students are required to shift their focus from tactical to strategic, looking at the management of businesses as whole entities within the wider business environment. Self-development continues, but this too develops a more strategic focus and students are encouraged to plan for their future careers and study.

2 and 3 modules, each worth 40 credits.

Modules within the 'business' and 'management' themes have been developed to satisfy the requirements of the QAA General Business and Management benchmark statements. There is some overlap between business and management as subjects, but the model shown in Figure 2 helps to clarify content under each of these themes.

The QAA *Framework for Higher Education Qualifications* guided the learning outcomes for each theme at each level. However, the development team felt that in this type of work-based programme it is also appropriate to encourage learners' development through the levels by escalating and expanding the students' outlook within their organisations and outside. Thus, the focus at each level can be explained in terms of the distinctions in Table 3.

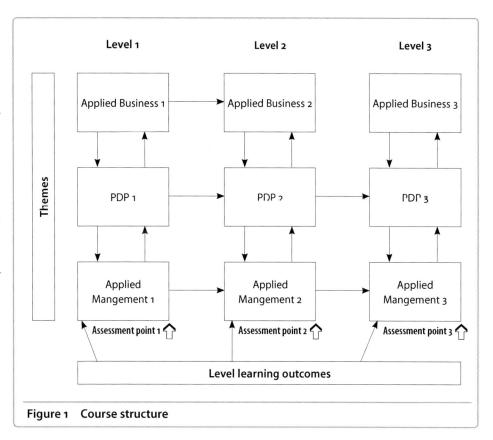

Figure 1   Course structure

Teaching, learning, assessment and programme delivery

We were keen to provide a programme that would have high workplace impact. To that end, the programme focuses on process much more than content and is outcome-based. The guiding principle for the programme is that the learning experience is designed to create graduates who are aware that there is a body of knowledge and theory about management in business and know how to locate and apply theory as appropriate to improve their performance as managers in varied situations throughout their careers. Implicit in this is that graduates will also be aware that knowledge is dynamic and they will therefore appreciate the need for continued learning and have the skills to continue their learning process independently after graduation.

This moved us away from the traditional discipline-based approach to course design, where subject content often takes precedence over the learning process. Modules take on an integrated nature to try to mimic the 'real world' as much as possible, and because their learning experience is predominantly within the workplace, our students can see the relevance of their learning and consolidate it much more effectively than can those studying by the traditional route. For much of the programme students work together in learning sets, comprising individuals from as wide a range of organisational types as possible. This provides them with the opportunity to discuss different perspectives and share experience and views.

Summative assessment takes place only at the end of each year and the main emphasis throughout the year is on formative work and feedback (though this is formally managed through both a learning log and a reflective task log, both of which contribute towards a student's final grade). Thus, we provide students with the opportunity to learn from their mistakes and to develop their understanding from feedback without the fear of being formally marked for everything they produce. Our focus is on the 'exit velocity' of our students, not how well they can write a report six weeks into the programme. We believe that this is a more realistic approach that better supports students attracted through widening participation routes.

If you come in here and just lecture to them and get them to write loads of reports and essays, they'll switch off

Business and management themes

Programme delivery takes place in formal workshop sessions on one day per month. These sessions currently run on Saturday, but alternative provision may need to be made to accommodate multiple cohorts. Students are required to prepare for these sessions by a mix of completing work-based tasks, reading and research, reviewing lectures provided electronically and completing exercises on WebCT. Through ensuring that students are suitably prepared, best use can be made of contact time with tutors to discuss, reflect, share and expand on learning. We anticipated that at level one a student would not have the appropriate

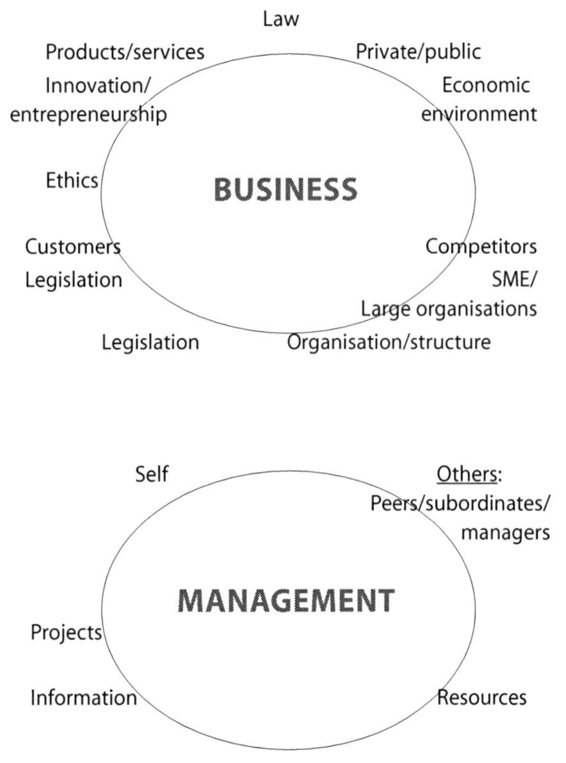

skills to complete detailed preparation before workshops, so this process starts slowly and escalates as the student progresses through the course.

By using this model, learning hours for each module comprise time spent on:
- weekend input
- development of PDP and learning log
- review of lectures
- assessment preparation (formative & summative)
- WebCT work
- private reading.

During development the programme team devoted some time to discussing how to ensure comparability of learning experience for students working in very different organisations (e.g. SMEs vs large organisations; public vs private sector). There was concern that some students would have much more scope than others for finding appropriate projects to help them contextualise their learning and complete assessment tasks and that some would get insufficient support from their management. Solutions proposed were:

1 Institute a formal 'pairing' system for students from different types of organisation, which we have termed 'buddying'.
2 Require students to arrange visits to their own organisations for others in their learning set.
3 Invite high-profile guest speakers from business, commerce and academia.

These features are particularly important for levels two and three when students are required to extend their learning beyond their own organisations.

Personal development theme

While the 'business' and 'management' themes provide the academic context for this programme, it is the 'self' theme embodied in the Personal Development Planning modules at each level that provides the 'capstone' to the programme. We think that the success of this theme is crucial to meeting the programme's

Figure 2 Business and management themes

aims. The tutor/student relationship is fundamental to this success, since it is through this relationship that reflection, deep learning and independent learning skills will be developed. Important to the success of the theme are the following points:

- The programme is 'front-loaded' with 'learning to learn' skills, including specific learning tasks.
- Staff involved as tutors for PDP **must** engage in training before taking on the role.
- No tutor has more than five tutees.
- Self- and peer-assessment form part of the learning process to develop independence.
- Staff who clearly do not 'buy in' to the ethos of this programme are not included in the programme team.
- Some effort is needed to encourage and support students who feel uncomfortable with the reflective process.
- The role name given to tutors is important to the definition of the staff/student relationship. 'Tutor' and 'supervisor' are inappropriate as they seem to imply a hierarchical relationship, but the term 'coach' defines the equal relationship that is needed to encourage a suitable degree of openness.

Progression and grading issues

During development a great deal of discussion centred on whether the award should be classified or simply be pass/fail. A strong argument for pass/fail was the problem of variability in students' organisations – i.e. some students may not have as much opportunity as others to conduct strong work-based projects and would therefore not have the same opportunity to receive a good grade. Grading might also be counterproductive in terms of promoting deep learning. However, experience shows that part-time students tend to be fiercely competitive (primarily with themselves) and prefer a grading system as it provides them with added motivation. We also felt that employers prefer to have some indication of how well students are doing and look to grades for this purpose. The decision was therefore to classify the degree. Given the nature of the programme and the relatively small number of summative assessments, we had to draw up programme-specific regulations to describe how this would be done.

Evaluation

We started with a pilot cohort of 27 in October 2003. Very quickly a few left because either they could not adapt to the learning process, or because of difficulties at work. Those who remained (22) have been successful beyond our hopes. In particular, feedback gathered again through the nominal group technique has suggested levels of meta-learning that have never been observed on a cohort-wide basis at this level.

Other outcomes that were raised by students, though they did not come out with top ratings when class scoring was completed, were nevertheless just as

> we agreed to start with a blank sheet of paper – to decide what we wanted the students to 'look like' when they graduated, while trying to avoid all the problems of traditional provision

encouraging, and indeed unique, for part-time feedback. For example, students mentioned:

- *Improved self-belief*
- *Being more contemplative*
- *Being able to apply learning*
- *Causing real visible improvement to my organisation.*

Employer feedback has also been impressive. Comments include:

- *Since Nicola commenced the course her management input has exceeded all expectations.*
- *X made a presentation to our bank manager on my behalf which was very impressive and undoubtedly above my own capabilities!*
- *This course has proved extremely valuable, not only to our employee, but to the future of our company*

Student performance was similarly impressive. Of the 22 students completing the pilot year, five gained marks in excess of 70%.

Discussion

The success of this programme in terms of students' learning outcomes has taken even the most dedicated members of the programme team by surprise and has led us to look in much more depth into what might be happening with our group of students. The intensely reflective nature of the learning process, along with the contextualised nature of programme content, are design features that have undoubtedly played a large part.

Our inclusion of 40-credits worth of personal development planning at each level raised some eyebrows amongst (perhaps less enlightened!) colleagues and was the source of intense scrutiny at the programme validation. However, our first-year experience has proved to us the value of this formalised approach to

> Our focus is on the 'exit velocity' of our students, not how well they can write a report six weeks into the programme

PDP. We have seen some remarkable results. Although not popular with some students (who found intense personal reflection uncomfortable) it forced them into true reflection mode and this even took some of the learners themselves by surprise. Perhaps the most extreme example is the case of one class member who, during her end-of-year presentation, described a tale of an abused past that had destroyed her self-esteem and made her believe that she was not capable of achieving anything worthwhile. The PDP process had somehow helped her to unlock all of this and she explained how she felt that she could now put all of it behind her because the process had restored her self-belief.

Most intriguing is the success of the student learning sets. Our students have taken the learning set approach very seriously. Most meet regularly to discuss their work and share ideas. Often, at the end of a hard day's session at the business school, sets will stay behind to reflect on the day together and to record their feelings and experiences for their learning logs. Feedback showed that they rated the learning set experience as the most valuable part of the learning process. This in turn started us reflecting on what was actually happening here and led us back to our original feedback from the traditional part-time students, whose main complaint was that we were not valuing what they had to offer. But what exactly was that?

Few, if any, of our part-time students had formal qualifications and many had not studied in any academic sense since leaving school. The vital 'student skills' such as using the library, referencing, report writing and so on, were absent. On the other hand, many were in management positions and they came from a wide variety of organisations: small and large enterprises, public and private sector, service and manufacturing. In terms of business and management knowledge, they represented a pool of resource on a much greater scale and more up-to-date than the business school itself could provide. The problem lay in the nature of the knowledge. This was largely *tacit* knowledge and, by definition, difficult to articulate and to transfer from one person to another.

The scientist turned philosopher Michael Polanyi (1966) explained the nature of such knowledge, developing a model of cognition showing knowledge as having two dimensions, the tacit and explicit. He commonly used the phrase 'we know more than we can tell' to introduce the idea of tacit knowledge. For example, we know the face of a close friend or relative, but we cannot say how we know it; we could not specify exactly its shape, colouring, or the measurement of its features. Another example that Polanyi gave is a skill. You know how to ride a bike, yet you cannot tell how you do it (Scott, 1985).

These ideas can easily be transferred to the management role; with time a manager builds a valuable stock of tacit knowledge. Eventually, with experience, a manager will know intuitively how actions or decisions will affect implementation in a range of different contexts. It has been suggested that tacit knowledge about the business environment, industry patterns and company abilities is a resource that can provide significant competitive advantage for organisations (Kogut and Zander, 1993), because it is experientially acquired and is, therefore, unique to each person. It therefore represents a valuable resource.

Back to our class of part-time students: if we accept the idea that tacit knowledge is an important part of a manager's ability to do their job effectively, it follows that if we can find a way to access and share the tacit knowledge of our class members then we are going some way to valuing what they have to offer and providing a richer resource for all involved. McNett, Wallace and Athanassiou (2004) have given this problem some considerable thought. They contend that the fundamental source of our teaching challenge lies

Things I have gained from doing the course	Score	%	Cumulative %
Learning set contact	77	48%	48%
Increased understanding of organisation	19	12%	60%
Being more reflective	11	7%	67%
Understanding why changes occur	7	4%	71%
Only opportunity to do degree	7	4%	76%
Taking a more objective approach to problems	6	4%	79%

Table 4 Nominal group items (positive issues, new programme), arranged in descending order of points allocated

in the dual nature of knowledge that a manager needs to develop and that tacit knowledge plays a significant, though not widely recognised role in the teaching of management (and other disciplines). They suggest a number of ways in which we can approach learning and teaching in order to tap into this valuable resource. First, they suggest that the more inductive the learning, the greater the role of tacit knowledge. The normal deductive theory-to-application model applied in most management classrooms, then, does little to recognise tacit knowledge. They also suggest that the curriculum must emphasise a high level of cognitive development; students must be confronted with the complexity inherent in meta-learning and concepts that require thinking at high levels of complexity and ambiguity: 'the security of the right answers lodged in the mind of the professor is no longer part of the classroom'.

Polanyi also provides some pointers for us; as he describes tacit knowledge, it requires intensive personal experience. The learner must be able to take new knowledge and integrate it with previous experiences and knowledge and this is done most effectively when the learner is immersed in *action* using as many senses as possible.

Somewhat unwittingly, we seem to have tapped into the pool of tacit knowledge that our students possess and provided a vehicle for them to share that knowledge. We have done that by designing a programme that asks our students to *do* things, that brings them into contact with as many alternative ideas as possible (mainly via the learning sets), that contextualises the learning and is inductive in approach. This leaves us, as academics, with a dilemma. If the strongest part of the learning experience is the acquisition of tacit knowledge by some process of sharing, reflection, or storytelling and yet tacit knowledge, by definition, cannot be articulated, how do we measure the full extent of students' learning? Certainly, none of our traditional methods of assessment can do this. It is a dilemma we have yet to solve, but it is perhaps not so important when we realise that we are helping our students to develop. In fact, the achievement of the programme can probably be best summed up through the words of one of our students, who said:

'*I can feel my brain grow!*'

References

Kogut, B. & Zander, U. 1993. Knowledge of the firm, combinative capabilities and the replication of technology *Organisation Science*, **3** (3), 383–97

McNett, J. M., Wallace, R. M. & Athanassiou, N. 2004. *Tacit Knowledge in the Classroom: A strategy for learning.* Paper presented at 29th Improving University Teaching Conference, Bern, Switzerland

Polanyi, M. 1966. *The Tacit Dimension.* London: Routledge & Kegan Paul

Rowell, A. 2002. *Learning and Skills in Tyne & Wear: Initial analysis of the Tyne & Wear Household Survey 2002.* Tyne & Wear: Learning & Skills Council

Scott, D. 1985. *Everyman Revived: The common sense of Michael Polanyi.* Grand Rapids: WB Eerdmans Publishing

Yorke, M. 1999. *Leaving Early: Undergraduate non-completion in higher education.* London: Falmer Press

GAIL SANDERS is Principal Lecturer responsible for Quality Assurance and Learning Enhancement for Sunderland Business School. She has extensive experience in the development and delivery of part-time programmes for practising managers, most recently focusing on innovative developments in work-based learning.

Gail's key research interest is in learning development and support, particularly as it applies to non-traditional and part-time students. She has a PhD in this area, and has delivered papers at a number of national and international conferences related to her field of research.

Embedding employability in th curriculum: enhancing students career-planning skills

Angela Maher

This case study describes and discusses the experience of developing and delivering a career planning module for final-year hospitality and tourism undergraduates at Oxford Brookes University. The story encapsulates both the philosophy and the practical aspects of adopting this approach to embedding employability in the curriculum.

Objectives

The stated aim of the bachelors' degree at Oxford Brookes is to:

develop effective and innovative managers for the international hospitality and tourism industries. (Student Handbook 2004/05)

In order to achieve this aim, the university not only needs to provide a programme of study that is current, academically rigorous and vocationally relevant, but also needs to help students acquire the confidence and appropriate skills that allow them to make an effective transition from education to work. Career Planning for Hospitality & Tourism is a final year undergraduate module designed to help students manage that transition successfully. It encourages them to know themselves, know what types of employment they are suited to and aims to provide them with skills to enhance their career prospects in a highly competitive labour market. Specific objectives addressed by the module are:

❑ To raise students' awareness of the career opportunities available in the labour market.
❑ To enhance students' understanding of the skills and attributes required for successful graduate employment.
❑ To provide students with tools that enable them to audit their own skills for employment and enable them to plan their personal and professional development.
❑ To encourage students to plan for their future

career via the development of individual career plans and strategies.
❑ To build students' self-confidence and encourage them to articulate their abilities to prospective employers effectively.
❑ To encourage students to value their work and personal experiences and acknowledge their achievements.
❑ To help students develop job application skills and provide useful feedback on their CV and career plan.
❑ To encourage students to develop skills that help them make an effective transition from university to work.

Context

Oxford Brookes University has a strong reputation for providing excellent vocational education within the framework of a well developed modular programme structure. The introduction of this new module came at a time of significant change at Oxford Brookes. In 2002 the university made a decision to change the structure of the academic teaching year and so began a two-year planning process involving a major redesign and revalidation of the university's academic course portfolio. The outcome of this was that, in September 2004, the university made the transition from a term-time structure of three ten-week blocks, to a semester structure of two 15-week blocks. In addition to ging the structure of the teaching year, the university also reconfigured the School/Faculty structure, an outcome of which was the merger of the School of Business and the School of Hotel & Restaurant Management. These changes initiated a major review of tourism and hospitality programmes and allowed the course teams to develop and update their provision to meet the needs of graduates and employers in the 21st century. The period of change provided an opportunity to reflect on our approach to developing the employability of hospitality and tourism students and to ensure that curricula reflected current thinking in this area. It also allowed us to address the wider institution's developing employability strategy and its approach to implementing PDP.

The hospitality and tourism course teams have long recognised employability as a core aspect of our undergraduate provision and colleagues shared a philosophy about how this might best be delivered. Within the formal curriculum, core or transferable skills

> in an attempt to source some form of industry sponsorship… those I contacted were, in the main, extremely enthusiastic and keen to help in any way they could

would remain embedded within compulsory 'subject' modules, with specialist work-based and work-related modules providing students with an opportunity to develop employability skills in realistic work environments. Thus the course employed a combination of the approaches to embedding employability advocated by Yorke (2004). The Career Planning for Hospitality & Tourism module therefore represents only one aspect of employability skills development within a student's programme of study and is designed as part of a comprehensive package of modules and extra curricular activities. This package incorporates a 40-week period of work placement, a work-based learning portfolio, several work-related learning modules (e.g. 'live' case studies, consultancy projects, entrepreneurship and events management modules) and a programme of complementary careers events and activities running alongside the formal curriculum. The Career Planning module was designed as a 'capstone' to the course, encouraging students to reflect on all four

years of their education and to begin in earnest to prepare themselves for entering the labour market.

Description

Having established that a Career Planning module would enhance the curriculum, the development progressed through a series of key stages.

Stage 1 incorporated both primary and secondary research

In addition to a comprehensive review of the literature on employability and career management, a small scale survey of Oxford Brookes hospitality graduates was undertaken to determine which employability attributes were important for career success. Funded jointly by the HE Academy subject network for Hospitality, Leisure, Sport and Tourism and Oxford Brookes University Student Services, the survey provided some interesting and useful data on which specific skills or attributes might be addressed by this module (http://www.hlst.heacademy.ac.uk/projects/networkfunded.html). In addition, we carried out a series of interviews with graduate recruiters, employers and employment specialists. This first-stage research was crucial in establishing the parameters of the module and what types of issues it could and should address. It was clear that the module needed to cover the following key areas:

- Awareness of labour market opportunities and skills required for success in employment
- Increasing students' self-confidence and awareness of their own capabilities
- Increasing students' capacity to adapt to change and plan for the future
- Enhance students' time-management and prioritising skills
- Improve students' networking skills
- Improve students' job-getting skills, including their ability to articulate their attributes and achievements to employers.

The module also needed to be pitched at the right level in terms of academic and intellectual development for a level-three honours module. It was very important that the module was seen by students (and colleagues) to be academically rigorous and appropriately challenging if it was to deliver its aims successfully.

Stage 2 involved the production of the module description for review and validation

The module description includes learning outcomes, indicative content and assessment requirements. It was decided that the module should be delivered over the final two semesters of the student's programme. The rationale was that students should start the process of career planning as early as possible in their final year of study and that this would also give them time to reflect on and develop their skills for employment over a period of months. It was proposed that the module be designated as one of four honours-level modules within the undergraduate programme, (worth 15 level-three credits from a total of 240 credits) and should be compulsory for students studying on the four-year programmes in hospitality and tourism (approximately 120 students per year). The module would involve a total of 24 hours of contact time per student delivered via a programme of lectures, interactive workshops and culminating in a mock graduate assessment centre. Total study time for the module would be 150 hours including independent preparation and study. The module was successfully validated in July/August 2003 and was planned to run for the first time in September 2004.

Stage 3 involved detailed planning and production of module documentation

In order to make the module more appealing (and useful) for students we were very keen to involve external speakers and employment specialists in its delivery and also to build in opportunities for students to experience 'real-world' activities such as employer recruitment events and networking and assessment centre practice. Much time was spent on the telephone in an attempt to source some form of industry sponsorship and those I contacted were, in the main, extremely enthusiastic and keen to help in any way they could. In addition to securing almost £3,000 from the Savoy Educational Trust, I was also able to engage a range of external specialists who were prepared to contribute their time and company resources either free or at cost.

Once this was accomplished, the next task was to put together the study schedule for the module. The study schedule is designed to help students move from a process of self-analysis to an understanding of labour-market opportunities so that they can match their skills to those sought by prospective employers. The second part of the module focuses on developing students' 'job-getting' skills (e.g. CV writing, selection tests, time management, career planning) so that they are equipped with the ability to secure employment. At this stage, a key task was to develop the module assignment and assessment criteria (see Table 1). The use of a portfolio for assessing student learning is consistent with the self-development and reflective practice philosophy underpinning the module (Kolb, 1984; Schön, 1983 and 1987). It is an approach that is also found useful for continuing professional development used in the workplace (Pedler, Burgoyne and

> I was also able to engage a range of external specialists who were prepared to contribute their time and company resources either free or at cost

Boydell, 1994). The inclusion of a CV and personal statement within the portfolio also meets the university's requirement for PDP. The assessment criteria grid in Table 1 is based on research conducted by Price and Rust (2004) and is designed to provide guidance for students in producing their assignment, as well as being a means of summatively assessing their achievement of the learning outcomes for the module. Although students were not in class every week, the module handbook contained weekly self-study activities and reading to help students build towards the production of their portfolio.

Table 1 Assessment criteria grid

Criterion	A (85–100%)	A (70–84%)	B+ (60–69%)	B (50–59%)	C (40–49%)	Refer (30–39%)	Fail (0–29%)
Reflection and analysis							
Reflection/ evaluation	Demonstrates an outstanding ability to critically reflect on and evaluate personal development and employability skills	Strong evidence of an ability to critically reflect on and evaluate personal development and employability skills	Evidence of an ability to reflect on personal development and employability skills	Evidence of an ability to collate information on personal development and make vlinks to employability skills	Limited evidence of ability to collate information on personal development. Reflections on employability skills may be weak or partial	Little evidence of ability to present a coherent evaluation or reflection on personal development or employability skills	An unbalanced response to the assignment task. Material of little relevance to personal development or employability
Critical reasoning and analysis	Consistently demonstrates application of critical analysis to concepts underpinning graduate employability	Clear application of theory on graduate employability through critical analysis of topic area	Demonstrates an application of theory through critical analysis of topic area	Some evidence of critical thought/ critical analysis on theories of employability	Can analyse a limited range of information on graduate employability	Little or no analysis of information on graduate employability	Fails to evaluate or analyse information on graduate employability
Content and knowledge							
Knowledge of theory	Assignment demonstrates a high level of integration and innovation in the selection and synthesis of theory	Assignment demonstrates integration and innovation in the selection and synthesis of theory	Insightful and appropriate selection of theory in key areas	Most key theories are included in the work in an appropriate and straight forward manner	Selection of theory is appropriate but some aspects have been missed or misconstrued	Lacks evidence of knowledge relevant to topic, inaccurate or inappropriate choice of theory	Little or no evidence of knowledge of appropriate theory
Use of literature/ evidence of reading	Evidence of an ability to read widely and critically and research independently	Strong evidence of independent research and a wide range of reading effectively used in assignment	Evidence of appropriate reading and ability to use a range of sources to develop own ideas	Evidence of an ability to select appropriate material from different sources and apply them appropriately in assignment	Evidence of selection of some relevant material but evidence may not be used accurately	No evidence of reading beyond minimum directed reading or course handouts. No analysis or interpretation	No evidence of literature being used or irrelevant to the assignment set

Criterion	A (85-100%)	A (70-84%)	B+ (60-69%)	B (50-59%)	C (40-49%)	Refer (30-39%)	Fail (0-29%)
Evidence of interpersonal skills development							
Self-presentation and self-development	Presents excellent quality CV, personal statement and career plan clearly developed from participation on self-development activities	Presents a high quality CV, personal statement and career plan. Evidence of participation in self-development activities is effectively presented	Presents a good quality CV, personal statement and career plan. Some evidence of participation in self-development activities will be presented in a coherent manner	Presents a CV, personal statement and career plan, although these may require further development. Evidence of participation in some self-development activities	Presents a CV, personal statement and career plan. These documents are in need of much further development. Evidence of participation in self-development activities is limited	Fails to present one or more of required self-presentation documents. Little evidence of participation in self-development activities	Self-presentation documents are missing or inadequate. Little or no evidence of participation in self-development activities
Presentation and style							
Presentation of assignment	Shows polished and highly imaginative approach to assignment presentation. Appendices used to maximum effect	Material is imaginatively presented, resulting in clarity of message and information. Appendices used very effectively	Material is carefully structured and logically organised with clear message. Appendices well-organised with relevant materials	Shows organisation and coherence in presentation of assignment. Some use of appendices for relevant materials	Shows some attempt to organise material in a logical manner, but lacks structure and/or is difficult to follow. Appendices not used/ not used to good effect	Material is presented in a disorganised or incoherent manner	Significant omission of relevant materials with unstructured and unfocused format
Clarity of expression (incl. accuracy, grammar, spelling, punctuation)	Articulate and fluent writing style appropriate to document. Grammar and spelling accurate	Clear and fluent writing style appropriate to document. Grammar and spelling accurate	Language fluent. Grammar and spelling accurate	Language mainly fluent. Grammar and spelling mainly accurate	Meaning apparent but language not always fluent. Contains grammatical and/or spelling errors	Language lacks coherence and meaning unclear. Frequent errors in spelling and/or grammar	Language significantly flawed and meaning unclear. Frequent errors in spelling and/or grammar
Conforming with instructions (incl. referencing and word length)	Assignment has been submitted within time boundaries, within word-limit and referencing is accurate		Assignment has been submitted within time boundaries, within word-limit and referencing is accurate		Assignment deviates slightly from word-limit (no more than 10%) and/or referencing is partially inaccurate	Assignment deviates significantly from word-limit (more than 10%) and/or referencing is largely inaccurate	Assignment deviates significantly from word-limit (more than 10%) and/or referencing is largely inaccurate/ absent

Module delivery

This section discusses the actual delivery of the module. My intention here is to highlight key aspects of the module and its impact on student development, rather than cover all the taught sessions in detail.

Self-analysis and self-awareness

The first session on the module reminds students of the concept of self-development and reflective learning. Students make connections between this approach and their own continuing professional development. An external training company provided students with the opportunity to complete an online assessment of their work preferences and work motivations (information on this test can be found at http://www.jobeq.com/applications.htm). A specialist from the company debriefed the students on their results and how these could be used to help them understand which

> a significant number of students revised their career aspirations as a result of understanding better their personal motivations and thinking about what might be a fulfilling career for them

types of organisation or work environment might best suit their profile.

Following this session, an employment consultant specialising in career coaching delivered a highly imaginative and interactive session, encouraging students to develop a clear vision of where they wanted to be in ten years' time. The session required students to write a series of very specific steps that would enable them to attain their vision or goal.

Both of these sessions produced some really interesting reactions in the students who found the sessions very engaging and useful in helping them clarify what it was they needed to be considering. One outcome was that a significant number of students revised their career aspirations as a result of understanding better their personal motivations and thinking about what might be a fulfilling career for them. Rather than focusing on securing a 'typical' graduate traineeship with a large company (which is how most had envisaged the 'right type of career'), some students now focused their research on smaller companies or on

niche occupations. This outcome, in my opinion, was significant as it meant that students were developing a better understanding of themselves and what they wanted from life (a crucial aspect of increasing their self-confidence). It also meant that students could adopt a job search strategy that would enable them to identify more accurately which skills they would need for successful employment in their chosen career.

Awareness of labour market opportunities

This was developed and encouraged in a number of ways. In addition to a session delivered by two international recruitment specialists in hospitality and tourism, students were directed to a wide range of resources that would help them assess career opportunities for graduates. The *Prospects* website was a particularly useful resource and provided students with a wide range of advice and guidance on job searching. In addition to this, students were offered the opportunity to attend employer presentations organised by our departmental Careers and Work Experience office. These weekly presentations were delivered by a wide range of hospitality and tourism employers, some of whom interviewed students for graduate positions on campus.

Students on the module were given the opportunity to 'host' at one of these employers events. This might involve meeting and greeting, taking the employer to lunch and/or ensuring the employer was shown to the right room and that all the equipment was in order. This provided students with a chance to meet one-on-one with an employer they might be very keen to work for and to develop their interpersonal and networking skills. Students were also required to attend two additional sessions organised by the Careers and Work Experience office. One, called Focus on Careers, involves a panel of senior employers from various industry sectors who each present for ten minutes on what they look for in graduate recruits. This is followed by a Q&A session where students can ask specific questions of the panel and, later, an informal wine reception where students can talk directly and informally to the employers. The second session is a networking evening which is organised in association with our departmental alumni association (Bacchus). The evening allows current students to speak with

Table 2 Aspects of employability

A Personal qualities

1 Malleable self theory: belief that attributes (e.g. intelligence) are not fixed and can be developed
2 Self-awareness: awareness of own strengths and weaknesses, aims and values
3 Self-confidence: confidence in dealing with the challenges in employment and life
4 Independence: ability to work without supervision
5 Emotional intelligence: sensitivity to others' emotions and the effects they can have
6 Adaptability: ability to respond positively to changing circumstances and new challenges
7 Stress tolerance: ability to retain effectiveness under pressure
8 Initiative: ability to take action unprompted
9 Willingness to learn: commitment to ongoing learning to meet the needs of employment and life
10 Reflectiveness: the disposition to reflect evaluatively on the performance of oneself and others

B Core skills

11 Reading effectiveness: the recognition and retention of key points
12 Numeracy: ability to use numbers at an appropriate level of accuracy
13 Information retrieval: ability to access different information sources
14 Language skills: possession of more than a single language
15 Self-management: ability to work in an efficient and structured manner
16 Critical analysis: ability to 'deconstruct' a problem or situation
17 Creativity: ability to be original or inventive and to apply lateral thinking
18 Listening: focused attention in which key points are recognised
19 Written communication: clear reports, letters etc., written specifically for the reader
20 Oral presentations: clear and confident presentation of information to a group
21 Explaining: orally and in writing
22 Global awareness: in terms of both cultures and economics

C Process skills

23 Computer literacy: ability to use a range of software
24 Commercial awareness: understanding of business issues and priorities
25 Political sensitivity: appreciates how organisations actually work and acts accordingly
26 Ability to work cross-culturally: both within and beyond UK
27 Ethical sensitivity: appreciates ethical aspects of employment and acts accordingly
28 Prioritising: ability to rank tasks according to importance
29 Planning: setting of achievable goals and structuring action
30 Applying subject understanding: use of disciplinary understanding from HE programme (e.g. marketing, finance, human resource management etc)
31 Acting morally: has a moral code and acts accordingly
32 Coping with ambiguity and complexity: ability to handle ambiguous and complex situations
33 Problem-solving: selection and use of appropriate methods to find solutions
34 Influencing: convincing others of the validity of one's point of view
35 Arguing for and/or justifying a point of view or a course of action
36 Resolving conflict: both intra-personally and in relationships with others
37 Decision-making: choice of the best option from a range of alternatives
38 Negotiating: discussion to achieve mutually satisfactory resolution of contentious issues
39 Teamwork: can work constructively with others on a common task

---

Oxford Brookes hospitality and tourism graduates over a meal in the Brookes restaurant. There are one or two graduates per table and students move around at regular intervals to talk to graduates about their career to date and to pick up top tips on how to make the transition from university to work.

This combination of employer presentations, labour-market research and advice and personal networking opportunities raised students' awareness of the graduate labour market and its opportunities and encouraged them to develop a suitable job search strategy, perhaps exploring career options they might not initially have considered. More important, this exposure to employers and graduates made students far more realistic about what to expect in terms of career opportunities (unrealistic and inflated expectations were a major criticism cited by the graduate recruiters and employers I spoke with as part of my initial research).

Awareness of graduate attributes

In addition to the exposure to employers and graduates cited above, students were required to evaluate critically the research that has been carried out into graduate employability and graduate attributes. The first part of the portfolio assignment is designed to focus attention on the types of attributes that lead to graduate success and how these relate to the industry or sector where the student is seeking employment. The students are encouraged to reflect on their own skills for employment by assessing themselves against graduate attributes lists (see Table 2) and using self-analysis tools such as those contained in the Windmills Programme (http://www.windmillsprogramme.com).

Students are encouraged to identify any potential skills 'gaps' and to plan for how they can overcome these by engaging in appropriate development activities. It is interesting to note that they reported an improvement

| students reported an improvement in their vocabulary about employability and felt better able to articulate their attributes to potential employers

in their vocabulary about employability and felt better able to articulate their attributes to potential employers (see CV-writing discussion below). Students were also able to see more clearly the skills they possessed and how their higher education experiences had enabled them to develop their attributes for employment. Helping students see the relationship between education and employment was a key objective of the module. It was very rewarding to see students begin to understand this for themselves.

Job-getting skills (including articulating and evidencing achievement)

Knowledge of their own employment skills, the career opportunities available and graduate attributes is perhaps of only limited use if the students cannot translate this in some practical sense to actually getting a graduate job. Students need to have an ability to sell themselves effectively in the employment market both on paper (e.g. excellent CV, cover letter, application, selection tests) and in person (e.g. great interview skills, interpersonal communication and networking abilities). Underpinning these practical skills is the need for students to be able to manage time and prioritise tasks effectively. Graduate recruiters and employers I spoke to were unanimous in their disappointment with the quality of job applications and CVs they received from students about to graduate and with students' inability to properly organise themselves and manage their time and tasks when they did start work.

The module provided a session on CV writing and applications delivered by a recruitment specialist followed by practical workshops on developing CVs and covering letters. Students were directed to a range of paper and online resources to help them develop their job application- and CV-writing skills and were offered feedback on their draft CVs by module tutors. To be frank, it came as somewhat of a shock to see for myself the very poor quality of students' first attempts at producing a CV; I was extremely pleased that tutor feedback and advice had been offered as part of the module prior to students submitting CVs to potential employers. Students were also given an opportunity to practise selection tests under test conditions and to engage in mock interviews with peer feedback. The portfolio assignment required students to produce a CV and cover letter or personal statement targeted at a particular graduate position. This enabled students to practise summarising their achievements and skills in a way that made their applications attractive to employers. Students were also required to reflect on how they could evidence their skills for employment and to incorporate this into the reflective commentary section of the portfolio.

The feedback from students was interesting. The majority had never really thought about how they might evidence their skills, and many assumed that employers would accept that having a degree was evidence enough of their abilities and skills. Although students struggled at first with evidencing skills, with some prompting and support, they became more confident about how they might do this. A really pleasing side-effect of this process was that it enabled students to see just how much they had to offer and what they had achieved both within and outside their formal study programme. Students were encouraged to celebrate their successes. Again this helped build their self-confidence and to made the important link between their educational and personal achievements and the world of work.

Mock assessment centre

Towards the end of the module a half-day mock assessment centre exercise was held off-campus at a local hotel. The focus of the assessment centre was to give students an opportunity to experience a 'real-world' exercise that would allow them to bring together their learning from various stages of the module. Amongst other things, the focus was on helping students develop their time-management, decision-making and prioritising skills and to feel what it was like to complete activities under time pressure (experiences difficult to emulate in the traditional classroom).

The assessment centre was organised by the teaching team and involved students in a series of team-building and decision-making activities, time-management/prioritising (in-tray) exercises, selection tests and one-on-one performance feedback. The fact that the day was delivered by very experienced human resource managers from the hospitality industry and held off campus, which really added to the authenticity of the event and gave students a taste of what it would feel like to experience the real thing.

The students' response to the day was hugely positive although they found the in-tray exercises difficult and many commented that the selection tests were something they needed to go away and practise.

It was very gratifying to witness the reactions of students both during and after the event – they found the day challenging, but really enjoyable. Many of them emailed me later in the year to let me know how much the exercise had helped them when they came to participate in a real assessment centre.

> they found the day challenging, but really enjoyable. Many of them emailed me later in the year to let me know how much it had helped them when they participated in a real assessment centre

useful' in preparing them for their career. The quality of portfolios submitted was very good overall and student achievement in terms of grades attained was above average compared to the average for other level three/honours modules (59% compared with an average mark of 54% across level three modules).

Tutors

Tutors were impressed with the enthusiasm demonstrated by the students studying this module and reported higher than average levels of attendance in the taught sessions. They were also impressed with the high quality of student assignments. The teaching team was initially concerned about whether students would engage with academic literature at an appropriate level, but it was encouraging to see some excellent analytical reports on graduate employability and the labour market. Many students also effectively used literature on career management and self-development in their assignment.

External examiner

The external examiner's comments were encouraging. He felt that this was one of the best modules he had examined on this topic. I quote:

> 'An interesting module with some innovative angles. The guest speakers in semester one represent an informative basis for the student's assessments in semester two.
>
> The module handbook is very thorough and the module is sound in terms of aims and objectives with relevant learning outcomes to the students' needs. The feedback is thorough and moderation apparent, resulting in fair and consistent marking.
>
> The self-reflection is in the main excellent and the better performing students made good use of the theoretical frameworks.
>
> The report structure worked well, with the focus on reflection and interpretation rather than just data regurgitation.'

Evaluation

Much of the discussion outlined above is based on informal feedback from students during the delivery of the module and my own observations. In addition, a more formal evaluation of the module was conducted using a questionnaire completed by students during the final taught session.

Students

The feedback from students was overwhelmingly positive: they reported good progress in the key areas of self-awareness, self-confidence, labour-market awareness, understanding of graduate attributes and job application skills. A high proportion of students (84%) agreed that the module had been 'very/quite

Discussion

This case study has presented one example of how Oxford Brookes University is developing the employability of its students by providing them with the skills and knowledge to plan for their future career. At the heart of this approach is the philosophy of creating a learning environment that values and promotes self-reflection and values experiential learning. This phiolosophy infuses the entire curriculum and is central to our approach to learning and teaching on this module.

References and URLs

Kolb, D. A. 1984. *Experiential Learning: Experience as the source of learning and development.* New Jersey: Prentice Hall

Pedler, M., Burgoyne, J. and Boydell, T. 1994. *A Manager's Guide to Self-Development,* 4th edn. Maidenhead: McGraw Hill

Price, M. and Rust, C. 2004. *Assessment Grid.* York: HE Academy http://www.heacademy.ac.uk/resources.asp

Prospects Website http://www.prospects.ac.uk/cms/

http://www.qaa.ac.uk/academicinfrastructure/progress-Files/guidelines/progfile2001.asp

Schön, D. A. 1983. *The Reflective Practitioner: How Professionals Think In Action.* New York: Basic Books

Schön, D. A. 1987. *Educating the Reflective Practitioner.* San Francisco: Jossey Bass

ANGELA MAHER is Senior Lecturer in Hospitality Management at Oxford Brookes University. Her research and teaching lie in the areas of human resource management and employability. Angela is currently Project Director for a HEFCE-funded project which focuses on enhancing graduate employability amongst hospitality, leisure, sport and tourism students. Angela teaches Career Planning and also manages work experience for both undergraduate and postgraduate hospitality and tourism students at Oxford Brookes.

Integrating and embedding employability 4

Graham Holden

Through the evaluation of BSc (Hons) Business and Technology at Sheffield Hallam University, we have identified core attributes – transferable to any course – that enhance student employability. Through practical examples, this case study demonstrates how these features have been implemented in an undergraduate programme of study.

The attributes of student employability are summarised by the Sheffield Hallam Employability Framework, which is combined with:

- a learning environment which encourages autonomy and personal development
- a student-centred approach to support and guidance
- a strong emphasis on Personal Development Planning (PDP)
- an innovative approach to learning, teaching and assessment
- a strategic and collaborative approach to curriculum design and course management, based on strong relationships with key stakeholders such as careers guidance, employers and external advisors.

This case study provides evidence that 'integrated embedding' of employability is the most effective way to achieve full engagement by students and to enhance their employability within the context of widening access to higher education.

Objectives

As part of the process of applying for a Centre for Excellence in Teaching and Learning (CETL) in Employability at Sheffield Hallam University, teaching programmes were evaluated. The evaluation team wanted to identify examples at Sheffield Hallam of excellence in embedding and enhancing employability. Courses selected through learning, teaching and assessment networks were rigorously evaluated through student outcomes and interviews with staff about practice. The evaluators looked for triangulation by reviewing evidence from course meetings and external examiners' comments, as well as consulting final-year students in a structured group session about what helped them.

Four programmes met the stringent criteria set by the team. For the business and technology degree, there were excellent key performance indicators on employability. Both students and employers provided unsolicited support and evidence of employability enhancement.

I have used the skills learned on my course and throughout my placement, time and time again. (Student)

It was evident that his [the student's] *perspectives during problem-solving and general discussions were wider and more comprehensive than one would normally expect from a business studies student.* (Employer)

This case study identifies the key features of the business and technology degree that have enabled it to yield such excellent outcomes. Similar features could be adopted by other courses across Sheffield Hallam and other higher education institutions.

Context

The BSC (Hons) Business and Technology course is a four-year sandwich degree, incorporating a year-long placement in industry in the third year of study. The course aims to enhance the employability of all its students by providing a vocational, commercially relevant programme of study developing technically literate, reflective practitioners for managerial roles in commerce and industry. The course has been specifically designed to be accessible to a diverse student population. The course has over 200 students drawn from diverse backgrounds and achieves excellent employability outcomes in relation to the modest entry qualifications required. It demonstrates outstanding retention rates, first destination statistics and good degree statistics in relation to the university and across the higher education sector.

The embedding of employability is integral to the culture of the course. This view of employability mirrors that of the university, focusing on the enhance-

> students' success (over 80%) in getting placements and jobs within six months of graduation … the range of jobs students are willing to consider … our observation that students more autonomous

ment of lifelong employability, reflecting research on the graduate attributes sought by employers: intelligent, flexible, self-aware lifelong learners with communication, interactive and teamworking skills, who add value to and transform organisations.

This course culture, developed over a number of years, can be summarised by:

❑ A learning environment in which mutual respect and honesty encourage autonomy and personal development.
❑ A student-centred approach to support and guidance.
❑ A strong emphasis on Personal Development Planning (PDP) linked strongly to learning from work, career management and the provision of opportunities.
❑ An innovative approach to learning, teaching and assessment – the course was an early adopter of e-learning.
❑ A strategic and collaborative approach to cur-

riculum design and course management building on excellent relationships with Careers and Employment Service, Learning and Teaching Institute, employers and external advisors.

Description

The framework builds on its definition of employability –

enabling students to acquire the knowledge, personal and professional skills and encouraging the attitudes that will support their future development

– by specifying curriculum features that, together, develop student employability. Its coherent conceptual base draws on a model of employability development and is firmly rooted in relevant literature, research and many years of practice. Brown and Drew (2005) discuss it in detail, but the framework's essential features are:

❑ progressive development of autonomy
    ❑ skills development (intellectual; subject; professional; key skills)
    ❑ Personal Development Planning (PDP)
    ❑ inclusion of activities similar to those required in external environments i.e. 'the real world' (to encourage transfer)
❑ reflection on the use of knowledge and skills (to encourage transfer)
❑ encouragement of career management skills
❑ engagement with learning from work (LfW)
❑ preparation for professions
❑ engagement with enterprise.

Evaluation

How does the business and technology degree enhance employability so well? We feel certain that it is through the integrated embedding of employability. Here are examples of how the course meets each aspect of Sheffield Hallam's Employability Framework with summaries of the supporting evidence.

The progressive development of autonomy

This is characterised by ongoing but decreasing student support, increasingly critical feedback, increase in peer support and tasks with more responsibility.

For example:

Year one: Through structured Personal Development Planning (PDP) sessions, embedded within a content focused module, students are supported to clarify expectations, identify strengths and weaknesses and submit personal development action plans which are assessed by personal tutors. Personal tutors provide structured feedback at key points throughout the year.

Year two: Students share coursework online, receive immediate feedback and present their final assessment to employers as well as to academic staff.

Placement year: All students are required to undertake a training year in which the need to work without close supervision is a key attribute required by all employers.

Final year: Students undertake a business-consultancy project where tutors role-play as employers. Students are also required to undertake a dissertation based on their work experience in which they apply academic theory from their course to a real-world problem.

Among the supporting evidence and outcomes, we cite: the students' approach to learning in the final year (e.g. use made of dissertation supervisors); improving grades against learning outcomes through the levels; good quality work in relation to modest entry qualifications; a final dissertation (which contextualises skills developed); formalised feedback from external examiners; workplace supervisors; employers and excellent (and rising) attainment statistics since 2000.

Skills development

There is a strong focus from day one on the continual development of skills. For example:

- Skills expectations are clarified at induction, e.g. the ESECT Employability Card Sort is used to help students to reflect on expectations, linking to PDP sessions and leading to first assessment.
- Intellectual skills are embedded in subject-learning outcomes at each level of the degree.
- Specified key skills learning outcomes/assessment criteria are applied in all modules, developing through the course. Assessment tasks require the development and demonstration of specific skills, with support and guidance (e.g. use of Key Skills Online).

Among the supporting evidence and outcomes are very good retention rates; high levels of student achievement against learning outcomes; students' success in getting placements and final employment; feedback from graduates and employers; external examiners' comments on performance; the Annual Quality Review and destination statistics.

Personal Development Planning (PDP)

The Dearing Report of 1997 recommended the adoption of student progress files at all levels of higher education as a 'means by which students can monitor, build and reflect upon their personal development'. They have been systematically built into the Business and Technology programme to support PDP and provide a coherent focus for the continual development of skills throughout the student's academic career.

PDP (see Figure 1) is supported and assessed across all levels and integrated into the preparation for and assessment of the training year. It is a support mechanism to enable students to:

- Develop skills of reflection on their academic, personal and professional development within clearly defined (safe) boundaries.
- Increase self-awareness of and confidence in, their own skills, qualities, attitudes and capabilities.
- Set goals and action plans to develop, monitor and review their own progress.
- Improve their own learning and attainment by developing as an autonomous learner.
- Compile a record of their learning experiences and achievements, progress reviews, personal reflections and action plans.
- Plan realistically and manage their own career development.

At each level of the course, a module provides the focus for development and assessment of PDP, for which students can access online materials in the university's virtual learning environment. PDP focuses on process (review-reflect-action plan), not just on the production of a progress file:

- **Year one:** Focuses on personal development. Students review and reflect on experiences and compare their action plan against personal expectations. Action plans are assessed against criteria (the whole staff team is involved).
- **Year two:** Focuses on work experience/placement preparation. Action plans reflect on students'

Figure 1 Personal Development Planning (PDP)

Key features

- PDP is embedded into a key module at each level
- Skills are assessed in individual modules – governed by a skills matrix for the whole course
- PDP assessment is focused on process of Review, Reflect and Action Plan, supported by evidence – not files
- Blackboard has been used to enable and support the process but the activities also make use of meetings and paper-based resources with some electronic submission and feedback
- PDP/Placements tutor co-ordinates the process from level 4 to level 6
- PDP is strongly linked to placements at all levels
- PDP assessment is performed by personal tutors at level 4 and visiting tutors (placement) at level 6

Year one

- PDP embedded within 20-credit module interfaces
  - → 30% of module assessment is based on PDP
  - → other assessed work in module relates to development of relevant skills
- PDP starts in induction and is 'front-loaded'
- Support materials for PDP accessed thro module Blackboard site
- Module co-ordinates support for key skills through a seminar.programme,seminar programme, personal tutor meetings and Blackboard site
- PDP assessment performed by personal tutors
- Skills audit and personal review
- CV and covering letter
- Progress review
- Reflection on level 4 and Action Plan for level 5

Year two

- PDP focuses on support for placement
- PDP embedded within 20-credit module Web Technology
  - → 20% of module assessment is based on PDP
  - → other assessed work in module relates to placement preparation
- Support materials for PDP accessed through module Blackboard site – electronic submission and email feedback
- Module co-ordinates placement support such as CVs, Application Forms through seminars and review meetings, links to careers
- PDP assessment focuses on action planning and reflection on placement process

Placement year

- Students visited twice by tutor
- Students are encouraged to keep a logbook or learning diary which might include:
  - → job description, roles, responsibilities etc
  - → notes of meetings with supervisors
  - → evidence of action planning
  - → evidence of meetings attended or workshops
- Employers required to assess the student at two points in the year
- Formal assessment in level-six module Professional Practice (10 credits)

Final year

- The focus and assessment of PDP is the ten-credit module Professional Practice – this has three elements:
  - → Placement report – a report which describes and reflects on the placement experience
  - → Poster Day – open to year one, year two, employers
  - → Employer assessments
- Input from Careers encouraging career management skills at the start of the final year

current position, identify goals and identify employability 'gaps', e.g. should they participate in Hallam Volunteering?

- **Final year:** PDP is located in the Professional Practice module in which students reflect on placement experiences and identify career action plans.

Among supporting evidence and outcomes we again cite the high retention rate (above 85%). Students demonstrate their ability to reflect and create action plans and they can articulate where this was located within their course. Comments received from tutors indicate how well focused these students are compared to those on other courses.

'Real-world' case studies and activities

We know that examples of these can be found at all levels, including reports, presentations and teamwork.

- **Year one:** Students undertake market analysis with information gathering, extensive use of IT (spreadsheets, databases, etc).
- **Year two:** Students evaluate new product development opportunities and develop customer database.
- **Final year:** Students participate in a year-long small business planning simulation assessed by externals – bank managers, 'business angels'.

Among supporting evidence

and outcomes we cite levels of achievement against learning outcomes: students' preparation for work activities; examples of students' work; feedback from workplace supervisors on students' performance in work tasks; and the fact that 10–15 externals take part in the final-year simulation – they come because it provides them with new ideas.

Reflection on the use of knowledge and skills

PDP runs throughout the course and includes assessed reflective activities. Some examples:

- **Year one:** Students do a 'mock' presentation, reflect on it and receive feedback before an assessed presentation.
- **Year two:** Students give peer feedback on reports prior to final submission.
- **Final year:** In their Professional Practice module, after placement, students display posters about their placement, how they got it and what they learned. Year two students and employers attend, assess the posters and give feedback.

Among supporting evidence and outcomes we cite their action plans that show that students are able to make connections between the course and work.

Encouragement of career management skills

PDP has a strong career management focus from the start. In each year employers are encouraged to participate by the careers and employment service.

- **Year one:** Students reflect on their position and goals, produce CVS and covering letters to a job specification.
- **Year two:** Students prepare an action plan for how to 'plug' any employability gaps (perhaps through extra-curricular activities). Students are supported in their job application skills by a Blackboard placement site which advertises opportunities, pro-

vides access to company and job specifications and offers other resources such as Key Skills Online; Careers Service website.

- **Final year:** In their placement report students are required to identify goals for the next five years and prepare an assessed action plan to achieve them.

As evidence we cite: students' success (over 80%) in getting placements and jobs within six months of graduation; the range of jobs students are willing to consider; our observation that students more autonomous; the effects of feedback on changing student behaviour and improvement in grades.

Learning from Work linked to a compulsory training year

The BSC (Hons) Business and Technology is a four-year sandwich course incorporating an industrial training placement which is typically 48 weeks long. Students with relevant prior work experience may be able to gain credit through the APEL (Accredited Prior Experiential Learning) process and can then complete the degree in three years full-time.

Figure 2   Year-one PDP activities

The following assessment activities contribute 30% of the assessment mark to a 20-credit year-one module which also focuses on the development of IT skills.

1   Skills audit and action plan

Students are required to submit for the first assessment a 250-word commentary reflecting on personal and academic achievements to date. The assessment must identify those areas in which students feel they need to improve and an action plan to explain how they will improve attainment in these areas. This is assessed and handed back in the first meeting with the student's personal tutor.

2   CV and covering letter

Students are required to write a CV and covering letter in application for the post of marketing assistant at a ghost company. This is handed back in the second meeting with a personal tutor.

3   Progress review and tutor assessments

Students are required to attend three meetings with their personal tutor and a formal progress review with their year tutor. These meetings include a discussion of marks and attendance as well as achievements and general overall progress.

4   Review of year one and action plan for year two

Students are required to submit a 500-word commentary reflecting on their personal and academic achievements in their first year in HE, . They are also required to submit an action plan identifying those areas in which they feel they need to improve, with appropriate actions, to gain the most from their second year of study.

During the placement year, the employer and the university share responsibility for supervising the student. The student's academic tutor and the course placement tutor monitor progress and provide support to the student, employer and workplace supervisor. Students gain credit for the placement (ten credits in the final year) by undertaking the module Professional Practice while on training placement.

The placement year is a vital element of the course (arguably the most important) in which students gain real work experience. The placement must involve responsibility, but it should also consolidate and put into practice students' prior learning, so that they practise and develop their skills and formulate career plans.

All students do a Placement and Professional Practice module or a module about learning from other work experiences (such as a year out, setting up their own business, multiple work experiences).

While on placement students have three mini-appraisals with their workplace supervisor. They must also submit assessed deliverables: a report, with an action plan for the next five years, the employer's assessment against stated criteria and a poster. Quality of the placement is ensured through moderation, tutor visits, other visits if there are problems – and email contact.

For those not on placement undertaking the Learning from Work module, there is a Blackboard site with peer support and tutor support online.

As evidence we cite: improvement in coursework after placement; students' ability to cope well with placements and to contextualise their learning; the high rate of employment on graduation; favourable external examiner and employer comments – and so are students' placement reports.

Enterprise

From the outset, Business and Technology has provided its students with a range of experiences during which to practise the skills and apply the knowledge gained in other parts of the programme. The enterprise theme is a series of elective units. There are no prerequisites to impede progression or students joining at various points along the way. These modules form a coherent series which, if taken completely, make up a mini-strand. As any engineer will know, the process of design is not linear, requiring iteration and invariably modification before an idea is realised.

The enterprise modules endeavour to break down the process into a number

---

Educational aims

The placement year will provide all students with:

- Preparation for a career in business and management by experiencing an extended period of training within an organisation.
- Relevant work experience providing the opportunity to put prior learning into practice, illustrating the level and extent required in employment
- Personal and professional development through exposure to a supportive work environment and professional colleagues.
- The context and focus for a final-year dissertation enabling the student to focus on the analysis of a real business problem.
- The opportunity to formulate future career plans based on experience of working in a commercial environment.

Learning outcomes

At the end of the placement year the student will be able to:

- Demonstrate an in-depth knowledge of organisations, their management and the changing external environments (economic, technical, social, political) in which they operate. (Knowledge and comprehension)
- Summarise essential and other important aspects of a business or technical subject, and synthesize information, making and justifying links between subject areas. (Cognitive)
- Make and justify decisions about information and situations which are complex and (maybe) unpredictable. (Subject-specific)
- Identify, justify and use methods of analysis and enquiry which are appropriate to solve business-related problems (including those self-initiated). (Subject-specific)
- Select and use appropriate techniques, process and terminology depending upon the task and the business or technical context. (Subject-specific)
- Extend and improve knowledge, learning and performance by applying methods and techniques, learnt for example in a new situation. (Professional)
- Draw upon the knowledge and experience of others to establish the range of skills and knowledge of workplace issues demanded in areas of employment relevant to their own future careers. (Professional)
- Articulate and reflect on the key elements of a successful job application procedure, within the context of developmental work on preparation for employment. (Professional)
- Evaluate, reflect on and form action plans to improve their own skills in relation to employability, within the context of the course and take responsibility for own learning

---

of stand-alone yet identifiable phases of the process, which – when combined and mastered – will provide the student with the tools to maximise the chances that a novel idea will succeed. If individuals are entrepreneurial, giving them the relevant tools will make them more successful. Likewise, if some individuals are not entrepreneurial, providing them with these tools will make them better employees.

For example, our students in year one identify opportunities to market a product. In year two, they explore how others identify opportunities and develop products and as a case study they innovate for a customer. In the final year they prepare a business plan for a small business. They also engage in extra curricular activities, such as the Learn to Lead course run by Sheffield Chamber of Commerce, or participate in the IBM business Planning Competition.

As evidence, we can point to students' willingness to work in SMEs (the placement trend is to work for an SME). Over the two years, five students have set up businesses during their placement year and after the course two students have started their own micro-businesses. Achievement of learning outcomes is reflected in improving grades through the levels, showing added value. We can also cite employers' comments on the commercial awareness of students and feedback from students and externals.

Discussion

This paper has identified practical ways in which the features of Sheffield Hallam's Employability Framework can be made to 'come alive' in a real programme of study. In addition, this case study also illustrates the types of evidence that can be gathered to determine whether employability has indeed been enhanced. The methods, summarised below, used by the Business and Technology degree to embed employability, offer a strong base from which to extend practice across Sheffield Ha[...] higher education institutions.

The programme shares the p[...] Employability Framework, referring[...] learning, to the 'reflective practitio[...] importance of context, with learning (e.g. skills development) situated in the subject, 'real world' activities and Learning for Work. There is a clear articulation of aims, learning outcomes and practices. The programme leaders believe in empowerment, in valuing students and their owning of their learning.

The programme uses a variety of learning, teaching and assessment methods in meeting students' differing

> The enterprise modules endeavour to break down the process into a number of phases which ... will provide the student with the tools to maximise the chances that a novel idea will succeed

needs (e.g. problem-based learning: a blend of direct contact, module tasks and Blackboard). Assessment is used for learning, with clear assessment criteria and extensive feedback.

The programme has a stable and effective course team with strong leadership, adopting team teaching, formal staff roles, funded projects and champions to develop innovation and support the embedding process. The team sees active collaboration with external contacts as crucial in embedding practice and there is extensive collaboration other faculties and Sheffield Hallam infrastructure elements (e.g. Careers Service).

Formal review and action planning points are embedded within the programme. At least every six years, revalidation provides a major opportunity for re-planning, involving employers and other stakeholders. Annual programme reviews draw on staff reflections, course team or moderation meetings and student, employer and external examiner feedback to identify actions and check progress from previous reviews.

Reference

rown, S. and Drew, S. 2005. Developing an employability framework: an institutional approach. ESECT Conference: Enhancing Student Employability, Birmingham.

GRAHAM HOLDEN The work for this paper was undertaken when Graham was Course Leader for a multi-disciplinary degree Business and IT. Subsequently he moved to the Learning and Teaching Institute at Sheffield Hallam University where he leads the University's Assessment for Learning Initiative.

A Nottingham Business School degree to enhance graduate employability

Vanessa Knowles

This case study is an overview of BA (Hons) Business Management (In-Company) – an undergraduate degree programme designed and implemented by Nottingham Business School – which specifically aims to enhance graduate employability. In addition to highlighting the distinctive features of the degree, it also provides key findings from research undertaken with students and graduates, academic staff and company representatives who sponsor the two-year 'in-company' period which offers a unique work-based learning experience.

Research conducted to date suggests that simply having a degree does not in itself secure employment. It is a combination of knowledge, skills and attitudes – developed here through the particular design features of the BA (Hons) Business Management (In-Company) degree – that has an impact on employability.

Objectives

The objectives of this case study are:

1 To provide an overview of an approach undertaken by Nottingham Business School (NBS) to design an innovative undergraduate level degree programme that aims to enhance graduate employability.
2 To highlight the key distinctive features of the degree design that distinguish the programme from traditional sandwich degree programmes in the UK.
3 To provide summary evaluative information on the key success factors of the degree to date which have been derived from a range of stakeholders: BABM students, BABM graduates, sponsoring employers and academic staff involved in the management and delivery of the programme.

Rationale

The BA (Hons) Business Management (In-Company) degree (BABM) was designed by NBS in a direct response to criticisms from graduate employers in the mid-1990s that, despite a significant increase in the number of graduates entering the graduate labour market, there was a lack of 'quality' in terms of the level of personal transferable skills which recruiters considered as valuable as a degree in terms of enabling graduates to 'hit the ground running'.

With its reputable history of vocational education, NBS considered this to be a challenge worth addressing. Hence in 1997, Professor Martin Reynolds, Dean of NBS, commenced the process of designing a business management degree that would not only deliver learning outcomes focused on the traditional knowledge and understanding associated with this wideranging subject area, but would also focus on establishing learning outcomes that addressed skill development and an assessment strategy that would have work-based learning as its central theme.

Context

The BA (Hons) Business Management (In-Company) degree programme was validated in March 1998 and its first cohort of students started in September 1998. The programme was designed in a partnership with a small number of blue-chip organisations, including Reuters Ltd, Marks & Spencer plc and British Sugar plc. The principal objective of the programme's design was to develop

> outstanding business graduates whose employability and performance in the work place will be enhanced by a unique work-based learning experience. (BABM, 2004/5: 2)

In essence, the degree aims to produce employable graduates who can 'hit the ground running', are equipped with a sound business knowledge and commercial awareness and have developed a set of strong transferable skills. The programme, therefore, provides students with the potential to develop awareness of both their self and their opportunities (Malkin et al, 1997) during the unique experience of completing the second and third years of their degree programme while based in one of the consortium companies that sponsor the programme (see Stewart & Knowles, 2001; 2003).

Within the university, the BABM course has become the most popular degree in terms of applications per place available. It has the highest average A-level-input measure. Its design places it out on its own in terms of preparing students for the world of work – which is acknowledged by students, companies and academics – and it involves sponsoring organisations in establishing and reviewing programme policy and

> graduate and student focus groups felt that two years' worth of company experience would lead to a robust CV at the end of the programme, enhancing both employability and faster career development

procedure for years two and three via the programme's Corporate Policy and Advisory Group, which meets twice in each academic year.

To date, 77 students have graduated from the programme. In June 2005 a further 15 students will graduate and in the academic year 2005/06 the course will consist of 50 new-start year ones, 28 year twos and 24 year threes. NBS decided to increase the intake in 2005/06 because of increased interest from sponsoring organisations wanting to offer two-year placements to BABM students.

In summary the course aims to:
- Recruit high quality students onto a unique business degree that will significantly enhance the employability potential of graduates through a programme of integrated learning and work experience.
- Develop students' knowledge and understanding of business and management issues from both a theoretical and practical perspective.
- Develop students' practical business and management skills necessary for effectiveness in a business organisation, with a particular focus on commercial awareness, professional skills and interpersonal skills.
- Develop students' self-awareness and skills in support of their own personal career development and lifelong learning.
- Fully exploit the benefits of a three-way partnership between the business school, the business community and students.

Description

Students enter the two-year in-company period having successfully completed a full-time first year university business studies programme. During the two years, students return to the business school for four intensive study blocks of three weeks each. The partnership approach to designing the programme led to employers encouraging an emphasis on skills development being an integral part of the curriculum throughout the three years of the degree, with the principal driver being the notion of the 'self-reliant learner'. The course was therefore designed to enable progressive development of students' commercial awareness, self-reliant learning, professional skills and interpersonal skills.

Such skills development is facilitated in year one by the taught module Developing Learning for Business and Management. In years two and three, the students have four study blocks (each of three weeks), each followed by a work period that focuses on a skills area:

- Communication – in work period one
- Teamworking – in work period two
- Adaptability – in work period three
- Leadership – in work period four.

Each of these is acknowledged as a key skill area for graduates entering those organisations that sponsor the programme in years two and three.

At the end of each work period, students have to complete a reflective piece of course work that documents and provides evidence of their development in the skills area and which includes a Personal Development Plan highlighting future courses of action. Each student is assigned a mentor from the Business School and within the company and it is through this support structure that students agree their skills priority areas at the beginning of each work period. The mentors from NBS and the company assess and agree the mark for the students' skills development reports and provide detailed written and verbal feedback to the students.

From the start, the course emphasises preparing students for future graduate employment. There is a particular focus on selection process at the end of year one, which determines the placement and company in which the students will be based in years two and three.

The Developing Learning for Business and Management module provides workshops that focus on both study and transferable skills and highlight the role they play in graduate recruitment and selection, with assessment centre type activities (e.g. competency-based interviews, negotiation exercises and group problem-solving activities) playing an important part in the reflective learning approach that not only underpins this module but also the skills process in years two and three highlighted above.

Additionally, taught inputs from the university's Careers Service on career planning, CV preparation and competency-based interview skills assist in preparing students for the rigorous selection practices that they will face at the end of year one. The fact that students experience early on in the degree programme a range of employers' selection procedures and practices, in order to secure a placement for years two and three, reinforces the learning and the emphasis that graduate recruiters place on transferable skills.

Evaluation

In 2003 a course review was undertaken by the programme management team, with the principal aims of investigating stakeholder perceptions of the positive and negative aspects of the course from a design and operational perspective and to gather views on how the course could be improved.

Stakeholders included graduates from cohorts one, two and three, students who were currently enrolled on the programme in years two and three, academic

> a company resourcing manager said that BABM graduates are more employable and linked their success in particular to the emphasis placed on skills development within the degree programme

members of staff involved in module management and delivery across all three years, academic mentors and company representatives. Students on the first year of the programme were excluded from the research because of their limited experience of the programme at the time the research was conducted. The evaluation methods included 12 focus group discussions:

- two with current students
- two with BABM graduates
- three with academic members of faculty
- one with company representatives who also act as mentors
- three with academic mentors
- one with course management and administrative staff.

The focus groups yielded three key themes: perceptions of employability; the degree as a fast track to a good career; and the importance of skills development in securing a job on graduation.

Employability

Graduates and students felt that they had a distinct advantage over standard graduates entering the labour market, which included traditional one-year sandwich graduates. The BABM experience was valued as enhancing employability in the graduate labour market. These opinions were further supported by the company mentor focus group where one company mentor stated that the BABM students 'grow up much quicker' and further claimed 'BABMs are more marketable'.

Fast track to a good career

A key aim of the degree is to enhance graduate employability so that, on completion of the programme, students can 'hit the ground running' and be suitable for management-level positions in a relatively short time. The graduate focus group said that the two-year in-company period 'makes the course different and enables progression to the world of work much faster than most' (BABM Graduate, Cohort two). A similar perception was evident from all the graduate and student focus groups which felt that two years' worth of company experience would lead to a robust CV at the end of the programme, thereby enhancing both employability and faster career development and progression. Research on BABM by Bateman (2003) established that 14 out of 22 respondents had secured a management role within one or two years and 16 out of 22 rated their jobs as being typically associated with someone with more experience than a relatively new entrant to the graduate labour market. In terms of progressing careers quickly, nine respondents had been promoted since graduation and 13 were aware of opportunities to be fast tracked and/or promoted in the near future. Such claims were supported with statements such as 'there is a five-year plan for me to become senior management if I stay with the company' and the reason for an early exit from a graduate scheme was claimed to be 'due to my previous experience which will constitute a fast track into a more senior management position'.

Skills development

The graduate focus groups linked the skills-development process with the design and delivery of the programme and saw the process as a vital component that helped prepare them for future interviews and performance reviews in their employing organisations. To quote a third year student, it provided 'good feedback, with continual assessments all being useful for graduate schemes'. (BABM Student, cohort 4).

Similarly, year-two staff and academic mentors considered the process to be supportive of future company performance management systems and a BABM graduate from cohort two claimed:

'Since graduating I have better interpersonal skills, self-assessment and commercial understanding than other graduates in the company. This is noted through appraisals.'

This emphasis on the role of skills development playing a key role in graduate employability was reinforced by a company resourcing manager (Bateman, 2003), who said that BABM graduates have a direct advantage over both standard and sandwich graduates and are more employable and linked their success in particular to the emphasis placed on skills development within the degree programme.

Discussion

Reviews of the BABM programme to date suggest that it is not simply having a degree that secures employment. Rather it is rather the combination of knowledge, skills and attitudes developed through particular design features of the degree that has an impact on employability. In addition, evidence suggests that BABM graduates secure positions and promotional opportunities traditionally associated with graduate jobs and careers. This is not common for all graduates (Pollard, 2004) and so it seems reasonable to hypothesise that the BABM degree affects the quality of employment as well as straightforward employability. This is, at least, the perception of BABM graduates.

This latter point has some connection with the notion of careers. Many employers involved with BABM engage with the programme in order to identify and develop candidates for their graduate schemes or graduate-related roles. In that sense BABM is perceived to be the start of a career development programme. Perhaps the idea of a long-term career, and indeed that of the internal labour market, is not entirely dead.

From the course review, it seems that many employers, students and graduates still operate with a traditional mindset in relation to 'careers'; a relatively high proportion of graduates remain with their sponsoring organisation and significant numbers experience promotion in a relatively short time. To date, Rolls-Royce plc, a major sponsor of the BABM programme, has an 80% retention rate, and British Sugar Plc, a 100% retention rate. These high rates could be attributed to the perceived high investment by sponsoring employers in the education and development of BABM students. Some graduates and company mentors have said that the degree effectively prepares individuals for company-based competency frameworks and performance management systems. It may be the case that such preparation and matching predisposes both graduates and employers to continue their employment relationship.

References

BABM, 2004/5. *BA (Hons) Business Management (In-Company) Degree Course Brochure.* Nottingham: Nottingham Business School, Nottingham Trent University

Bateman, V. 2003. *Tackling Contemporary Higher Education Issues. Is BABM the model for the future?* Unpublished Final Year Dissertation. Nottingham: Nottingham Business School

Malkin, J., Allen, A., Hambly, L. & Scott, F. 1997. 'Rational Career Planning', *Perspectives on Career Planning, Occasional Papers in Careers Guidance*, **1**, Institute of Careers Guidance

Pollard, E., Pearson, R. & Willison, R. 2004. *Next Choices: Career Choices Beyond University*. Brighton: Institute of Employment Studies

Stewart, J. & Knowles, V. 2001. Graduate Recruitment: Implications for business and management courses in HE. *Journal of European Industrial Training*, **25** (2/3/4), 98–108

Stewart, J. & Knowles, V. 2003. Mentoring in undergraduate business management programmes. *Journal of European Industrial Training*, **27**, (2/3/4), 47–59

VANESSA KNOWLES is now Early Career Development Advisor on the Rolls-Royce Engineering Graduate Leadership Development Programme and at the time of writing this case study was Programme Director of Nottingham Trent University Business School's BA (Hons) Business Management (In-Company) degree programme.

6 Preparing Aston Business School students for placement

Helen Higson and Etta Parkes

Aston Business School (ABS) has offered four-year sandwich degrees (including a year-long placement) for over 30 years and ABS has often been ranked top for graduate employability. This report outlines the activities ABS uses to meet its ever-increasing placement targets.

Aston Business School builds relationships between theory and practice in students' thinking and this has implications for their study, the placement period and beyond. Developing these links has certainly been a factor in the enhanced employability of ABS graduates, resulting in ABS having been ranked top for graduate employability for many years.

The eight employability skills used as the basis for the placement preparation objectives originate from Smith et al's work on employability (2002). We were encouraged to find that these employability skills overlap with the benchmark of the 'Profile summary for Business and Management' outlined by Hawkridge (2005).

In this case study we provide a rationale for the placement preparation period and then its objectives, followed by specific details of the preparation process. The evaluation highlights key achievements and areas for development and the discussion is future-focused.

Readers should note that the ABS undergraduate curriculum is aimed at preparing students for employment but this case study focuses on the role of the placements team.

Rationale

The key role of the ABS placements team is to place second-year undergraduate business students within organisations. Work placements can be viewed as a 'win-win' situation, with employers having the chance to 'road test' potential recruits, while enabling ABS to maintain its excellent links with industry. The current commercial environment, characterised by increased levels of competition, is leading recruiters to seek employees who will be both effective and efficient. Taylor describes the main goal of organisations participating in graduate recruitment as

> reaching that elusive creature – the well-qualified, well-motivated, intelligent, energetic and mobile graduate with management potential. (Taylor, 2003: 150)

It is up to ABS to prepare students to meet the above criteria and enable students to market themselves effectively throughout the selection process.

Objectives

The broad performance measure for the placements team is the number of students who secure high quality placements. However, this would be a somewhat short-term and mechanistic objective. More intangible long-term measures need to be used as the placement preparation period also seeks to prepare students to fulfil the learning objectives once on placement. These are outlined below. And beyond this, the preparatory stage should also positively influence the first graduate destination, the position five years on and an individual's potential in the workplace throughout working life.

The Aston Business School placement year carries a set of explicit, robust learning objectives:

a   To benefit from the integration of university study and work experience in ways that facilitate critical reflection on each.

b   To experience the responsibilities, tasks and relationships involved in managerial work at a level appropriate to a third-year undergraduate student in a business school.

c   Where students are specialising in a particular functional or professional area, to gain greater practical understanding of their chosen specialism.

d   To gain an understanding of the ways in which their placement organisation operates and how this might relate to other organisations and management processes.

e   To build personal awareness of their own interests, competencies, values and potential.

f   To develop the ability to share their work experience and evaluations with peers and with academic staff in order to gain more from the final year of study and to assist others to do likewise.

g   To increase the ability to make informed career choices.

Figure 1   Learning objectives for students on placement

To have an opportunity to fulfil the objectives in Figure 1, students must develop skills during the placement search. The eight employability skills (skills beyond subject knowledge), outlined by Smith et al (2002), offer the starting point for the team's objectives during the placement preparation period:

❏ Skills (1) **teamworking**, (2) **independent working** and (3) **working without direct supervision** are skills which all students will have had the opportunity to develop prior to commencing their placement search, all three being embedded in the curriculum. The role of ABS lies in encouraging self-reflection and skills analysis so that students are equipped to identify examples of where these skills have been developed in order to market themselves effectively. As Rhodes asserts (2004): *Any experience is experience; the key is to reflect on what has been achieved so these achievements can be articulated.*

❏ Skills (4) **business awareness** and (5) **an understanding of the world of work** are vital. Students must develop an ability to recognise the key issues facing organisations plus a knowledge of how they can add value and the part they will play in help-

ing companies to meet current and future challenges. As selection procedures become increasingly sophisticated and employers' expectations rise, this area is highlighted as a weakness among undergraduates, who often have limited industrial experience.

❏ Skill (6) **communication** is developed through curricular and extra-curricular activities. Both written and verbal communication are crucial elements in the students' success. Effective communication must always follow from a thorough self-analysis plus an understanding of the business context, in order to prove clear links between the candidate and the post. However. students often struggle to identify these links and articulate them.

❏ Skill (7) **planning one's own development** includes planning one's development around any skills gaps which become apparent prior to securing a placement. The gaps may be limited work experience, for example, or poor interview technique. But employers also seek students who are proactive and are able to seek out opportunities once on placement.

❏ Skill (8) **job-search** is an important focus throughout the placement preparation as students learn key sources for placements and how to assess a match between their skills/competences and those required by an employer.

Context

The three full-time staff of the ABS placements team manage the placements process from student preparation to employer relations. The team successfully placed over 400 students in 2004/05 and 475 in 2005/06. Figures for 2006/07 indicate that similar numbers are seeking a placement. This figure includes single honours and combined honours students (those who combine business with study of another subject). There is a high percentage of international students, averaging 21% across ABS undergraduate programmes for 2004/05. They have a variety of needs which the team also aims to meet.

The current context is changing. With the introduction of student tuition fees and an impending increase in fees we feel a student-centric approach is vital so that students feel confident that they are receiving a high quality service. Competition is fierce, with increasing numbers of institutions now offering industrial placement opportunities. This is in part a response to the Dearing Report, which asserted that:

global competitiveness requires that education and training should enable people to compete with the best. It is recommended that all institutions should identify opportunities to increase the extent to which programmes help students to become familiar with work and support them in reflecting upon such experiences. (cited in Booth, 2002: 6).

In addition, the CIPD Quarterly Labour Market Outlook (Spring 2005) indicates a substantial negative balance (23%) of employers expecting to employ fewer people by spring 2006 over those expecting to employ more people, demonstrating a deviation from previous years' trends.

The above factors have influenced the level of assistance and support students have required in order to secure good quality placements in an increasingly challenging labour market and will continue to do so.

Description

Table 2 outlines the main activities students are offered to meet the programme objectives from the first year up to their successful placement year.

First-year counselling

The counselling session aims to demystify the placement process for the first-year students, plus provide practical guidance on how students can start to prepare for their placement from this early stage. This session begins to focus students' thoughts on their own development.

Second-year counselling

This session is designed to answer the more specific queries that second years will have as they go through the placement search process. It allows further one-to-one guidance, which students value and a chance to address students' specific queries.

Placements fair

The placement fair takes place annually in November; the format enables students to speak to final years about their placement experiences. This provides students with an understanding of the world of work, and practical guidance on job-searching skills.

The fair is split into three main zones:

1 **Functional Zone**, where final year students represent their organisations and functional areas; this zone includes representatives from voluntary organisations and SMEs to assist in raising the profile of these important opportunities.

2 **Skills Zone**, where students are helped to forge and strengthen links with both internal and external representatives. This raises the profile of the ABS placements scheme and highlights the opportunities students have to develop their skills prior to and during their placement search.

3 **International Zone** is split into two main areas. The team felt that, given the increased numbers of international students, the presence of successful role models who had completed their overseas placements would be critical in this zone. Second, more and more students, domestic and overseas in origin, enquire about placements overseas. The international zone contains a plethora of information about overseas placements.

Placements website

All placement positions from September to June are advertised on a website that enables students to search by criteria such as location and function. All events throughout the placement search period are advertised here too.

The website contains comprehensive advice sheets relating to the major selection techniques, plus advice on how students should search for their own placements. Student profiles and placement reports provide the students with an insight into the roles and companies available from the perspective of past placement students. A links page gives students instant access to sites they may find useful, such as *Doctor Job*, *Hobsons*, and *Fledglings*.

The placements website also offers a tracking facility. This is used to identify students whose level of activity is deemed low, enabling barriers to be addressed early on in the placement search process. In many ways, the website limits the extent to which students are required to develop independent job search skills. However, owing to increased competition, ABS is increasingly placing the emphasis on students seeking their own placement.

Timing	Activity	Skills objectives met	Target audience
Second Term	1st Year Counselling	7	1st Years
Second Term	2nd Year Counselling	1,2,3,4,5,6,7,8	2nd Years
First Term	Placements Fair	4,5,7,8	1st and 2nd Years
Continuous	Placements Website	8	2nd Years
Continuous	Resources Room	2,3,45,7,8,	2nd Years
First Term	Timetabled sessions (2 identical sessions run each week)		
	Week 2 – Briefing Session	2,3,4,5,7,8	2nd Years
	Week 3 – CV/Cover Letters		
	Week 4 – Application Forms (employers present)		
	Week 5 – Interviews (employers present)		
	Week 6 – Assessment Centres (1): Overall Process (employers present)		
	Week 7 – Assessment Centres (2): Psychometric Tests/Presentations		
First Term	Student Charter	2,3,7	2nd Years
First Term	Employer Presentations and Practical Sessions	4,5	2nd Years
First Term	International Student Session	5,7,8	International 2nd Years
Second Term	International Placement Opportunities Session	4,5,7	2nd Years
First Term	Mentoring Scheme	5,7	2nd Years (particularly International Students)
Continuous	One to one support	1,2,3,4,5,6,7,8,	2nd Years
Continuous	Surgery Sessions	1,2,3,4,5,6,7,8	2nd Years
Several sessions each term	Psychometric Test Sessions	8	2nd Years
End of First Term	Tracking sheet plus provisional feedback in order to inform 2nd term activities	7	2nd Years
Continuous	Email Contact		2nd Years
Second Term	'Finding Own Placement' session	1,2,3,4,5,6,7,8	2nd Years planning to conduct their own search
Third Term	'Send-Off' meetings	4,5,7	2nd Years who are successfully placed
Third Term	Briefing Pack	2,3,5,7	2nd Years who are successfully placed
Third Term	Summer Scheme	1,2,3,4,5,6,7,8	2nd Years who are still to secure their placement
September	Motivation Event	1,2,3,4,5,6,7,8	2nd Years who are still to secure their placement

Table 1 Placement preparation: main activities

Resources room

This is a dedicated environment where students have all the resources they require for a successful placement search: PCs, printer, hard copies of placement reports and company literature. It is open during normal office hours and students also have access to the placements team five days a week.

Timetabled sessions

The first session sets the scene for the academic year, outlining the resources available and the process students need to follow. A 'Student Charter' is also introduced, which sets out expectations from the start, encouraging students to undertake independent working, to begin reflecting on what they have achieved to date in order to plan their future development and to voice their achievements and experiences effectively to employers.

The sessions which follow cover the major selection techniques and, in order to provide a 'real-world' perspective, representatives from recruiting organisations are invited to outline how they select students. These sessions undoubtedly increase students' business awareness and enable them to hone their job-searching skills to match employer requirements.

Employer presentations and practical sessions

Many employers visit the campus for company presentations and practical workshops. This benefits both students and employers, as the students receive credible guidance and the employers have an opportunity to promote their schemes. Students can gain an insight into the organisations they plan to apply to.

International student session

ABS has many international students, with additional and different needs. This session offers guidance on translating grades from home countries, the visa and fee implications of taking a placement and how best to gain work experience. International students must understand clearly the placement search process and the role that effective written and spoken communications will play in securing their placement.

International placement opportunities session

Students are increasingly interested in working overseas and, with over 100 international positions advertised so far this year, it is essential that students should have a thorough understanding of how they should approach the selection process, including the procedures and preparations that working overseas will entail. The session includes talks from students who have successfully completed an overseas placement.

Mentoring session

The mentor scheme offers second-year students direct contact with the returning final-year students. The process is managed informally and allows students to gain in-depth advice and guidance from students who have worked in the organisations/functions that they are interested in.

One-to-one support

Appointment slots are available to students daily and provide a valuable opportunity for specific queries to be addressed. Appointments cover a wide variety of areas, including:
- advising on skills audits and matching skills/competences to positions

- mock interviews
- practising presentation skills
- assessment-centre advice
- students' own placement searches
- career guidance
- psychometric test guidance.

Surgery sessions

One-to-one student appointments get booked up very quickly, so drop-in surgery sessions are also provided to make optimum use of resources. Surgery sessions focus on 'hot topics' at given points throughout the placement cycle, allowing current queries to be addressed. As with the one-to-one appointments, specific student queries dictate the objectives which the surgery sessions aim to meet.

Psychometric test sessions

Twenty-seven per cent of employers use general ability tests and 23% use some form of numerical/verbal psychometric testing in their selection process (CIPD Survey, 2004). It is therefore helpful for students to gain experience in order to demystify the tests and assist them to perform to their optimum level when faced with the test 'proper'. In addition to having a focused timetabled session on testing students are also invited to sit the psychometric tests which are used most commonly by employers in undergraduate recruitment, followed by a 15-minute feedback session where they are advised on their current performance and actions they can take to increase their chances of success during their placement search.

These sessions have been an excellent addition to the ABS offering. Psychometric testing often worries students who may not perform to their full potential without previous experience of these tests. Two members of the team are BPS (British Psychological Society) level-A qualified (the minimum qualification required to administer and feed-back on psychometric tests) and can give advice and guidance.

Student tracking and feedback exercise

With such a large number of students, it is important that their progress and activity levels are monitored rigorously, in order to keep down the numbers of 'late

> The process is managed informally and allows students to gain in-depth advice and guidance from students who have worked in the organisations/functions that they are interested in

placed' students. Students are issued with a tracking and feedback form. Their feedback directly informs activities over the following terms, allowing resources to be channelled effectively. The form (and the placements website) also provides the placements team with information on who is least active. Those students who do not appear to be looking for placements are then contacted and any difficulties are addressed.

Email communications

This is one of the key tools used throughout the placement search period. It allows the team to inform students of new opportunities and services. Most important, it maintains constant contact with a large number of students and helps motivate them.

'Finding own placement' session

This session was first offered in direct response to the tracking exercise. It covers areas such as identi-

> It is, therefore, helpful for students to gain experience in order to demystify the tests and assist them in performing to their optimum level when faced with the test 'proper'

fying opportunities, networking, speculative letters and personal PR, all of which seek to meet the programme's objectives. Also a large part of the placements team's role is to motivate and equip students to find their own positions, and this is a vehicle for doing so. Competition is fierce. Pursuing personal opportunities and taking responsibility are therefore high on ABS' agenda.

'Send-off' meetings

Students are invited to attend a 'send-off' meeting prior to commencing their placement. The meeting aims to equip students with the information they need for a productive placement experience. The following topics are covered:
- employer, student and university expectations
- finances including tuition fees, tax, national insurance, council tax etc.
- keeping in touch with university/fellow students
- employment legislation

- health and safety information
- how to deal with any problems
- how Blackboard (VLE) can support students
- the role of the placement tutor
- assessment requirements and deadlines
- final-year accommodation, module options and outlines.

Placement-year briefing pack

During the 'send-off' meeting, students receive a briefing pack. This provides detailed information on the learning objectives of the year, the assessment package, students' key responsibilities, key contact details plus brief information on finances, fees, health and safety and other employment legislation.

Summer scheme

At the end of June, the placement website closes and the system changes to that of a recruitment agency. Placements team members work closely with students and employers to match students to vacancies. The scheme benefits students who are late in securing their placement, as well as employers who have additional or late requirements.

All unplaced students are invited to attend a workshop session that identifies their skills gaps and equips them with the information and practical skills they require for their placement search. Perhaps most importantly, this session also prepares students to work independently, with no direct supervision.

Motivation event

In early September, about three months into the summer scheme, those students who remain unplaced are invited to attend a motivation event. The invitation process requests feedback on any areas in which the students are still struggling and the session is designed specifically to meet their needs.

Common areas covered are as follows:
- job-search activities (practical groupwork)
- time-planning (examples of a well-utilised week)
- cold-calling (role-play)
- networking and identifying opportunities (group-brainstorm plus positive examples from previous students)

- interview skills (students see the process from the interviewers' perspective as they sit on a mock interview panel)
- personal PR.

We require students to prepare beforehand, so that the four-hour workshop is as productive as possible.

Evaluation

Student feedback

The main evaluation tool used to assess the above activities is the student evaluation questionnaire, distributed at the end of the students' placement. For 2003/04 the response rate was 37%. Students are asked to reflect on their placement experience and the preparation period.

Table 3 shows students' ratings of the services offered by the placements team in 2003/04. There is no data for some 2004/05 activities described above as these were developed in direct response to feedback received in 2003/04. Similar feedback has been collected for 2005/06.

Positive comments on the team's service in 2003/04 included:

Very supportive to me on a number of occasions.
Summer placement scheme was excellent.
Website is fantastic – well organised.
They were always very helpful. Even during the summer when the placements website was closed.

Service type	% of respondents rating services as excellent or good
Placements website	92
Advice sheets on website	7
Timetabled sessions	77
Employer presentations and practical sessions	59
One-to-one support	53*
Placement Fair	44
Resource room	63
Student reports	58

* The relatively low rating is possibly because an increase in overall student numbers meant that less one-to-one contact time was available for each student.

Table 3 Students' evaluation of the placement process 2003/04

Students' suggestions for improvements

In answering the 2003/04 questionnaire, students made suggestions for improvements and these are being addressed.

'Presentations from post-placement students would be welcomed'

We now have the Placements Fair, mentoring scheme, profiles on the website plus involvement at the international placements session. We have developed and used alumni links throughout the 2005/06 year.

'More international placements'

Well over 100 international positions have been advertised in 2004/05 and 2005/06, compared to 23 in 2003/04. International placements fit well into the increasingly international perspective of ABS's undergraduate programme, allowing students an insight into working overseas and the various challenges and opportunities that this presents.

'Difficult to book an appointment'

Anecdotal feedback suggests that students find the appointments immensely helpful. Although the facility is advertised formally, it is often word of mouth, following a successful appointment, which leads other students to use the facility. It is worth noting that appointments are not always the appropriate channel for students (often their enquiries can be dealt with and answered face-to-face during office hours). In direct response to this suggestion, surgery sessions have been used successfully for the first time this year, with high rates of attendance and repeat attendance. The additional post of placements adviser will allow more contact time to be offered to students where this is necessary and will further advance the student-centric focus.

Placements Fair

In direct response to feedback received from students, several changes were made to this event in 2005. The fair will be rebranded to reinforce its main aims, namely to share experience. In addition, a 'speed-dating' style question and answer session will be piloted next academic year to help students gain maximum value from attending.

Involving first-year students proved a real success: it helped to demystify the placement process at an early stage and showed them a variety of ways to improve their employability in the 'Skills Zone'. It enabled students to reflect, very early in their university career, on their potential skills gaps, allowing time for these to be addressed.

Timetabled sessions

A key determinant of success is attendance, which overall was excellent and helped by offering students two sessions from which to choose each week. Given that these sessions are not mandatory and ABS do not offer credit for placement preparation, it is vital that the sessions take a highly practical, 'real world' perspective in order to engage students; this is where employer involvement is so valuable.

Employer presentations and practical sessions

There has been historically poor turnout at employers' sessions which has had implications for continued relations with employers. Students are therefore now charged a £5 deposit prior to employer events, following the Careers Service example. This has not been found adversely to affect the number of students signing up for events and has increased the attendance rate to 100%.

International student session

Placements are not mandatory for international students because the level of fees paid are much higher compared with those of UK/EU students, which increases the financial burden of the placement year. A key indicator of success for both the specific international student session and other support given to this cohort is the number of international students who successfully secure a placement. The figure is already impressive at approximately 50% and with additional services targeted at this cohort we hope this figure will rise.

Mentoring scheme

Mentoring was offered to all international students based on research which suggested they responded very well to one-to-one support (Higson and Jones, 2002). The scheme was also used by a number of EU and UK students. The uptake rates were superb.

Owing to the informal nature of the schen no formal feedback figures, but anecdotal suggests that students have found it very val

Summer scheme

The success of the summer scheme is evaluated primarily on the number of students who are placed via the scheme, which is always very high. The level of support the scheme offers throughout the summer is vital to ensure that students remain focused.

Motivation event

For those not placed via the summer scheme the motivation event with its developmental and motivational focus has proved a great success. Many students gain placements shortly after attending the event.

All respondents indicated that the session had either met or exceeded their expectations. Students were also asked to indicate the main idea/key skill they felt

> 97% of employers stated that the placement student either met or exceeded their expectations …the overall picture from employers is exceptionally positive

they had gained from the event; selected responses were as follows:

- how to contact companies and the need for open questions
- confidence when contacting companies
- being more organised with job searching
  I feel I have gained in motivation and will act on it.

Partnership working

An additional measure of success is the extent to which the placements team work effectively with both internal and external representatives in order to offer a comprehensive service to students.

Students have been found to make good use of the excellent facilities available via the Careers Service. These include the Careers online self-help package and careers skills sessions that are advertised to students seeking a placement via the placements website events section.

The placements team also takes an active role

.1 publicising short-term employment opportunities and skills sessions offered by Graduate Advantage, Schools Liaison, SIS (Students Industrial Society/CRAC), AISIEC, Students Guild and Job Shop. These play a vital role in preparing students for their placement and their success can be measured by the volume of students who are involved in extra curricular activities such as university committees, sports and short-term work placements.

Employer evaluation questionnaire

It is also important for ABS to ascertain employers' levels of satisfaction, as placement preparation plays a part not only in helping students secure their placement but also to help them integrate and add value once placed.

An evaluation questionnaire was sent in 2003/04 to all placement supervisors to canvas their opinion relating to the students, their work and the university (see Table 3). This data has been collected in subsequent years, with broadly similar findings. Nearly 97% of employers stated that the placement student either met or exceeded their expectations; the overall picture from employers is therefore exceptionally positive.

The questionnaires also asked about the recruitment

Employer	Feedback
WAA	The placement process was good and everyone at the university was very helpful.
3M	This is the first year our group had used a placement student… I personally see everything as working well and beneficial. A professional and well-run process.
Oxfam	I've been grateful for the straightforward approach Aston takes towards placing and supporting students. The few queries I have had have been very quickly and easily sorted out. The quality of students Oxfam has received this year has been excellent. I am looking forward to welcoming more students in the forthcoming academic year and in developing this relationship in the longer term.
IBM	Better and more active involvement than we have seen from other universities.
Comag Magazine Marketing	Aston will continue to be our first call when finding suitable placement students.

Figure 4 Examples of employer comments on the recruitment process and university support 2003/04

process and university support (see Table 4).

Specific feedback on the students' contribution included:

- *Student is a valuable member of the team. His commitment and motivation have been outstanding.*
- *Her commitment and loyalty will be missed when she leaves as will her positive communication skills with my clients and suppliers. She has proven herself within my company and I have no hesitation in recommending her to future employers unless she wants to come back – the door is open.*
- *Her energy and enthusiasm generally created an environment of activity and helped others to positively apply themselves.*
- *(Student X) immediately impressed with his positive, enthusiastic attitude and his friendly and outgoing personality. Consequently, he has been a popular member of the finance team. His work has been of a high standard and he has quickly grasped the nature of the work he has been asked to do, with minimal supervision. Certainly, in the last nine months particularly, I have come to think of X as one of the most able members of the team, rather than as a work-placement student. His contribution has been excellent.*

The overall picture from both employers and students is very positive but future developments and increasingly high expectations mean that ABS must continually review these processes and ensure they continue

Skill area	% of employers responding who rated student as excellent or above average 2003/4
Application of skills and abilities	68
Effort made during placement	82
Communication skills	68
Managerial duties	65
Working relationships	76
Taking the initiative	76
Contribution made	69
Attitude	78
Effectiveness in accomplishing tasks	76
Motivation	80

Table 3 Employers' evaluation of students' skills 2003/04

to meet the varied needs of key stakeholders.

Discussion

This case study has demonstrated the work the placements team do in order to meet the short-term, target-driven objectives and, no less important, the development of longer-term employability skills.

A high level of investment is made in the development of ABS placements team and, with the imminent introduction of a new post, the team is able to offer a flexible and truly value-added service. Development within the team will also play a key role in building on already impressive international links.

The placements team must prioritise working in partnership with employers, internal departments such as the Careers Service and government initiatives, to ensure a thorough understanding of what employers expect, and to use resources within higher education to prepare students effectively. The team also needs to remain up-to-date with developments within the selection field, so that students are well versed in common techniques they may face.

One-to-one contact can make all the difference. But with finite resources and increasing student numbers innovative solutions are required to meet escalating employer and student expectations. This is where IT support plays a vital role. The placements website already offers flexibility, but further enhancements in IT provision, such as skills analysis packages and interactive advice sheets, will enable students to access guidance around the clock.

We have made increasing use of returning students but this is to be extended to alumni. Positive role models can provide students with motivation and impetus which is hard to instil via other methods. It is also vital for ABS to identify any barriers to placement which students may encounter and to help them successfully overcome these. Focus groups will be introduced for students who are placed later in the cycle to explore any themes which may have led to this happening.

In conclusion, ABS placements team must be alive to new challenges and continue to offer an approach which is flexible for both employers and students and will enable evolving needs to be met.

References

CIPD Survey Report, Spring 2005. *Quarterly Labour Market Outlook*. London: CIPD Surveys

CIPD Recruitment. *Retention and Turnover 2004*. London: CIPD Surveys

Hawkridge, D. 2005. *Enhancing Students Employability: The national scene in Business, Management and Accountancy*. The Higher Education Academy Subject Centre for Business, Management and Accountancy. Milton Keynes: The Open University

Higson, H. E. & Jones, K. E. 2002. 'Your students have excellent knowledge and skills but they don't think about them…' Paper at Learning and Teaching Support Network, BEST Conference, Edinburgh

Honey, P. and Mumford, A. 1986. *Learning Styles Questionnaire*. Peter Honey Publications

National Committee of Inquiry into Higher Education, 1997. *Higher Education in the Learning Society/The National Committee of Enquiry into Higher Education* (the Dearing Report) London, NCIHE cited in Booth, J. 2002. *Briefings on Employability 6: Good learning and employability: issues for HE services and careers guidance practitioners*. Milton Keynes: ESECT, The Open University

Rhodes, L. 2004. The transition from learning to earning. Keynote Lecture, Aston University, The National Council for Work Experience

Smith, H. and ESECT colleagues, 2002. *Briefings on Employability 1: Issues for employers*. Milton Keynes: ESECT, The Open University

Taylor, S. 2003. *People Resourcing* London: CIPD

HELEN HIGSON is Director of Undergraduate Studies at Aston Business School and is also Director of the Research Centre for Higher Education Learning and Management (HELM).

ETTA PARKES recently joined Graduate Advantage, a regionally funded government project. She co-ordinates the graduate-focused side of the project. Having taken an industrial placement year with British Nuclear Fuels as part of her BSc (Hons) degree in Psychology and Management, she exemplifies the value of work experience and continuing development.

7

Encouraging Aston Business School students to reflect on their employment experience

Helen Higson and Nicola Bullivant

This case study shares with a wider audience of placement officers, tutors and people involved in the management of placement students or employment of graduates the approach taken to encourage reflective learning in undergraduate placement students at Aston Business School.

Reflective learning forms an important foundation of the placement year at Aston Business School, where a professional placement is a mandatory element of the four-year degree, for all home/EU students who are taking a single honours degree (i.e. a full business programme). The placement year is not compulsory for international students and students taking a combined honours degree (i.e. a degree where two unrelated subjects are studied), although approximately 50% of combined honours students opt to take a placement year.

Students spend their year out undertaking a 'proper' job within a company or public sector organisation. They are normally paid a reasonable salary for their work (in 2005/06 the average advertised salary was £14,000 per annum). The placement year is assessed, and carries credits which contribute 10% towards the students' final degree. The assessment requires students to submit an academic essay relating theory to practice, a factual report about the company which can be of use to future students and a logbook, which is the reflective piece of work.

The Aston Business School placement year carries a set of explicit, robust learning objectives. Encouraging reflection on the placement year has always been an important feature of Aston Business School's approach to learning. More recently, however, feedback from employers has indicated that, although our students have excellent employability skills, 'they do not think about them' (Aston Business School Advisory Panel,

2001). We, therefore, began some activities which would encourage students to go beyond the mere acquisition of skills and knowledge. This work became the basis of a programme of introductions to reflective learning, mentoring and awareness of different learning styles written up in Higson and Jones (2002). The idea was to get students used to the idea of reflecting on their experiences well before they entered the placement year.

Objectives

The logbook's objective is a developmental piece of work, rather than an academic assignment, aiming to meet the ABS objectives b to e (possibly also objective a). See Figure 1, Chapter 6, p 43.

Rationale

The logbook is students' record of their development during the placement year. It is a tool for students to use to reflect upon their experiences, opportunities, aims and objectives and to encourage critical evaluation of their achievements.

According to Christine Fanthome (2004):

Although the practical and cultural skills that can be acquired in the workplace are very important, arguably an even more valuable aspect of work placement experience is the opportunity it offers for reflective development and analysis… students can

hone the technique of critical reflection that is fundamental to developing the skill of organising one's own learning...in contemporary society, the notion of 'lifelong learning' has superseded the view that education ends after school or university. (p 4–5)

In 2004, Alan Johnson, then Minister of State for Lifelong Learning, Further and Higher Education, gave the keynote address at the 2004 Association for Sandwich Education and Training (ASET) Annual Conference, at Fitzwilliam College, Cambridge. He stated:

whatever HE qualifications students are aiming to achieve, let's not forget life skills. Again, we have listened to the pleas of employers, to their repeated requests that each and every young person brings to a job these skills which may be less tangible but are nevertheless essential. Skills like initiative, leadership and problem-solving, that employers so often inform us are so often lacking in even the most highly qualified and gifted of graduates.

The reflective practice that Aston Business School placement students undertake enables them to explore more deeply the experiences they have been exposed to (and actively sought out) during the course of a professional placement year and can help to reveal skills such as those outlined by Alan Johnson.

For the purposes of this article, a definition of reflective practice should be offered:

Reflection, if managed in an ordered way, can provide great opportunities for learning, understanding and clarifying thought, both in one's personal life and in learning and professional development. (Moon, 1999)

Aston Business School supports the view of Moon: by giving students a framework upon which to pin their reflections, we can aid an often difficult and ultimately challenging process – that of critical self-reflection and analysis.

Context

In 2005/06, 475 Aston Business School students embarked upon the placement year as part of their degree programme of study. The school's placement office has links with over 800 employers across the world. Students are employed by organisations which span employment sectors and the globe. This year they are in the UK, of course, but also Italy, France, Germany, the Netherlands, the USA, China and Belgium. The range of countries where placement contacts and partners exist has been expanded quite significantly recently and 2005/06 will also see students undertaking placements in Canada, India, Greece, Brazil, Sweden and Hong Kong.

The intercultural experiences of students working for global organisations offer opportunities for personal and professional development. This is shown in the written reflections set out by students in their logbooks. With this in mind, along with the phenomenon of culture shock, Aston Business School equips students for the intercultural learning dimension of their placement year, through sessions on international placement and, more specifically, through an online intercultural training package. Aspects of the course

The idea was to get students used to the idea of reflection on their experiences well before they entered the placement year

are delivered through a web-based system, complemented by face-to-face interactions – for example, role play with French and German nationals. One of the many aims of this training is that it can help students to make better sense of their new experiences and learning.

The Foundations of Management module, delivered in year one to all Aston Business School students, includes lectures and workshops on reflective learning. The learning outcomes of this module provide:

❑ an idea of what reflective learning is
❑ an understanding of how reflective learning is important to their studies
❑ an understanding of the importance of a reflective approach to managers
❑ an introduction to how the topic will be explored in tutorials.

Students are encouraged to appreciate the differences between 'surface' learning and 'deep' learning (Fry et al, 1999), with those involved in deep learning being individuals who:

❑ have ideas that change

- regard information flexibly
- question materials
- hold ideas that are linked
- are active
- are able to retrieve information
- have concern for meaning
- have wide views on a topic
- compare and contrast
- consider ideas which conflict
- transform information.

Description

Aston Business School's placement office introduced a logbook as part of its assessment of the students' placement several years ago. This was initially graded on a pass/fail basis but, more recently, the marking scheme was adapted to include merit and distinction ratings, to reward those students who fully engage with this piece of work and who demonstrate that they have developed the ability to self-reflect. Certificates are awarded to students on the basis of this achievement.

The logbook requires the students to keep records of their experiences and how these link to their learning, thus developing their ability to be critical and reflective. The structure of the logbook is as follows:

Section One Framework

Here the students put together a framework for their placement employment upon its commencement. The students arrange a meeting with their placement supervisor to discuss and agree a framework for the placement. During this process they are advised to address, at least, the following basic questions:

- What is your role in the organisation? What will this entail? What are your responsibilities?
- What are you aiming to achieve?
- What personal skills do you wish to develop/gain?
- How will your progress be appraised by your supervisor?
- What training/learning/development opportunities will be provided?

The meeting is then documented by the student and they and their manager sign this record. This then completes section one of the logbook and sets a framework for the placement year.

Section Two Regular reflections

This section of the logbook is written over the course of the placement year, month by month.

Students meet with their placement supervisors regularly during their placements – meetings may be frequent during the early stages (e.g. daily, weekly) and then perhaps less frequent as they settle into their role (but ideally monthly).

The meetings should enable the student to:
- Gain feedback from their placement supervisor on their performance.
- Reflect on what they have achieved, and how.
- Reflect on any difficulties that they have encountered, highlighting any particular problems or areas of difficulty there might be and agreeing what could be done to resolve these.
- Decide on a course of action for the next stage of the placement, taking into account progress so far.

Students are advised that such meetings will be more effective for all parties if they prepare for them thoroughly beforehand. The following checklist is provided to assist the process:
- Reflect on what you have been doing.
- How you have done it.
- Identify problems, constraints and opportunities.
- What went well?
- What went badly?
- Who helped you?
- What obstacles did you face?
- How did you overcome these?
- What have you achieved?
- What have you learnt?
- Do you feel as if your skills have been developed? In what way?
- Would you change your approach if faced with a similar situation in the future? How?

Each meeting is then recorded by the student as a monthly entry in section two of the logbook. At the end of the placement year each student's logbook should contain 12 entries for section two – one for each month of the placement. They may, however, include more entries if the student or his or her supervisor or tutor think that more regular meetings are required.

Each of the monthly entries should include comments on:
- the activities the student has been involved in
- reflection on any problems they faced and what action they took to try to resolve the issue

- their learning – they should also reflect on the skills and knowledge gained and any personal development from the experiences
- an outline of their objectives for the next month
- the supervisor's signature, comments, if appropriate and the date
- the student's signature and date.

Students are encouraged to include additional entries. For example, if the placement company has an appraisal process, the reports or documents from appraisal meetings could be incorporated into the logbook as these are complementary reflective processes.

Reflection is often highly personal. Students are advised that they may write about a particular event or learning situation a second time, perhaps at a later date, after their supervisor has signed off the original entry for that month. Students are reassured that this is acceptable in situations where they wish to write very openly and honestly – perhaps about a personal situation or an event involving the supervisor, for example. In these circumstances, students are encouraged to submit both the original signed entry and the second version.

at the beginning of your placement (answering queries over the telephone perhaps). How do you think you acquired this new found confidence or expertise?

- Think of a mistake you made in your work or a situation that did not go to plan. With the advantage of hindsight, how would you react to a similar situation now? What has this experience taught you?
- Have you encountered an especially difficult or tricky situation or experience at work? How did you cope with it? What was the outcome? What did this experience teach you about the best way to deal with these sorts of situations? Did you learn anything about yourself and your working relationships through this experience?
- Have you any problem in getting on with or being accepted by any individual in your workplace?

> they may write about a particular event or learning situation for a second time, perhaps at a later date, after their supervisor has signed off the original entry for that month

Section Three Summary

The final section of the logbook is a summary of what the students feel they have individually gained from the placement in terms of skills, new learning, knowledge, experience, training, etc. This is the overall, holistic reflection on their placement: what they have learnt; how they have developed as a person; what skills they have gained; how they have developed as a student.

They evaluate their performance against the objectives outlined in section one and are asked to reflect on whether these objectives were met. Did they develop further than anticipated? We encourage the students not to worry if they did not meet all of the aims and objectives they set out to achieve in section one. They are not penalised when the summary is reviewed by a tutor. However, we do ask them to reflect on and comment on why they did not meet these goals.

We give students examples of this kind of development:

- You may find that you can now quite happily deal with a task which would have worried you

Why do you think this might have been and how have you dealt with it? Has this difficulty helped to develop your interpersonal communication skills, understanding, tact, insight etc?

Aston Business School degrees are accredited by a number of professional bodies, including The Chartered Institute of Personnel and Development (CIPD), the Association of Chartered Certified Accountants in England and Wales, the Chartered Institute of Marketing, the Chartered Institute of Public Finance and Accountancy, the Chartered Institute of Management Accountants, the Institute of Chartered Accountants in England and Wales, the Institute of Chartered Accountants in Scotland, the Institute of Chartered Secretaries and Administrators, and the Chartered Insurance Institute.

For students who embark on professional careers and develop their membership levels within these professional bodies, the skill of reflective practice is essential. For example, CIPD members are required to practice and be able to demonstrate continuing professional development in order to upgrade their membership. Members complete an application form which states:

The important aspect here is that you are able to reflect on your learning and show how you have added value in a professional capacity. (CIPD, 2005)

As a developmental piece of coursework the logbook echoes and supports the notion propounded by Fanthome (2004):

You are most likely to learn from your work placement if you spend some time reflecting upon each aspect of it and particularly if you then analyse your response and reaction to the various situations you encounter and think through how your behaviour and performance could be improved. (pp 4–5)

Alongside the briefing given to students as they commence their placement, the workplace supervisor has an important role to play in the development of the student's reflective ability. The supervisor is asked to assist the student in compiling his or her logbook and to sign off the log at the end of each month. As well as developing reflective skills, the log also facilitates joint-objective setting, the regular review of these goals and to generally ensure that developmental dialogue occurs regularly between supervisor and student. Many organisations' existing performance appraisal schemes dovetail with meeting some requirements of the log.

As stated earlier, employers' feedback to Aston Business School indicated that they believed students were not spending time thinking about the skills they had or needed. An employer who recruited one student into a housing association on a 12-month professional placement, for example, felt as a placement supervisor that:

•*The monthly log was very useful feedback for me so I could appreciate some of the thoughts and problems the student may have had.*•

Each student has a placement tutor, who, along with visiting the student (and his or her supervisor) while on placement, also provides academic guidance and will 'liaise with the student throughout the year by whatever method is appropriate to help their development and maximise learning opportunities' (Aston Business School Placement Briefing Pack 2005/06).

This reflective approach is now being further developed via the university-wide scheme for Personal Development Plans (PDPs). A total of 130 students from across the four schools at Aston University and all years, participated in the 2004/05 pilot project on a voluntary basis. Among them were nine ABS placement students.

The PDP used in the pilot contained a skills audit and a reflective log. The briefing to students on the reflective log in the pack stated that it is:

a process of thinking about your experiences on a week by week basis. You consider how you responded to the tasks performed, how you interact with your fellow students or colleagues, what progress you make, what strategies you employ and if you need to modify them and how all this relates to your personal development. (Thompson, 2004: 6)

The personal element in reflection was recognised and in the materials provided to students for the PDP pilot, the author commented on personal feelings:

this is often one of the main differences between your university studies and this type of learning. In this PDP you are allowed to reflect in a personal way… It is OK to say 'I' or 'my'! Discussing personal attitudes is a way of unravelling your responses and discovering your strengths and weaknesses. (p 17)

The pilot was completed in May 2005 and was evaluated through an online questionnaire, with 29 questions completed by 50 students. A number of questions related to reflection and asked students about their reactions and thoughts on this process throughout the PDP and also their perceptions of reflection and the need to reflect and how they went about this.

Students were asked: 'Why did you volunteer to do this PDP?' One student responded that it would 'help reflective thinking.'

Responses to the question 'Did you find the template provided to help you be more reflective useful?' included:

•*It helped me reflect on my experiences and aided my understanding of my strengths and weaknesses in dealing with particular situations.*•

•*I could look back at things, which then helped with the monthly reviews.*•

•*It made me understand myself more.*•

•*It was useful when completing coursework, learning from past errors.*•

•*This was particularly useful as I had an unsuccessful placement. Rather than dwell on the negative aspects it helped me to see instead not only what I was learning but where I was going wrong.*•

I was able to reflect on my week critically and high-light some areas of concern. I was able to reflect upon how I could deal with certain situations in the future. It also made me think about what I had learnt and areas that I haven't learnt and would like to.

Students were also asked: 'What was the most positive aspect of undertaking the PDP?' Responses to this included:

The reflective thought it provided.

Having some structure to base my reflective diary on.

To see how skills can develop.

The reflective log.

What you learn and how you apply it to your work.

Help us to achieve our goal, more specific and think critically.

It actually helps you to structure your development and the recording of the progress of that development.

I am able to think about what I have learned from each experience. It motivated me towards a better self.

Being able to look back and see how I have developed, throughout the year.

Being able to see just how much I had achieved during the year.

It allowed me to critically reflect on my placement to write up my logbook.

We are hoping that the feedback will enable us to combine the Personal Development Plan with the Reflective Learning Journal. At the same time, perhaps it could be presented to students in electronic form, rather than paper form – or even both. The research undertaken by Thompson asked students which format they preferred the PDP to be available in. The results are shown in Table 1.

Almost half of the students surveyed indicated a preference for an online or web-based means of completing the PDP.

With technology being used to great advantage by Aston Business School's placement office in other areas of student support (i.e. Blackboard, a placement intranet and discussion board), the use of technology in the development of the logbook will be looked at in more detail in the near future.

Discussion

All students who went on placement in 2003/04 were asked about their placement when they returned to university in October 2004. A similar survey was undertaken in October 2005. The 2004 survey showed that some students felt that the advice given to them on the logbook was insufficient: 'more information on logbook should be available'; 'more straightforward guidelines for the logbook'; 'more detail on each piece of coursework'; 'examples of logbooks should be made available' and 'the placement report and logbook should count towards final year grade'.

Students on placement from 2004/05 have benefited from the use of the Blackboard virtual learning environment (VLE). A placements module has been developed which incorporates the functionality of student discussion boards. These boards facilitate student discourse, along with offering quick access to

> …particularly useful as I had an unsuccessful placement. Rather than dwell on the negative aspects it helped me to see instead not only what I was learning but where I was going wrong

a member of the placements team, with whom students can raise queries. A range of topics has been discussed through the boards, including the issues surrounding writing up their logbooks.

Key questions posed on the discussion boards from July 2004 to April 2005 related to students' unease with writing in the first person, writing descriptively and not reflectively, simply not recording experiences at source and so on.

Anecdotal feedback and evidence from placement tutors also suggests that students are more challenged by the log than by a 5,000-word academic essay

Table 1 Which of the following formats would you prefer?

Options	%
Online or web-based	44
Paper-based PDP	32
Blackboard or WebCT	14
Paper-based and online PDP	2
CD-Rom or floppy disk	2
Other	6

linking theory to practice.

A further barrier for some is the need to involve their supervisor – supervisors are required to sign off the monthly entries. As a development piece rather than an academic one, the logbook facilitates regular discussions between the student and their employer. This means that in even the busiest of commercial enterprises, the supervisor has an obligation to sup-

> the logbook facilitates regular discussions between the student and their employer… in even the busiest of enterprises, the supervisor has an obligation to support the student's development

port the student's development and learning and this is underpinned by the logbook. However, this does not always occur, for some of the following reasons:

❏ The student has not developed a relationship with their employer.
❏ The student wishes to write about an incident involving the supervisor.
❏ The student feels that the level of reflection is too personal and they do not wish their supervisor to read the piece.
❏ The supervisor does not make time for these developmental meetings.

While the nature of the reflective process is personal, the involvement of the supervisor helps to support the agreed framework and provides further credence; confirmation that the learning and development activities the student has described and reflected upon have taken place.

With a range of intrinsically linked issues, the logbook (as a piece of coursework) has been examined. The information provided to students in their placement year briefing pack was scrutinised. It was felt that some of the information could be ambiguous. Some students were also misinterpreting the guidance provided, which led to too many descriptive pieces being written and submitted. In other words, students were 'logging' their activities and were not spending enough time identifying the learning which had actually taken place – therefore they had not reflected on it enough or at all.

For students embarking on their placement for the academic year 2005/06, we decided to revise the title

of this piece of placement year coursework: logbook will become Reflective Learning Journal. We acted on students' feedback and feedback from tutors involved in marking the log. We believe that effecting a simple change in the title of the piece will be an important step in making the concept of reflection a much more explicit and tangible practice. This seemingly cosmetic change was backed up by structural changes and clearer guidance on what being reflective is and what it involves.

Furthermore, the authors carried out extensive reading on refection, reflective learning and the use and value of logbooks and journals in learning. Staff also attended a training course on reflective learning which will enable improved guidance for students. In addition, the authors' personal and professional experience through continuing professional development in their individual fields has led to a deeper insight into reflective practice and ways in which this life skill can be developed.

Overall, we felt that some students demonstrated either a lack of ability or willingness to engage wholeheartedly with the task. For some, the term logbook conjured up the notion of the piece as descriptive (i.e. literally logging what they did, what happened) despite clear instructions provided. Critical self-reflection to only a basic level was being carried out by some students.

The difficulties associated with reflection were also experienced by students who took part in the PDP pilot. Participants were asked: 'Did you find it easy or difficult to reflect?' See Table 2. Only 14% of students surveyed stated that they had found it easy or

Table 2 Did you find it easy or difficult to reflect?

Responses	%
Found it difficult at first, soon got the hang of it	33
I did not find it a problem	12
Felt it was easy as I'd done it before	2
Other	3
Found it very hard; felt out of my depth	5
Difficult; never done it before	5
Hard: not sure what is meant by reflection	2
Could have done with more tuition	7
Did not know what to write	19
Did not have enough opportunities to reflect	12

not problematic.

The structure for the reflective learning journal outlined in the discussion section shows the revised information that has been prepared for the placement year briefing pack and this has been presented to students (and tutors and supervisors) undertaking their placement in 2005/06.

The new cohort of student placements commenced in summer 2005 and hand in their logbooks in October 2006. Therefore, at the time of writing, there is no structured feedback on the success of the implementation of the revision. Feedback will be sought using the suggested following methods:

❑ The discussion boards on Blackboard will be monitored for frequently asked questions relating to the reflective learning journal during the course of the placement year.

❑ Tutor input will be actively sought as the placement year progresses, for example, through placement visits undertaken and reports written by placement tutors on each student (these are reviewed by the placements manager, with action taken as necessary.)

❑ An evaluation questionnaire will be issued to all students at the end of the placement year and feedback will be sought on the placement year coursework, including the journal, along with students' thoughts on the guidelines for this piece of work contained in their briefing pack.

❑ A sample of company supervisors will be contacted during the year and their input on the reflective learning journal will be sought.

In future, the broader aims of the project are to develop reflective practice activities and to encourage reflection by students across the four years of the undergraduate degree programme, not solely during the placement year. The art of reflection should become a truly integral part of the student experience when studying for an undergraduate degree at Aston Business School.

This could be combined with PDP project development, so that being a reflective thinker becomes part of our students' approach from the first year on and indicative of a shift in culture. As professionals are required to go through the process of stepping back from their daily work with some regularity for continuing professional development purposes, we too are striving for this to become simply part of what our students do – ultimately, better preparing them for seeking graduate employment and indeed, professional life.

References

Bullivant, N. 2005. *Briefing Pack for Students, Company Supervisors and Tutors – Placement Year 2005/2006*

Chartered Institute of Personnel and Development, 2005. *Chartered Membership Simplified Application Form.* London: CIPD

Fanthome, C. 2004. *Work Placements – A Survival Guide for Students.* Hampshire: Palgrave Macmillan

Fry, H., Ketteridge, S. & Marshall, S. 1999. *A Handbook for Teaching and Learning in Higher Education.* London: Kogan Page

Higson, H. E. and Jones, K. E. 2002. 'Your students have excellent knowledge and skills but they don't think about them…' Learning and Teaching Support Network BEST Conference, Edinburgh

Johnson, A. 2004. Keynote Address. ASET Conference, Cambridge

Moon, J. 1999. *Learning Journals.* London: Kogan Paul

Thompson, D. 2004. *Aston University Student Progress File & Personal Development Plan* (PDP)

HELEN HIGSON is Director of Undergraduate Studies at Aston Business School and is also Director of the Research Centre for Higher Education Learning and Management (HELM).

NICOLA BULLIVANT is Placements Manager, Undergraduate Programme at Aston Business School. She liaises with organisations across the UK, Europe and beyond, in the private and public sector, to ensure that a broad range of relevant professional placements are available to over 600 undergraduate students. Her own experience is in human resource management and recruitment and selection; she is a Chartered Institute of Personnel and Development member.

8 Embedding employability at London South Bank University: a process of evolution or design?

Helen George

This case study describes and discusses the experience of embedding employability into the curriculum of the business programme at London South Bank University (LSBU). It outlines what we were trying to achieve in the area of graduate employability, how this was underpinned by our philosophy of learning and teaching and the methods we used to achieve our objectives.

This case study uses two modules to illustrate our approach to embedding employability within the learning experience on the business programme. These are a level-two core module, Management Skills, and a level-three optional module, Life Career Development. The case study discusses and evaluates our experience and lessons for our own and others' practice.

Objectives

In addressing employability in the business curriculum and developing these modules, our objectives were to:

- Raise awareness in undergraduates of the need to develop work-relevant skills while studying, in order to move successfully into graduate careers.
- Ensure that individual students were empowered to reach their full potential,
- Ensure that students were equipped with the skills to identify and address their personal and career development needs.
- Ensure that graduates were well-prepared to meet the expectations of future employers and able to make a significant contribution both to the economy and the wider community.
- Develop a range of 'framework modules' at different academic levels for use of, or sharing by, different programmes. Capable of being contextualised for particular student cohorts, these modules would be supported by fully developed student and tutor resources, as well as assessments.

Rationale

At the heart of our approach to embedding employability is the understanding that employability and effective learning are closely aligned (Yorke & Knight, 2004). Attributes, skills and attitudes that contribute to academic attainment correspond closely with the qualities rated highly by employers, namely: management of self; engagement and interaction with others; information literacy; and management of task. Our institution has a very diverse student profile; we are committed to enabling such students to 'become what they want to be', not least in the area of employability.

Our commitment to widening participation means that we may offer opportunities to individuals who have to strive particularly hard to reach the level achieved by university graduates. This leads to pressure on LSBU and programme teams to adopt learning and teaching strategies to support student achievement and contribute to improving retention rates.

As in many other HEIs, there is increasing pressure on resources and increasing demands on academics' time for scholarship, research and managing larger classes. Solutions to the problem needed to be effective, and also to be resource efficient. This led to the development of framework modules and shared reuseable learning resources.

LSBU's vision, stated in its Strategic Development Plan 2003, is of

a university... focused on the needs of its students and the needs of the London economy and its global counterparts. (LSBU)

This recognises not only the aspirations of individuals to access higher education, but also the university's role in contributing to the provision of a skilled workforce.

Graduate employability, for us, is about far more than gaining a 'graduate' job. We believe that it also involves the ability to perform successfully in that job and to have the capacity and willingness to engage in ongoing personal and professional development. Our graduates should move into the world equipped with subject understanding, personal qualities, skills and the capacity to see how these aspects relate to each other to inform their future learning. This meta-cognitive understanding of learning and self-development has been evolving for some time in the literature (Flavell, 1976; Lawrence, Roberts & Erdos, 1993; Yorke, 2004).

Context

LSBU is a large, post-1992 institution with a strong tradition of providing vocational education and of engaging in widening participation. It has one of the most diverse student bodies in UK higher education: 60% of students are from ethnic minorities and 44% from social classes IIIM, IV and V. Five per cent of students have declared disabilities and only 20% of entrants are aged under 21.

The business programme evolved during the 1990s from the highly successful BA in Business Studies, originally launched in 1971. It is a significant part of the undergraduate portfolio of the recently formed Faculty of Business, Computing and Information Management (formerly the Business School). The programme consists of a BA in Business Studies, with a placement year and a BA in Business Administration, with no placement. Level one consists of eight core modules (known as units), including a Business Skills module; these introduce the functional areas of business. The remainder of the programme provides a high degree of flexibility and choice.

At level two there are two core modules, Management Skills and Research Skills for Business. Students may then begin to specialise in preparation for a functional pathway at level three. In the final year there is only one core module, Strategic Management, and a double-credit project. The remaining level-three modules consist of three specialist pathway modules and two option modules from within or outside the specialist curriculum.

There are currently 600–700 full- and students across the programme. Significant transfer in at level two and level three with credit from other LSBU programmes or from other institutions. The profile of this intake is consistent with that of the university in general, with a high proportion of overseas and European Union students.

Approximately 130 students are registered for an HND in Business Studies, which shares the two core modules at level two. There are also three combined honours fields, in Human Resource Management (HRM), Management and Accounting, with a combined cohort of 250 who share the majority of their modules with single honours students. The programme is therefore highly complex in curriculum structure, delivery, pattern of recruitment and diversity of intake.

This case study tracks how two modules, Management Skills and Life Career Development, are used to embed employability in the curriculum. They have been chosen because developing student employability is an explicit learning outcome of both units. They are not, however, the only way in which employability is addressed in the programme. Other modules, placement opportunities and a range of extra-curricular activities also allow students to prepare for transition into the workplace. In some cases, however, the employability aspects are currently implicit, rather than explicit.

These two modules were not designed in isolation. They were set within an evolving programme structure, informed by powerful external drivers such as the Dearing Report (1997). It became clear that, in addition to providing knowledge and understanding of business, our curriculum needed to broaden out. It needed to incorporate both the traditional intellectual skills associated with graduate education with a range of transferable skills valued by both the individual learner and future employers.

Description

The two modules chosen for this study are typical of an approach to the design of this type of employability module at LSBU. Such 'framework modules' exist at all three levels and are offered on programmes both within business and in other disciplines such as Computing and Applied Science. Originally used to develop programme-specific modules for business, this approach has now been applied to employability modules that are centrally validated and can be taken 'off the shelf' by programme teams and contextualised to particular cohorts of students.

The consistent features of these modules, regardless of level, are that they all:

- Have explicit outcomes related to personal development.
- Have at least one element of assessment that requires the student to write reflectively on where they are, where they would like to be and how they might get there.
- Use an enquiry-guided learning approach and are usually delivered in a workshop style.
- Come with a fully developed set of resources for tutors and students, that can be used, adapted, shared and passed on.

In each case, core values underpin the design of the learning experience: the need to stretch students to engage with current personal and intellectual capacity and to support them in purposeful reflection on how they can develop themselves to reach their personal and career goals.

Management skills

In 1997 the programme planning team considered that, while necessary and worthwhile, the inclusion of specific outcomes for transferable or key skills was problematic.

Module development

Personal development, interpersonal communication and teamworking were seen as examples of lower-order outcomes relative to subject content and 'proper' academic skills such as critical thinking, analysis and academic writing. Challenging for staff to deliver, they were not easily explicitly addressed or assessed in 'academic' modules. The solution was to put them into the 'black bag', as it was called – the broadly based Management Skills module. The specific development and delivery of this unit could safely be handed over to 'evangelical' skills tutors!

The programme team was satisfied that, together with a pre-existing level-one module, Business Skills, this core unit would deliver all the skills students

needed without encroaching on the more traditional academic content in the remainder of the programme. The other function of Management Skills, in conjunction with a business research module, was to form an essential element in the 'ladders and bridges' progression route between the HND in Business Studies and the degree programme. The explicit 'skills-based' approach envisaged in delivering the modules was seen as appropriate to both constituencies.

Aims

The module is concerned with developing the critical, interpersonal and organisational skills needed by a potential manager to function effectively in both internal and external organisational environments. Students are expected to reflect on experiences in the facilitated workshops and to consider how they need to develop their own skills in order to prepare to move into the workplace. Since the central theme of the module is personal development, it is relevant both to students who have little work experience and to those who are already familiar with the working environment prior to choosing to study further.

Management Skills addresses employability through Personal Development Planning, emphasising self-awareness and the importance of personal effectiveness in managing key business functions. It also develops employability in a broader sense, requiring students to engage with the ambiguity and uncertainty of the business environment. It provides an opportunity to fit subject understanding into the broader context of their own learning, aspirations and beliefs.

Outcomes

The module builds a practical skills base on the foundation of knowledge and competencies gained in other course modules. It provides an important link to the working environment for those students taking the industrial placement year, as well as forming a basis for all students' longer term career planning. It lays conceptual foundations for the final year, by introducing students to business strategy. Specific outcomes are that students will be able to:

- Recognise the qualities, capabilities and skills that can contribute to effective management in today's competitive business environment.
- Relate to the importance of innovation and creativity in the management of change.

- Recognise and select appropriate strategic techniques for application in solving business problems.
- Select appropriate sources of information in order to carry out business-focused research.
- Reflect on their personal effectiveness as learners and assess their own career development needs.
- Demonstrate and reflect on their own capacity to work independently and with others, to complete a set of tasks and to communicate their solutions effectively, orally and in writing.

Learning and teaching

The learning and teaching is delivered through seven one-day face-to-face workshops, each focusing on a particular skill area or theme. These workshops are designed to replicate management training with activities that are student-centred and learner-oriented. They are organised around group exercises designed to be participative with lots of interaction to develop the individual student's skills base.

In addition to the workshops, students have to undertake a range of self-managed individual and team-based research and activities that feed directly into the module assessment. The module now has a fully developed set of student and tutor resources, which have been collected, adapted and packaged over the seven years that it has run.

Assessment

The workshops, small group activities and private study tasks are designed to provide many opportunities for tutors, students and their peers to give formative feedback. Module outcomes are summatively assessed through a problem-based, real-life business case study, with an individual and team element and a short portfolio that links what students have learnt about their current capabilities, development needs and career aspirations to what they have discovered about employer expectations.

The assessment is designed to allow students to investigate complex real-life questions, identify and collect appropriate evidence, and present, analyse and interpret their results. In each element of assessment, students are asked to reflect on and evaluate the effectiveness of their approach to the tasks. In this way, assessment is a tool to encourage and support their learning and provides students with an opportunity to see for themselves how they can improve their performance.

Module evaluation

The module has now run for seven years with an annual cohort size of 200–400 students. The success rate has been consistently high; the small number of module failures is mainly confined to students who have not participated sufficiently in the workshops or the team project. Student attainment is usually slightly higher than the overall average for the cohort, with performance for individuals in line with, or slightly ahead of, that on their other modules.

Early feedback from both students and the external examiner led the module leaders to reduce significantly the amount of assessment and with each successive offering to refine the assessment tasks, the input and the delivery of the module. Adjustment to

> Our graduates … equipped with subject understanding, personal qualities, skills and the capacity to see how these aspects relate to each other and inform their future learning

the assessment levels has resulted in consistently positive feedback from students, externals and the teaching team.

- Students appreciate **the workshop resources and the guidance** provided on completing assessment tasks. The day-long workshops are tiring for some, but this is alleviated by the fact that these run on alternate weeks. Most students say they feel stimulated by the reality of the assessment tasks and consider that the practical skills they gain in accessing and using real-time information will be useful elsewhere in their studies and in future employment.
- **Teamworking**, predictably, gets more mixed feedback. Many students value the opportunity to work with a diverse range of individuals (teams are not self-selecting); most feel that the learning experience will pay dividends in the future. A small number of interpersonal difficulties arise

each year and the students affected may feel this has a negative impact on their learning and their attainment.

- External examiners have commented on **the impressive quality of the work produced by many students**. They have also commented positively on the relevance and utility of the module for students, the clarity of assessment material and the quality of the learning resources.

- **Tutors generally find the module interesting to deliver** and the resources supportive and useful in guiding, but not constraining, the students' learning. The creativity and standard of work produced by students often impress them. The module leaders ensure that there are opportunities across the semester for tutors to meet and share experiences and function as a team themselves, which again the tutor team has appreciated. Along with the workshop resources and clear assessment criteria this is one way of ensuring a reasonable level of consistency in the student learning experience. It also models appropriate team behaviours to the students – who do note them!

- **The content and learning approach** on the module make it possible for tutors from any subdiscipline within the business programme to be part of the teaching team. In practice, the module leaders and most of the tutors come from the HRM Department. We have also had tutors from Strategy, Marketing, Finance, Information Systems and even Languages in the team over the years, all of whom have contributed to and gained from the richness of the experience.

Life Career Development

Life Career Development had an altogether different genesis.

Module development

This unit was designed in 2000 as a level-three option for a combined-honours field in HRM that could also be taken by students on the Business degree. As such, it is firmly rooted in the undergraduate Human Resources curriculum, sitting alongside other gener-

alist and specialist HR modules.

The common link between this and Management Skills is that one of the module leaders developed both modules. Personal and professional learning from developing Management Skills was brought into the design and development of Life Career Development. Enquiry-guided learning, the team-based approach to delivery, the workshop format (although in this case a half, rather than a full, day) and the early development of a set of learning resources for each session are all replicated in this module.

The guiding principle in developing the module was to put the learner at the centre of this experience. We tried to see life and career development theory through the eyes of the individual students: to help

> the practical skills they gain in accessing and using real-time information will be useful elsewhere in their studies and in future employment

them understand how and why they became the person they are and to discover what this tells us about ourselves, others and the world we live in.

It is of particular interest to HRM students that the way in which the module has been developed makes it suitable for students from any discipline to take as an option. The student needs to be prepared to examine and engage with their life journey and their future aspirations in a way that is personally developmental and has critical and academic rigour.

The module provides a theoretical framework in which to discuss the process of career management and development. It considers this process in the context of individual development, the work situation and the wider social environment. Learners are required to be able to apply career theory to analyse the development of others' careers and the planning of their own. They engage with current changes in work patterns and the impact on careers and individuals' career development.

Aims

The aims of this unit are both academic and practical. Throughout the unit and assessment, learners are asked to reflect on the implications of career theories and concepts for organisations and the individuals within them. The unit sees career planning as a means of systematically preparing the learners for their next career transition from student to full-time employee. It therefore also allows the learner to plan and critically reflect on their personal career plan.

Outcomes

The module develops students' skills in analysis, critical thinking, problem-solving and task management. It develops their communication skills – written and oral – as well as explicitly engaging them in understanding their own learning process. Specifically, the outcomes for the module state that on completion learners will be able to:

❑ Explain some of the meanings work has for different individuals.
❑ Identify the major factors that affect occupational choice and career development.
❑ Explain the concepts of occupational choice and career development.
❑ Assess the implications of career theory for the management of careers in the context of current organisational practices.
❑ Critique the relevance of theoretical approaches to career development.
❑ Apply career planning techniques to facilitate their own and others career development.
❑ Critically reflect on their personal development needs.

Learning and teaching

Based on Lee's enquiry-guided-learning approach (2003), the module offers the opportunity for individuals to decide which aspects of career management they particularly want to explore as they develop their ability to evaluate and apply theory in practice. To a large extent, the learners determine individually which aspects of the syllabus are most interesting and relevant for them. They take this decision in the light of their individual circumstances and aspirations in relation to the Personal Career Plan and their chosen subject for the career development interview and report.

The tutors' primary role is to introduce the broad area of contemporary career management, theoretical concepts, models and issues. They also develop the

learners' ability to analyse, challenge, evaluate and apply these skills, both in class-based activities and completion of assessments. They help students frame and find answers to 'good' questions. Two tutors team up to teach each session. Formats vary, but each session has no more than 30 minutes continuous tutor-led input. In some self-discovery sessions after a 10–15 minute briefing, the learning activity becomes entirely student directed, with learners working in triads and tutors moving around as a resource.

Assessment

Formative assessment takes place throughout the unit via exercises and progress reports in class on which there is tutor, self and peer feedback. Summative assessment consists of two elements: the first is a Personal Career Plan with self-analysis of previous experience, current employability skills, personal interests, values and aspirations, as well as research

> The student needs to be prepared to examine and engage with their life journey and their future aspirations in a way that is personally developmental and has critical and academic rigour

into future career opportunities. The other element of assessment is a career development interview and report that requires learners to identify, interview and write a report on the life career development of an individual of their choice. This incorporates pre-interview research and preparation, a record of the interview and a post-interview report giving an analysis of the subject's career choices using appropriate models, theories and knowledge of career management.

Module evaluation

Life Career Development has run for five years with seven cohorts of students, full-time and part-time. The cohort size has grown from 25 to 65 for the current intake. Overall the experience has been a very positive one for both students and staff: the quality of much of the work produced has been outstanding and most students achieve marks ahead of their overall average.

Issues have been raised about the scalability of the module, especially this year. Experience has shown that the maximum staff/student ratio should be 1:20. The first assignment has proved difficult for students in every cohort. They have been able to rise to the challenge, however, and produce thoughtful, reflective pieces that have practical value for them. We always return this work, with feedback designed to help them develop their second, major piece of work.

> every effort is made from the outset to ensure that students are clear that this module is concerned with academic study and not a form of career counselling

Most students are able to use this as a learning experience and produce work of an even better standard for the second assignment. Feedback from students, external examiners and the experience of the teaching team has been used to refine the delivery and assessment of the module.

- **Student evaluation has been overwhelmingly positive**, with individuals finding their learning enlightening and practical. There is, however, one (but never more than one, regardless of cohort size) who rails vociferously against 'a lack of theory' and finds the delivery style and content 'inappropriate on a university course' and lacking any merit. Fortunately, this is counterbalanced by the majority who find it stimulating, challenging and often one of the most interesting modules they study on their programme. At each offering there are students who report that their learning on this module has 'changed the way they see themselves and the world', an experience that resonates with the notion of threshold concepts developed by Meyer and Land (2003).
- **External examiner feedback was initially concerned with the balance of practice and theory**, given that this is a level-three module. After the first offering, more theoretical resources were provided by the development of a set of journal readings to supplement the recommended texts. An additional task requiring an evaluation of the theoretical content was also introduced into the first coursework. Since this adjustment was made, the feedback from the external examiner has been

exceptionally positive, citing the challenging and innovative assessment method, the quality of work produced by students and the high quality and sensitivity of the feedback provided by tutors.

- **Tutors find it challenging to maintain the balance between the academic content and demands of the developmental aspects of the module**. It is particularly challenging to provide feedback and a grade for the first assignment. This needs to focus on the process and depth of reflection without appearing to be judgemental or insensitive to the individual learner. We have considered making this purely formative but students say that without a grade they doubt they would take the module seriously enough. Overwhelmingly, they say that completing this work for themselves enables them to understand the relevance of the underpinning theory in writing up their subjects' life and career choices.

Ethical issues are important in the design and delivery of such a module. Tutors need to provide guidance to students who, if prompted, may be able to engage with aspects of their experience that they have been avoiding or were unaware of. While every effort is made from the outset to ensure that students are clear that this module is concerned with academic study and not a form of career counselling, boundaries can become fuzzy. Experience has taught us that we need to be very clear about mutual expectations and assumptions of tutors and students. At the very beginning of the module we share evaluations from past students as well as agreeing a set of ground rules with each new cohort. Despite this challenge, teaching – or rather facilitating – this module has been a privilege and has proved to be a shared learning experience between tutor and student.

Discussion

Early discussions of employability concentrate heavily on students' acquisition of transferable skills. Since 2000, the discussion around skills has been subsumed into the wider arenas of employability, Personal Development Planning (PDP) and lifelong learning. The shift has been helpful in moving from a tick-box competence model of discrete skills (e.g.

Edexcel's Common Skills framework) to a far more holistic model, such as the USEM model of employability (Yorke 2004) that recognises the possibility of differing levels and continuous development for both learning and future employment. This shift has helped in moving the discussion at LSBU away from a predominantly 'deficit' model of the skills students lack, particularly on entry.

The focus now is increasingly on personal and learning development, offering an opportunity for students to enhance their achievement throughout their programme of study and beyond. It is something that fits much more easily within HE and begins to break down the 'ghetto' that designates skills courses as an area that is different and remedial. By broadening the scope of employability, consideration is given to ongoing skills development, alongside knowledge and understanding, within the curriculum.

In order to mainstream the importance of employability, however, it is necessary to demonstrate that this area of curriculum development and practice is underpinned by sound education theory. Why?

> because, without [theory], education is just hit and miss; …we risk misunderstanding not only the nature of our pedagogy but the epistemic foundations of our discipline. (Webb, 1996: 23)

> Theory allows us to engage in scholarship; to solve problems in our practice in a focused and logical manner; to share the insights from reflection and peer review through a common language; and to justify, promote and explain our practice to colleagues, managers and other stakeholders. (Carlile & Jordan, 2005)

Learning and teaching philosophy

Lewin (1943) asserted that there is 'nothing as practical as a good theory'. Consciously or unconsciously, our theories of learning have developed and refined through our own years of study, discussion, debate and reflection on our practice. Writing this case study has provided a useful opportunity to stand back and see whether my views on what constitutes a good learning experience are coherent. It gives a reflection point to test the congruence, or otherwise, between my conceptions of 'learning', 'teaching' and my practice.

Perry (1970) identified a hierarchy of k that describes the progressive developm student's thinking through higher education. This developmental trend involves moving from a simple belief that knowledge is finite and there are 'right' and 'wrong' answers, through the acknowledgement of many relative answers that can be justified by evidence, to a commitment to a reasoned interpretation that fits with the individual's values and ethics. At its

> By broadening the scope of employability, consideration is given to ongoing skills development, alongside knowledge and understanding, within the curriculum

highest level, which he termed Stage 9, knowledge is the evolution of awareness, expressed as levels of consciousness, in which the individual breaks through to new perspectives and discards those no longer useful. At this stage, students as learners are able to transform information and ideas and to engage in deep, rather than surface learning (Entwistle, 2000), thereby making sense of the world and developing as a person, the condition that is necessary for Yorke's 'meta-cognition'.

We can facilitate this learning journey for our students by taking a constructivist approach that assumes that students are capable of finding and want to understand meaning in situations and experiences. As teachers we cannot be in charge of our students' learning; we must accept their autonomy, allow for their diversity and work with their experience. This does not mean abandoning them!

Our purpose in designing these learning activities and assessment is to facilitate, prompt and guide their journey. There is a limit to what the student can learn unaided and there is a limit to the resources we can devote to them as teachers. We can encourage and provide prompts and material to move them on. We can design in opportunities for collaborative work and peer-tutoring.

We must approach material from the learner's perspective, helping them to build on what is already known and providing a scaffold to support and help them to a higher level. This is often a challenge when so much of the curriculum is reduced to the content of interchangeable and self-contained modules.

Conclusion

This case study sets out to tell the story of how our approach to embedding employability in the business curriculum has evolved. It would be wonderful to say that it came about through some grand design, however this would be less than truthful! The author hopes that colleagues elsewhere will find it helpful to share our experiences and would welcome feedback.

The debate about employability and the essential characteristics of the LSBU graduate continues: through the development of a further iteration of our Learning and Teaching Strategy; the implementation of initiatives aimed at embedding employability across the whole of LSBU's curriculum (that have arisen from a Change Academy Project in 2004); and the mapping of PDP across all current and future programmes.

References

Dearing, R. (1997) *Higher education in the learning society. Report of the National Committee of Inquiry into Higher Education.* HMSO, Norwich

Carlile, O. & Jordan, A. 2005. 'It works in practice but will it work in theory?' The theoretical underpinnings of pedagogy. In *Emerging Issues in the Practice of University Learning & Teaching* All Ireland Society for Higher Education http://www.aishe.org/readings/2005-1

Entwistle, N. 2000. Promoting deep learning through teaching and assessment: conceptual frameworks and educational contexts. Proceedings of the Teaching and Learning Research Programme Conference, Leicester

Flavell, J. H. 1976. Metacognitive aspects of problem solving. In Resnick, L. B. *The Nature of Intelligence*, **12**, 231–235

Roberts, M. J. & Erdos, G. 1993. Strategy selection and metacognition. *Educational Psychology*, **13**, 259–266

Lee, V. 2003. Promoting learning through inquiry in *Essays on Teaching Excellence, Towards the Best in the Academy* **15**, 3 The Professional & Organisational Development Network http://www.podnetwork.org

Lewin, K. 1943. Forces behind food habits and methods of change. *Bulletin of the National Research Council* **108**, 35–65

Meyer, J. & Land, R. 2003. Threshold Concepts and Troublesome Knowledge: linkages to ways of thinking and practising. In C Rust (Ed.) *Improving Student Learning Ten Years On.* Oxford: OCSLD

Perry, W. G. 1970. *Forms of Intellectual and Ethical Development in the College Years: A scheme.* New York: Holt, Rinehart & Winston

Webb, J. 1996. Why theory matters. In J. Webb & C Maughan (Eds.) *Teaching Lawyers Skills.* London: Butterworth

Yorke, M. 2004. *Employability in Higher Education: What it is – what it is not.* Learning & Employability Series 1. York: Higher Education Academy

Yorke, M. & Knight, P. T. 2004. *Embedding Employability into the Curriculum.* Learning & Employability Series 3. York: Higher Education Academy.

HELEN GEORGE is Head of the Learning and Teaching Enhancement Unit at London South Bank University. Her remit includes leading on the implementation of learning and teaching developments, including e-learning and employability, as well as other policy and curriculum initiatives aimed at enhancing the quality of the student learning experience. Helen continues to teach each semester. Her particular areas of interest are Personal and Career Development, Employability and Change Management. She is a member of the co-ordinating team for the HEA Change Academy initiative.

Work-based learning in the University of Ulster embedding employability in business studies

9

Gillian Armstrong, Una McMahon-Beattie and Kate Greenan

This case study highlights how the business studies degree programme in the University of Ulster incorporates the development of employability skills as an integral part of the preparation for, monitoring and assessment of work-based learning (WBL). The case demonstrates how employability is embedded into the learning outcomes for work-based learning and reviews the challenges of developing and maintaining opportunities for employability within business studies.

Formal supervised work-based learning is one of the most powerful tools in developing employability skills among business studies students. Based on Purcell and Pitcher's categorisation of employability skills (1996) (traditional academic skills, personal development skills and enterprise or business skills) the course team has agreed the following objectives for WBL:

1 To develop and extend the study of academic disciplines.
2 To further develop the ability to relate theory to practice.
3 To reflect on their experience within the world of work and evaluate their own performance and learning
4 To reflect on experiences within this environment.
5 To improve their interpersonal and social skills.
6 To demonstrate innovative thinking and creativity, knowledge of future trends in the subject area and be able to communicate new ideas effectively.
7 To make informed career choices and consider the professional requirements of those careers.

Additionally, these objectives are advancing the personal development planning agenda within higher education. In this context, the issue of employability acts as a spur to students to see the relevance of their learning to their future career development. Work-based experiential learning within the programme provides the optimum level of connectivity with the world of work (SEDA, 2004). Despite the fact that 63% of graduates in Northern Ireland were reported to be in employment in 2003 (HEA, 2003), according to the Higher Education Statistics Agency's data for 2003 almost a third of graduate workers have previously been reported to be in non-professional jobs six months after leaving university. The need for graduate employability has never been higher; teaching it can help ensure that graduates have the ability, motivation and adaptability to fit the increasingly competitive graduate jobs market.

Support for the development of employability skills within the curriculum and the centrality of WBL in promoting employability is further evidenced within the University of Ulster formal committee structure. At faculty level, a placement tutor's group formally reports to Faculty Board, via the Teaching and Learning Committee. This group facilitates the exchange of best practice across subject discipline areas, such as accounting, marketing, human resource management and hospitality and tourism. At university level, a sub-committee on work-based learning takes responsibility for considering strategic

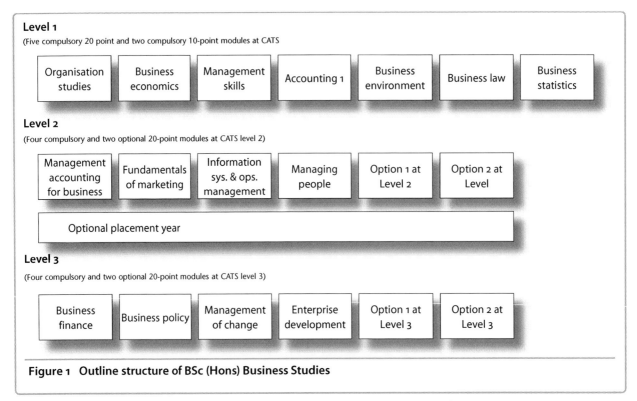

Level 1
(Five compulsory 20 point and two compulsory 10-point modules at CATS

| Organisation studies | Business economics | Management skills | Accounting 1 | Business environment | Business law | Business statistics |

Level 2
(Four compulsory and two optional 20-point modules at CATS level 2)

| Management accounting for business | Fundamentals of marketing | Information sys. & ops. management | Managing people | Option 1 at Level 2 | Option 2 at Level |

| Optional placement year |

Level 3
(Four compulsory and two optional 20-point modules at CATS level 3)

| Business finance | Business policy | Management of change | Enterprise development | Option 1 at Level 3 | Option 2 at Level 3 |

Figure 1   Outline structure of BSc (Hons) Business Studies

developments in the area.

The case will highlight how the programme objectives are achieved through an active partnership of student-university-employer within a formalised assessment process. This process adheres to the QAA Code of Practice on Placement Learning and is based upon the Faculty of Business and Management Placement Learning Handbook.

Rationale

Figure 1 shows the programme structure for Ulster's Business Studies degree and illustrates a holistic approach to the development of academic and employability skills. The course team has actively embedded opportunities for the development of employability skills within module teaching, learning and assessment strategies. For example, within the module entitled Fundamentals of Marketing, student skills in teamwork, presentation skills and business and organisation awareness are assessed via a sector-based product/service development group assignment. Work-based learning then enhances these types of skills in a realistic working environment.

Context

The development and promotion of employability at Ulster is central to the institution's *Vision and Strategy to 2010* and has underpinned teaching and learning across all faculties for many years. The university is characterised by a strong sense of a regional mission, placing it in the forefront of social and economic development in Northern Ireland. Many programmes of study are strongly vocational and reflect active and mutually rewarding links with industry, commerce and the professions. Students cite the opportunity to develop employability skills as a reason for applying to their programmes of study.

Of the university's full-time undergraduate students, 45% are enrolled on programmes of study which include a year out, which is generally paid, compared to 8% for the UK as a whole (University of Ulster, 2004). Of students on the business studies programme 60% currently spend the third year of a four-year degree programme on placement. On successful completion of their programme, students are awarded an additional qualification known as a Diploma in Industrial Studies (DIS). The business studies degree is viewed internally as a flagship programme for building experience with employers and business through proactive partnership.

The work-based-learning (WBL) process and assessment strategy

WBL preparation, monitoring and assessment of the period of work and WBL debrief spans a period of three academic years. The process can be viewed diagrammatically in Figure 2.

Employability and the online (WBL) preparation unit: Year two

Placement preparation sessions commence in year two in association with the careers service. These involve a series of lectures, workshop presentations from the placement tutor, employers, past and present placement students, careers specialists and advisers. Within this preparation there is a clear focus on developing the student's understanding of the need to develop their employability skills and this is supported by a university-wide online work-based-learning system (WebCT). This incorporates a preparation for WBL unit and a CV builder. The unit not only provides information and guidance on the WBL opportunities available, but also offers the students an opportunity to develop their own vocational profile through self-assessment and career decision-making.

For a student considering the range of opportunities available and to take advice on how to use the recruitment process, information is provided on CV development, writing covering letters and on interview technique.

A CV builder uses information from the student record/PDP system to assist students in the development of an appropriate undergraduate CV. Students can select a CV format to suit the needs of their professional area.

WBL opportunities are brought to the attention of students, through student noticeboards and web-based media, to allow students to indicate their interests. CVs and/or application forms are sent to the company and the company shortlists in accordance with its normal

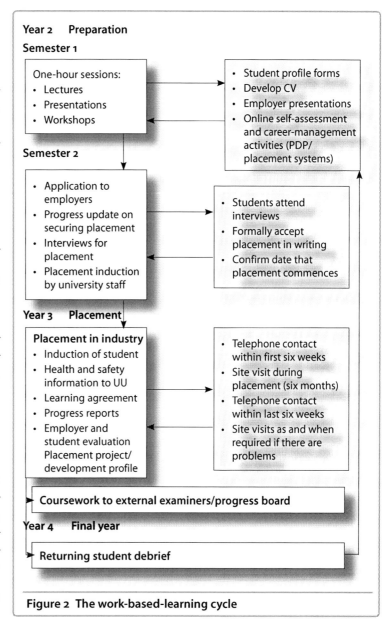

Figure 2 The work-based-learning cycle

recruitment procedures. Organisations which support the university's activities are drawn from both the private sector, ranging in size from small local indigenous SMEs to large international companies and the public sector. These employers have a central role in helping Ulster develop WBL policy and practice. The SME sector has particular significance for Northern Ireland in increasing much needed work-based learning opportunities. The university over many years has engaged in a range of activities to create links with and support the development of local companies. A recent initiative, for example, supported by the Higher Education Innovation Fund, involves a three-year project to raise the competitiveness of the SMEs in Northern Ireland by developing various models of WBL to meet the specific needs of that sector. Work will also focus on providing SMEs with online support for the recruitment and supervision of students.

On-placement and assessment process: Year three

Supervision is viewed as a shared responsibility between the employer and the university represented by the business studies course team. On each student's appointment to an organisation, an industrial supervisor/mentor is nominated by the employer to monitor the student's progress. A provisional training programme is formulated, which clearly identifies job/personal-related objectives and employability skills that are to be developed during the WBL period. Each student is also assigned an academic supervisor, who is a member of the business studies course team, as well as their industrial supervisor/mentor.

The business studies monitoring format (UK and Ireland) is as follows:

1 On arrival at their organisation, the student completes a contact details form (particulars of placement), a health and safety checklist and a learning agreement (this formalises the employability skills to be developed).
2 The academic supervisor makes contact with the student, normally by telephone/email and an on-site visit:
   ❑ The first telephone or email contact takes place within the first six weeks of placement
   ❑ The visit normally takes place midway through the placement
   ❑ The second telephone or email contact takes place within the last six weeks.

The purpose of the on-site visit is to allow the three parties involved – the student and the industrial and academic supervisors – to review the student's progress in meeting identified employability skills. The academic supervisor completes a report form that forms part of the academic assessment of placement.

To support students further on international placements (outside UK/Ireland), contact will be made formally (either by email or by telephone) on a further two occasions. Wherever possible, the university endeavours to visit students on international placements. Where this is not possible, alternative arrangements are made and students are advised of these where appropriate.

A review of contact between the business studies students and the academic supervisors is carried out twice in the year, to ensure that students are maintaining an appropriate level of contact and are progressing satisfactorily in the placement.

The elements of assessment are as follows:		
Element 1		
Academic evaluation:	Academic supervisor's report	Pass/fail
Element 2		
Industrial evaluation:	Industrial supervisor's report	Pass/fail
Element 3		
Student written work:	Project Personal and professional development profile	100%

Figure 3   Assessment strategy

The assessment strategy recognises the importance of employer feedback on student progress. In order to ensure consistency in employer feedback across placements, the faculty issues guidance notes for employers which clearly outline the assessment criteria for identified employability skills. Any queries regarding assessment can be discussed during the on-site visit. In addition, clear channels of communication are encouraged between academic and industrial supervisors. This helps should any issues arise regarding the assessment process.

The development of generic assessment criteria for both project and personal and professional profiles has become essential in order to maintain consistency across the high number of internal examiners (academic supervisors) involved in placements. The ability to ensure consistency in assessment when dealing with a large number of employers and academics has been cited as a key strength by the external examiner for placement.

Business studies programme – student written work

Having established the learning agreement outlining their job-related and personal objectives at the start of the placement, the student completes an interim and final report reflecting on progress and performance during the period. This is one of the key methods used to encourage students to reflect critically on the development of their employability skills and to develop appropriate action plans.

At the end of the placement year, students submit a personal and professional development profile. The aims of this profile are to:

❏ Provide an opportunity to set objectives and critically reflect on personal and professional development.
❏ Provide an opportunity to critically reflect on management of self and business impact.

On review of these profiles, within the business studies programme, skills such as communication, confidence, teamwork and organisational ability feature frequently as desired objectives for placement. The value of placement is evident in the reflective commentaries provided by the students. One current student in a food-and-drink-marketing organisation reflects as follows:

From reflecting back since I first began on placement and looking at myself now, I can see a vast change. I am not only confident, but I have grown to become much more independent, also by simply having my own car to travel to and from work has definitely made an impact in this area. I now have the ability to decide what I want with my career. I have interacted well with my work colleagues on a professional basis which too has resulted in a change in my personality.

Students also complete a project of 5,000 words, based either on an aspect of the their work, or on their overall placement experiences. The aims of the project will be to:

❏ Provide an opportunity for a research-based in-depth study or critical reflection of personal/professional development to include employability skills.
❏ Encourage innovation where appropriate.

❏ Display an ability to integrate information from a range of sources and research techniques.
❏ Provide an opportunity for students to synthesise information and apply to organisation or self.

The subject of projects can be quite varied and has included such areas as:

❏ The impact of low-cost airlines on the travel industry.
❏ An assessment of quality-control programmes for food-and-drink manufacturers.
❏ The role of event management in the marketing of the NI food-and-drink industry.
❏ A review of employee-appraisal systems in the local council.

Debrief

In association with Career Services sessions in their final year, business studies students are encouraged to reflect on the WBL experience in the formulation of graduate career plans. Students are normally required

> better performance in the first class and second class upper division categories for those students who elected to complete industrial placement

to present a snapshot of their placement experience to the students preparing for placement.

Evaluation

As with any module of study within the faculty, placement coursework is subject to the standard procedure for double marking and is moderated by an external examiner. Students receive detailed feedback on their placement performance using relevant assessment pro-formas prior to their final year studies.

Students evaluate the work-based learning programme by completing a questionnaire. They generally see the value of work-based learning and in many cases their attitude to work has changed. Having said that, many students have felt that the placements were not what they expected and their initial career plans have changed as a result. Employers tend to evaluate the work-based learning process in their ongoing communication with academics and feedback is generally positive after the initial few months. Issues that have arisen over recent years tend to be concerned more with international placements and students continuing their professionalism outside the work environment. In relation to academic feedback, academic supervisors can find the assessment of student reflection difficult and appreciate guidance and cross-marking from the placement tutor as and when required.

University placement activity has received positive comment from QAA subject review teams, with both the general organisation of placement and arrangements for student preparation recognised as being of a high standard. Placement activity is also considered as part of the university's Programme Approval Management and Review and Annual Subject Monitoring processes. For example, as part of the 2002/03 Annual Subject Monitoring process, an evaluation of business studies degree awards noted a better performance in the first class and second class upper division categories for those students who elected to complete industrial placement (see Figure 4). This type of information is invaluable in highlighting to students the added-value element of work-based learning.

In addition, Higher Education Statistics Agency benchmarks for 2003 indicate that the percentage of business and management graduates taking up employment was 76.1%. In comparison, 81% of graduates of the business studies programme entered employment in 2003, the majority of whom had completed a WBL assessed period. A further ten per cent were in further study and only four per cent were classified as unemployed and seeking work.

A review and evaluation of teaching, learning and assessment strategies associated with WBL across the university is currently underway. A key focus of this is the need to further enhance the methods by which employability skills are developed, measured and reflected upon. A review of placement learning outcomes across faculties revealed a common emphasis on developing employability (transferable/key) skills and, to a lesser extent, in developing subject-specific skills and knowledge of professional practice. As both the QAA code and relevant literature on developing employability support this focus on generic employability skills and the use of placement as part of personal development planning (PDP), the university feels that the learning outcomes of placement should focus on generic employability skills to help ensure relevance and consistency in assessment across faculties. This focus on employability skills is particularly relevant to the business studies programme, where the associated graduate market is highly competitive and requires students to possess the 'softer skills' to succeed in a business environment.

Discussion and challenges

The benefits of work-based learning are widely recognised in Northern Ireland and the University of Ulster continues to be the third largest provider in the UK of such programmes. Programmes such as business studies are long established as key providers of work-based learning opportunities within the university, providing benefits to a company such as:

- The cost-effective employment of a business-studies undergraduate for one year to contribute to a specific business project.
- Close liaison with academic staff who will support the student and supervise the project to completion.
- Highly motivated and skilled undergraduates who are willing and eager to learn.
- Undergraduates who have been exposed to the best in research-informed learning and who are up to date with the latest in business and management theory and practice.

WBL remains one of the key tools for adding value to a business studies student's university experience and ultimately to graduate employability. However, there remain several key challenges facing the course team:

1 Employers want graduates 'to hit the ground running', but there are fewer opportunities within

	Total % 2003	With placement % 2003	Without placement % 2003
First Class	9.21	13.58	4.23
Second Class: Upper Division	60.53	70.37	49.30
Second Class: Lower Division	26.32	16.05	38.03
Third Class	0.66	0.00	1.41
Others	3.29	0.00	7.04
Total	100.00	100.00	100.00

Figure 4 The effect of WBL on degree classifications awarded 2002/03

the major blue-chip companies. Only 20% of graduates were employed by the major blue-chip companies in 2003. Opportunities within the SME business sector are becoming more important, despite the fact that this sector needs additional support in professionalising student supervision.

2 Graduate numbers are expanding faster than the market for traditional graduate jobs. Graduates are more diverse in age, social background and motivations, while the labour market they enter is more complex and volatile. Against this background, the need for lifelong learning as the ultimate employability skill needs to be integral to the design of teaching, learning and assessment strategies associated with WBL.

3 An increase in part-time working and student fees is beginning to decrease student motivation for a full-time one-year placement. However, the fact that all placements on the business studies programme are paid may mitigate the impact of increasing student fees.

4 Many higher education staff in the course team may perceive the development of WBL as not generally associated with real institutional rewards – in contrast to the perceived rewards for research activity and RAE performance. Awareness and recognition of the value of developing employability within programme design could be more formally embedded within appraisal and promotional activities at higher education level.

References

BMAP, 2004. *BEST Student Employability Profiles 2004*. Milton Keynes: Business, Management and Accountancy Subject Centre, Higher Education Academy, Open University Business School

Higher Education Authority (HEA), 2003. *First Destinations of Award Recipients in Higher Education*. Dublin: Higher Education Authority

Higher Education Authority (HEA), 2003. *First Destinations of Students Leaving Higher Education Institutions*. Dublin: Higher Education Authority

Higher Education Academy (LSTN), 2003. *Graduate Employability*. Circular 5, Briefings for Senior Managers in Higher Education. York: LSTN Generic Centre

Prospects, 2003. *Prospects Directory*. Manchester: Graduate Prospects

Purcell, K, & Pitcher, J. 1996. *Great expectations: The new diversity of graduate skills and aspirations*. Manchester: Association of Graduate Careers Advisory Services and the Higher Education Careers Services Unit (CSU)

Quality Assurance Agency for Higher Education (QAA), 2000. *Honours Degree Benchmark Statements: Business & Management (General)*. London: Quality Assurance Agency for Higher Education

Staff and Educational Development Association (SEDA), 2004. *Employability: Learning through partnerships with employers*. SEDA Special 15, Birmingham: SEDA

University of Ulster, 2004. *Self-evaluation Document for QAA Institutional Audit Visit*. Belfast: The University of Ulster

Yorke, M. & Knight, P. 2004. *Embedding employability into the curriculum*. Learning and Employability series 3, York: Higher Education Academy

GILLIAN ARMSTRONG is a Lecturer in Marketing at the University of Ulster and Chair of the Placement Tutors Group for Business and Management. She has an interest in online learning, and has been actively involved in the development of a web portal for work experience, in collaboration with the Careers Service.

KATE GREENAN started lecturing in 1983 and is currently Professor and Head of School of Accounting at the University of Ulster. She is a member of the Advisory Board of the Higher Education Academy subject centre for Business Management Accountancy and Finance and of the Programmes Steering Committee of the Association of Business Schools.

UNA MCMAHON-BEATTIE is a Lecturer in Marketing at the University of Ulster and is currently the Subject Unit Co-ordinator for Business and Management. She was a placement tutor for 13 years and is still actively involved in the supervision, monitoring and assessment of students on placement both nationally and internationally.

10 Integrating employability and management skills into the tourism curriculum at Leeds Metropolitan University

David Hind

This case study explains how employability skills are integrated into the tourism curriculum at Leeds Metropolitan University. Employability skills are not just developed at level one – they are integrated and embedded into the curriculum at all levels of the course.

From day one of level one, semester one, all undergraduate tourism students at Leeds Metropolitan University start developing their portfolio of employability skills. A new level-one module – Employability and Management Skills – has been developed to initiate this process. This module includes a variety of innovative assessment, learning and teaching strategies to facilitate the students' skills development. Micro-teaching is a key component of the learning strategies used with work-related management scenarios, providing the focus for a theatre role-play exercise. Peer-assessment is used creatively to provide rapid and immediate feedback to the students on the development of their skills.

Objectives and context

The purpose of employability and management skills training on undergraduate tourism courses at Leeds Metropolitan University is to:

❏ Make students aware of the employability skills that employers expect of the graduates they recruit from universities.

❏ Provide structured learning opportunities for tourism students enabling them to develop further and reflect on their portfolio of employability and management skills.

❏ Encourage tourism students to transfer employability and management skills developed at

university to the world of work.

It is apparent that the careers marketplace has changed from being dominated solely by the bright, academically gifted person, to the domain of the person with management aptitude, displayed in their employability skills, in addition to intellectual abilities (Hind and Moss, 2005: 2).

In response to this change many university courses now include employability skills training and development as part of their curricula. The highly vocational nature of tourism courses at Leeds Metropolitan University necessitates the integration of employability and management skills training into the undergraduate curriculum. This case study explains how this is achieved.

It is the contention of this case study that to develop the employability skills of students a programme of learning needs to be devised that is fully integrated into the curriculum. This paper explains how such a training programme has been integrated into the undergraduate tourism curriculum at Leeds Metropolitan University.

Developing employability skills

When conceiving an employability skills development programme it is important to consider the teaching and learning strategies to be used. Developing employability skills is a four-stage process:

1 Making students aware of and sensitive to the employability skills to be developed

The first step in the process is to build students' cognitive awareness of the skills they must develop and the constituent elements of those skills. This can be achieved in a number of ways: demonstration; tutor-led presentation and discussion; independent study (e.g. text books – see Hind and Moss (2005) www.employabilityskillsforstudents.co.uk); observation, analysis and evaluation of the skills used by other people in videos or DVDs.

2 Practice

Once the students become aware of the employability skills to be developed and what constitutes a competent level of performance, strategies have to be developed whereby the students can apply these skills.

One teaching strategy that is particularly effective for skills development is micro-teaching. Micro-teaching, as the term suggests, involves breaking the class down into smaller sub-groups which are then the focus of attention. In these groups, a variety of learning strategies can be implemented which will involve all the group members participating in employability skills development. A frequently used learning strategy for skills development is role-play exercises. When the role-play is video-recorded, constructive feedback can be provided to students on the development of their skills.

3 Feedback on the practice

Just as important as practice is the feedback that the students receive on the strengths of their employability skills and the skills they need to develop further. Feedback is essential and should be provided through peer- and self-reflection, as well as by the tutor. As mentioned above, recording role-play exercises can significantly improve the quality of feedback that the students receive, particularly if well-prepared instruments are used for structuring the feedback.

4 Further practice in the light of feedback

To consolidate the progress that has been made so far and to develop further the employability skills of students, additional practice and feedback is required. This might be within the curriculum being studied but more realistically within a practical work-related setting. Feedback will now probably be through the student's self-reflection, and supplemented by formal or informal feedback received from a supervisor in the workplace.

When integrating a programme of employability skills development into the curriculum, course teams have three options to choose from:

1 Integrate employability skills development into the curricula of a number of modules. Modules that develop academic subject knowledge could have learning outcomes relating to employability skills development.

2 Design a specific module that specifically focuses on the development of employability skills.

3 Utilise both 1 and 2 above.

The approach adopted on undergraduate tourism courses at Leeds Metropolitan University is option 3. It is felt that this approach maximises the learning that students gain from a programme of employability skills development.

To determine which employability skills should be developed within the 'employability module', all the skills it was considered that students should develop as part of their course were identified. A mapping exercise of all tourism modules was then undertaken to identify and establish which employability skills could be most effectively developed within the 'academic modules'. Each module team took responsibility for developing these skills in addition to the academic subject content of their module. For example, the module entitled Travel Industry took responsibility for developing students' report writing skills, while Principles of Tourism provided opportunities for students to develop further their oral presentation skills. Part of the assessment for these modules involved students writing reports and making formal presentations.

The employability module – Employability and Management Skills – was then designed to incorporate a number of high-order employability skills that would not be developed fully within the other academic modules. Within the new module, time could be devoted to utilising the four-stage process identified above. This process would facilitate the students' development of their problem-solving, creativity and management skills, as well as giving opportunities for students to enhance further their learning and study, communication, groupwork and career management skills.

The Employability and Management Skills module

In designing the module, three principles were acknowledged:

1 Skills are developed through active participation – thus in this module the students should be as 'active' as possible.
2 Students learn through feedback – a number of opportunities should be taken to provide formal feedback to students on the development of their skills.
3 Immediate feedback improves motivation and enhances learning – assessment strategies should be devised that facilitate this.

Employability and Management Skills is a level one, semester one module delivered over a 12-week teaching period. It was felt that incorporating the above three principles into the design of the module would create an interesting and stimulating learning experience. In addition, through micro-teaching, students would establish friendships with their peers that would help them adjust to university life, contributing to their retention and loyalty to the course. It was designed around four broad themes that reflected the learning outcomes for the module:

❏ learning and study skills
❏ communication skills
❏ career management skills
❏ groupwork skills.

Within the above four themes, assessment strategies were devised that enabled the students to develop their:

❏ problem-solving skills
❏ creativity skills
❏ leadership and management skills
❏ reflective skills.

The first assessed exercise occurred in week four.

CV and covering letter

Tourism courses offered at Leeds Metropolitan University include a 48-week industrial placement that takes place in year two. To help students develop skills in applying for placements (and other employment opportunities) the first theme within the module is career management skills. After receiving guidelines on how to write effective CVs and covering letters, the students were required to apply for a 'mock' industrial placement. Six advertisements for tourism-industry placements were posted on the Employability and Management Skills WebCT site and students were asled to apply for one of them with a covering letter and CV.

To provide immediate feedback to the students in week four on the success of their CVs and covering letters, peer-assessment was used. Each student received a copy of another student's CV and covering letter and had to assess them from the perspective of the industrial placement employer using clearly designed marking criteria. Students were encouraged to write their feedback both on the CV and covering letter as well as on the assessment sheet. However, to develop students' skills in providing feedback to others, once the CV and covering letter had been assessed, each student also had to provide oral feedback to the person whose CV and covering letter they had assessed.

Interview skills

The assumption was then made that each student had been successful in applying for the industrial placement and had been offered an interview for the job. In week six of the semester the interview skills of the students were assessed. Once again, prior to the assessment, instruction was provided on how to be successful in interviews. Unfortunately, because of the number of students on the course, it was not possible to conduct lengthy oral interviews with each student. Instead, two learning and assessment strategies were devised. First, each student was asked to write answers to questions that are frequently used in job interviews. After writing their answers each student was given another student's responses and was required to adopt the role of the interviewer and to assess the answers given. Each assessor was asked to provide as much feedback as possible on the answers to the various questions. When this had been completed, the assessor had to explain to the interviewee how he or she rated the responses.

Then each student, in private with their tutor, was asked orally one of the questions posed in writing to give them an opportunity to communicate verbally their answer to the question. At the conclusion to each mini-interview, the tutor provided immediate feedback to the student on his or her response.

This exercise concluded the career management element of the module.

Theatre role-play

After week six of the semester, the content of the module progressed to consider groupwork skills. Instruction was provided for the students on a variety of different elements and aspects of groupwork before they embarked on a major assessment that would give them the opportunity of developing and practising a number of employability and management skills.

The students were broken into small groups and each group was given a tourism management scenario. Examples of the scenarios are:

1 Late check-in

Passengers arrive late for a flight check-in and the airline staff have to manage the situation.

2 Whiteknuckle shaker

Employees at a theme park feel that one of their team members is underperforming. The team members have to resolve this problem.

3 Club 18–70

In error, a tour operator books 18–30 guests into a hotel used by more elderly customers. The tour rep has to handle the complaints of both groups of guest.

4 Campsite challenge

An English family arrives at a foreign campsite on the back of a breakdown truck – their car has broken down. The campsite manager speaks little English but needs to help the family overcome their problem with a local garage owner who speaks no English. This management scenario required the students to communicate in another language (one of the option modules on the tourism courses enables students to develop their foreign language skills).

The briefing notes provided for the students on all the management scenarios were very simple. The management scenario was outlined and they had to devise the storyline and write a script that illustrated how the management challenge could be resolved. Each member of the group had to play a role in the exercise that would be video-recorded.

The exercise took place in week 11. After each group completed their role-play they were given the video tape on which their role-play had been recorded and the opportunity to play back and review their performance using the assessment criteria that tutors use to formally assess the role-play. This allowed them to overcome in private any embarrassment they might experience about seeing themselves on screen. This facilitated the next stage in the process – feedback.

Tutor feedback and the mark for the assessment was provided to students in week 12. A sensitive approach was adopted to this important part of the developmental process. Short clips from the videos were played back to the class and students were asked to highlight what was particularly impressive about the management scenarios. No comments about specific individuals were made; instead, comments were encouraged about behaviours that were in evidence within each role-play scenario. Aspects of the scenarios that could have been handled differently were explored, and the tutor took the opportunity to reflect on the approach that each group took to solving the management challenge.

Learning and study skills

The final assessment for this module took place in week 13, one of the assessment weeks after teaching had finished. The purpose of this assessment was to ensure that students had developed some of the learning and study skills that were considered to be essential for successful study at university.

An assessment day was planned in week 13 that would assess the students':

- notetaking skills
- Harvard referencing skills
- comprehension skills
- academic writing skills.

The assessment day started with a lecture (including a video playback) on a topic relating to one of the academic modules, Principles of Tourism. The students were required to take notes from both the lecture and the video. Following the lecture, students were given a question they had to answer, using their lecture notes and notes they had previously taken from academic journals or textbooks. The assessment criteria for this exercise reflected all the skills involved.

Integrating employability skills throughout the tourism curriculum

The Employability and Management Skills module proved to be an effective means of introducing the concept of employability skills development to the students. To reinforce the fact that employability skills are developed over time, a number of other teaching and learning strategies are deployed within the tourism curriculum at Leeds Metropolitan University. These are briefly summarised below:

- In semester two, level one, students study the module, Management in Tourism Organisations.
- Students have the opportunity of gaining practical work experience in year two on a 48-week industrial placement.
- During level two, students continue to reflect on and develop their employability skills in the module, Personal and Professional Skills for Managers.
- At level three, students work as tourism consultants to solve work-related problems that are set by real tourism businesses on the module, Tourism Consultancy Ventures.
- Students complete progress files and develop Personal Development Plans to support their learning and skills development at each level of their course.

Discussion

An innovative approach has been adopted towards the integration of employability skills into the tourism curriculum at Leeds Metropolitan University. Starting on day one of semester one, level one, students study the innovative module, Employability and Management Skills. At each subsequent level of the course there are modules that further enhance the students' portfolio of employability skills. Considerable opportunities are available for the students to transfer their learning at university to the world of work. A key focus of all the assessment, learning and teaching strategies referred to in this case study is that students arc involved as active learners and peer assessors, frequently through micro-teaching.

So what lessons have been learned?

- Employability-skills training needs to be integrated and embedded throughout the curriculum, with clear progression between the skills developed in each module and at each level of the course of study.
- For skills training to work, the students need to have confidence in their tutor. The tutor needs to create an environment where the students do not feel threatened by the learning strategies that are

employed. Thus, the tutor needs to appreciate and empathise with the concerns of the students and filter feedback so that it does not have a negative impact on the student.

- When planning a programme of employability skills training it is essential to devise learning situations that simulate as closely as possible scenarios that students will face in their future careers. This will add to the credibility of the programme and help motivate the students.
- Careful consideration has to be given to what is actually going to be assessed in the employability skills training programme and the means by which the assessment is to take place.
- While students initially find peer assessment daunting, in reality they are able to assess the work of their peers accurately. This is achieved by having clearly designed assessment criteria that are explained to students before they assess others' work. Tutor moderation of a sample of peer-assessed work indicated that the students were (on the whole) accurate in their evaluation and marking of work.
- Although learning strategies can be designed that are purely classroom-based, the opportunity to use special facilities such as video-recording studios helps to encourage greater commitment and professionalism – students rise to the challenge of being recorded.
- Students respond in different ways to the participative nature of employability skills training. Some students feel threatened by role-play exercises and being video-recorded. To reduce such anxiety, it is essential to stress the benefits of these learning strategies and to be sensitive to their concerns. Some students also find it difficult to watch their own performances on video. The role of the tutor in such circumstances is once again critical. Tutors need to reassure such students that comments in feedback sessions will not be made about individuals, but about how the role-play exercise worked as a management scenario.
- The management scenarios used for the theatre role-play exercise helped demonstrate to the students the relevance of the Employability and Management Skills module. All management scenarios were based on situations which previous students had encountered on their industrial

placements. By providing realistic management scenarios, students should be able to transfer the skills they are developing through this module to situations they face in employment.

❏ Feedback to students on the development of their employability skills is critical. Students will not always enjoy receiving feedback on the development of their skills. It therefore has to be offered in a tactful and constructive way, coming from the student, his or her peers and the tutor. However, at the end of this module the employability and management skills of the students had been developed further. Learning was achieved and the constructive feedback provided to the students was felt to be a key element of the learning process.

❏ The commitment of the tutor to innovative modes of assessment, learning and teaching is also important. The teaching team selected for the Employability and Management Skills module were colleagues who, it was felt, would be able to adopt a different style of delivery and assessment. These tutors could then act as catalysts for change to other colleagues, demonstrating that innovative modes of teaching and learning are effective.

❏ Employability skills cannot be developed solely within one module. The Employability and Management Skills module described in this case study is considered to be just one stepping-stone in the students' understanding and awareness of their need to develop a portfolio of employability skills. Integrating employability skills throughout the curriculum, at all levels of the course, is essential for enhancing the skills of the students. This also helps students to appreciate the transferability of the skills they are developing, both to other modules within their course and, we hope, also to practical work-related situations.

❏ The biggest challenge of all in employability skills training is encouraging students to be reflective learners, whereby they reflect on and assess the skills they use in a variety of different work-related and social encounters. Progress files and Personal Development Plans provide a structured and formal means of doing this.

❏ Feedback from students indicates that they enjoy the variety of learning, teaching and assessment strategies used for employability-skills training: they are daunting, challenging, motivating, but also add fun to a programme of study.

Conclusion

All university courses need to develop further the employability skills of their students. However, developing employability skills does not occur overnight; it is a lifelong process. Students do not necessarily find skills development an easy process; it can be just as challenging as developing academic subject knowledge and understanding. To facilitate skills development, course teams need to consider a variety of strategies for integrating skills training into the curriculum. The combination of these strategies will result in students developing skills that will enhance their employability.

References and URLs

Hannam, K. 2004. *Tourism employability and the European Social Fund*. Proceedings of the 2004 conference of the Association for Tourism in Higher Education

Hillage, J. and Pollard, E. 1998. *Employability: developing a framework for policy analysis*. Research Brief **85**, Department for Education and Employment

Hind, D. and Moss, S. 2005. *Employability skills*. Sunderland: Business Education Publishers

DAVID HIND is Head of the Centre for Tourism Management at Leeds Metropolitan University, one of the leading providers of tourism education in Europe. A major part of David's teaching, research and publications has centred around employability skills training. In 2005 he co-authored *Employability Skills*, a text book for students on how to develop further their portfolio of employability skills. For more details visit www.employabilityskillsforstudents.co.uk

11 Embedding employability and making it explicit within the learning experience: the language routes at Sheffield Hallam University

Gudrun Myers

The language courses at Sheffield Hallam University (SHU) combine the study of one or two languages with the study of a business-related subject with the aim of creating graduates who are able to take advantage of the opportunities that a global employment market offers.

The language routes at SHU have been designed to provide high quality professional training for linguists wishing to apply their language skills to business-related disciplines. They comprise the following named degrees:

BA (Hons) International Business Studies with Languages

BA (Hons) Languages with International Business Studies or Marketing or Tourism

The specific educational aims of these courses are to:

- Provide students with an education which prepares them for a career and enhances their prospects in the globalised economy.
- Develop competent linguists capable of operating successfully within and across cultures.
- Allow students to progressively acquire an increasing measure of critical understanding of the countries where the students' chosen languages are spoken.
- Provide students with the opportunity to develop a detailed and in-depth knowledge and critical understanding of a range of selected areas and key issues relating to International Business, Marketing or Tourism.
- Foster the students' ability to research effectively and analyse critically specific issues and to apply the outcomes of this analysis to a range of problem-solving activities.
- Provide students with the opportunity to develop independence and self-reliance through the development of communication skills, through working with others and problem solving within the context of language learning and study and work placement abroad.

Rationale
Employment market and pedagogical considerations

As far as the employment market is concerned, graduates with language skills are extremely sought after and in short supply. One of the main findings of the Nuffield Languages Inquiry (2000: 6) is that:

> The UK workforce suffers from a chronic shortage of people at all levels with usable language skills. Companies increasingly need personnel with technical or professional skills plus another language and often their only option is to recruit native speakers of other languages. Mobility of employment is in danger of becoming the preserve of people from other countries.

An overarching aim of the SHU language routes is therefore to provide opportunities for UK students to acquire the skills and attributes they need to compete in the globalised employment market, which does not restrict itself to companies abroad but also embraces those based in the UK.

In this context it was important for the languages team to build into the degree structure a study and work-placement element abroad because the acquisition of intercultural capabilities is as important as the attainment of high levels of linguistic competence. It is best acquired through first-hand personal and professional exposure over an extended period of time.

Referring to employer expectations, Lee Harvey (2003) states that:

> Employers want recruits who are going to be effective in a changing world. They want people who can deal with change – indeed who thrive on it. They want intelligent, flexible, adaptable employees who are quick to learn.

Being optimally flexible and adaptable in a global marketplace means understanding at an experiential level how other (business) cultures operate and how best to engage with them in order to further a company's competitiveness.

A further imperative was the encouragement of a positive attitude to lifelong learning. In a world where change is the only constant, everybody needs to be aware that learning is something that continues throughout life and that professionally we will find ourselves in situations where we will need to change direction and re-orient or even re-invent ourselves. It was therefore important to the languages team to build in a mechanism whereby students were encouraged to take charge of their learning by reflecting on their progress and performance and, where necessary, make adjustments to their initial action plans. Our underlying intention was to allow students to become more autonomous and develop positive self and efficacy beliefs.

David Little (2003: 1–2) offers the following observations about learner autonomy in the context of language learning:

> First, if they [the students] are reflectively engaged with their learning, it is likely to be more efficient and effective, because more personal and focused, than otherwise; in particular, what is learned in educational contexts is more likely to serve learners' wider agendas. Second, if learners are proactively committed to their learning, the problem of motivation is by definition solved; although they may not always feel entirely positive about all aspects of their learning, autonomous learners have developed the reflective and attitudinal resources to overcome temporary motivational setbacks.

In the particular case of second and foreign languages there is a third argument. Effective communication depends on a complex of procedural skills that develop only through use; and if language learning depends crucially on language use, learners who enjoy a high degree of social autonomy in their learning environment should find it easier than otherwise to master the full range of discourse roles on which effective spontaneous communication depends.

Learning a foreign language is a huge investment in terms of time and effort. Companies that operate internationally and globally appreciate this fact and are more likely to recruit competent linguists who have a good grounding in a business-related subject than spending valuable resources on raising the level of linguistic competence of existing staff. Our discussions with local companies in Sheffield revealed that if our graduates had a sufficient grounding in business-

those who had high levels of linguistic and intercultural competence would have a clear advantage when applying for jobs

related subjects, those who had high levels of linguistic and intercultural competence would have a clear advantage when applying for jobs.

In summary, four interrelated factors were considered important for underpinning the development of employability, resulting in a close alignment to the USEM model in Yorke (2003: 5), i.e. the development of subject-specific understanding, language and transferable/key/generic skills, positive self-belief and autonomy, and the ability to direct learning, reflect on it and take appropriate action.

Context
External and internal challenges
Nationally, the context within which languages operate has been complex. While there is a need for graduates with high levels of linguistic competence, recruitment to language degrees has declined steadily over a considerable period. This development is thrown into even sharper relief by the fact that it has been happening during a time of HE expansion (Footitt, 2005).

The decline in the number of language students at university is a direct consequence of falling numbers of A-level candidates opting to do languages in the secondary sector. The situation will probably be exacerbated by the government's decision to remove languages from the required diet of GCSE subjects. As individual languages are affected to differing extents it is important to maintain a range of languages and entry levels at university if we are to address the linguistic needs of commerce and industry and make good any shortcomings in the secondary sector.

Internally, the challenge consists of achieving efficient and cost-effective delivery by optimising student numbers per group.

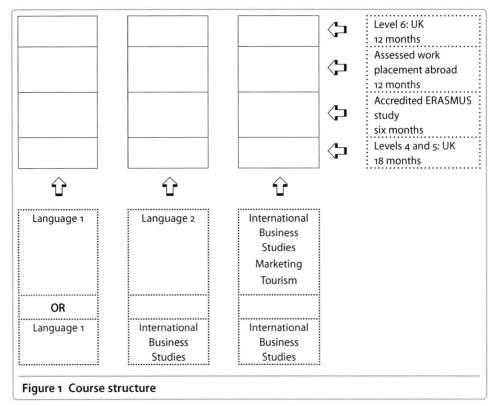

Level 6: UK
12 months

Assessed work placement abroad
12 months

Accredited ERASMUS study
six months

Levels 4 and 5: UK
18 months

Language 1

OR

Language 1

Language 2

International Business Studies

International Business Studies Marketing Tourism

International Business Studies

Figure 1 Course structure

Strengths

Fortunately, at an institutional level the languages team can draw on a number of strengths. These include a thriving institution-wide language programme, the University Language Scheme (ULS) and the well-established forerunner of the current degree routes, the BA (Hons) International Business with Languages (BAIBL). On the ULS the areas of expertise centre on the use of portfolios and the attention paid to learner training, while the team delivering on the BAIBL degree bring with them a well-established and successful tradition of placing students with well-known foreign companies, a proven track record in preparing students successfully for their period abroad and an extensive network of ERASMUS partner institutions. Further supporting factors for the development of the current degree routes were SHU's commitment to sandwich education and the location of the languages subject group in the business area.

Description

Structure and content

The language routes offer choice in terms of the amount of language study a student wants to undertake and which non-language subject he or she wishes to combine this with. In the case of the Languages with… routes the course comprises the study of two languages (L1 and L2) amounting to 80 credits and of either International Business Studies (IBS), Marketing (M) or Tourism (T), each contributing 40 credits. On the International Business Studies with Languages route 80 credits are made up of the study of International Business (80 credits) and one language (40 credits). The languages on offer are French, German, Italian and Spanish. See Figure 1 for illustration.

As far as the vertical structure is concerned, students spend the first 18 months at SHU in preparation for their 18 months abroad, which includes six months assessed ERASMUS study at one of our European partner institutions and 12 months on an assessed work placement abroad. In the case of two languages being studied the 12 months are divided into two six-month placements. The final 12 months of the course are again spent at SHU.

Each languages strand is made up of two types of

module: University Language Scheme modules, content-based business, society and culture modules and an international consultancy project in the final year. The ULS modules have as their focus the teaching of language skills and the development of independent, reflective language learners, while the non-ULS language units are content-oriented and concentrate specifically on providing students with an in-depth knowledge of the political, economic and social environments of the countries in question. At levels four and five they also prepare students thoroughly for study and work placements abroad. Both ULS and non-ULS language modules contributing to the different awards provide mechanisms that require students to integrate their language study fully with their chosen specialism.

The combination of modules from the institution-wide language programme and from a limited number of bespoke content modules enables us to consolidate class sizes, while at the same time providing a varied mix of student backgrounds and interests. The *ab initio* students, i.e. students who have no previous knowledge of their chosen language, follow an accelerated programme during the first 18 months and join the A/AS level students after the placement period in the final year.

All modules on the languages route are mandatory, apart from a very limited choice between two modules in the final year. The non-language subject modules are carefully selected to fit into the three levels of study. They are also reflected in the module choice a student has while studying abroad and the type of company where he or she is placed.

However, in our view, employability does not only reside within modules. As Yorke (2003) says:

It is reasonable to ask what a module contributes to student employability but wise to recognise that many outcomes derive from the set of modules that comprises the programme.

Therefore one important step in bringing the individual modules together into a coherent and effective course of study was the decision to undertake curriculum auditing. This means that we took a very co-ordinated approach in clearly articulating the learning outcomes at all levels of study. This has been an iterative process and has resulted in the learning outcomes of all modules (language and relevant business units) having been determined in such a way that they achieve meaningful horizontal as well as vertical integration.

In other words, modules complement and reinforce each other across each level of study, as well as allowing for progressive development of students' knowledge, skills and level of autonomy as they progress through their course. The result is a holistic programme design whose defining elements are closely interlinked and cannot be disaggregated. Furthermore, tutors take great care to explain the relevant documentation and refer to it in classroom sessions, thus stimulating a feeling of ownership of the learning and assessment process.

In addition, we have embedded further mechanisms to integrate and link the various elements that develop employability. These are:
- ❏ The use of portfolios at all levels of study (including a placement diary while on work placement).
- ❏ The creation of safe environments and opportunities for personal, professional and intellectual growth, and success in these environments via the use of real world activities.
- ❏ The use of final-year modules to support the transition to the world of work.

The portfolio as a means of developing autonomy and reflection

As part of the language skills modules, the languages programme requires students to submit a portfolio of language-related exercises at all levels of study. Via the portfolio, the course team endeavours not only to enhance the student's linguistic ability, but also to develop the student's awareness of his or her strengths and weaknesses as a learner. This process of learner development consists of a number of steps. Each student starts by completing an individual needs-analysis and then formulates an action plan of how he or she intends to improve in terms of linguistic competence. At the end of each semester, having completed the language tasks they have selected themselves, the learners reflect on their progress and make the necessary adjustments to their action plans. The language portfolios, which form part of the students' official diet of assessed work, are marked for content (50%), degree of independence (20%), level of planning and reflection (20%) and the overall quality of presentation and organisation (10%). A student in the upper second range, for example, would be characterised by the following descriptors.

- **Content:**

  The tasks chosen are generally at an appropriate level for the stage of study, are relevant to the needs analysis and action plan and completed to a high standard. There is some evidence of follow-up work and of progress made.

- **Independence:**

  A substantial degree of initiative and some originality is evident in the choice of materials. Appropriate resources and activities have been selected and exploited.

- **Planning and reflection:**

  There is clear evidence of the learner's ability to identify needs and to plan work accordingly. There is evidence of reflection. The tasks have been completed fairly regularly.

A further significant feature of the portfolio is that the students are required to build links between their non-language modules and the languages studied by developing the appropriate lexis and register of their specialist field. In other words, through the choice of texts appropriate to their non-language subject the learners will be able to acquire the relevant vocabulary and also become familiar with the particular ways in which different types of text are written, cf. the academic style of writing on marketing versus practical examples of marketing texts aimed at promoting a particular product or service. This gives students an ideal opportunity to integrate the study of the foreign language with the study of their business subject.

The effectiveness and success of the portfolio element rest to a large extent on staff commitment with regard to maintaining and constantly updating existing banks of suitable learning materials in the Language Learning Resources Centre as well as in the university's Adsetts Learning Centre. The whole process is further enhanced by the teaching-and-learning opportunities offered by digital technology.

Creation of safe environments, support and opportunities for practice

Embedded in the course structure is the expectation that students move from a period of supported prepa-

ration (the first 18 months at SHU) to operating largely on their own on work placement after acculturation during their ERASMUS semester. Going abroad to live, study and work is a daunting undertaking for anybody and students often have doubts about whether they will actually have the required courage and spirit of enterprise to cope. This is why the languages team has adopted a tailor-made personal-development review (PDR) system. This system means that students on the Languages plus… routes are grouped together and tutored by a member of the languages team.

During the first year, apart from inducting students into the university and their chosen course, PDR sessions also serve as a platform for disseminating information about the ERASMUS study semester and the work placement. The information provided by tutors is complemented and, more important, verified by final-year students, who are invited to specially organised sessions. The second-year PDR tutors are also the placement co-ordinators, who maintain the links with our placement companies abroad. This means not

> students, by now well-known to the languages staff, can be carefully matched in terms of their own strengths and aspirations to a company's specific requirements and demands

only that students have access to the specific knowledge that these members of staff have about the various companies in question, but also that students, by now well-known to the languages staff, can be carefully matched in terms of their own strengths and aspirations to a company's specific requirements and demands. A further element in the preparation for the work placement is the ERASMUS semester. The period of study abroad allows students to acculturate and to get their first taste of living abroad, while still being tied into the supportive network provided by our partner institutions.

Students continue to be supported while on placement via telephone and email and, crucially, are visited at their placement company by a member of the languages staff. Normally this will be a colleague teaching in the relevant language area, who will be thus well equipped to resolve any difficulties the student may be encountering. The purpose of the visit is to check that the student has settled in, is functioning within the work environment and is given appropriate tasks. Feedback from both the student and employer are taken into consideration and any areas of potential disagreement or unhappiness can be addressed. The visit also provides an opportunity for the tutor to give feedback and comment on the placement diary and its content.

Real-world activities

Within the language skills modules, in addition to the portfolio work, students are required to undertake a number of further language skills assessments, all of which are related to the world of work and increase in difficulty and the level of challenge throughout the course. At level four, for example, assessed tasks include the oral presentation of a product or service, while at level six students engage in detailed and complex business negotiations conducted in the target language, as well as liaison interpreting and written translation.

The bespoke content modules aim to familiarise students with the political, economic, social, technological and environmental issues of their target language countries. This module consists of a general introduction at level four and the specific study of the higher education sector and the world of work at level five. As in the language skills modules, the target language is the medium for teaching, learning and assessment. All assessed work in the content modules closely focuses on the preparation of the students for placement abroad, e.g. the production of a written CV, the completion of a job/placement interview, the oral presentation of information gathered on the town/region where they will be undertaking their ERASMUS study, as well as schooling in some of the likely tasks students may need to undertake while on placement, such as providing written and oral summaries of English texts/communications in the target language.

Final-year modules and transition to the world of work

The third stage in developing the students' employability skills is the final year of study at Sheffield Hallam University. All level six language modules incorporate

an assessed element which specifically requires the students to reflect on their placement experience and gives them the chance to debrief. Within the Business, Society and Culture module three students prepare and deliver an oral presentation where they link their placement company and their own experience while there with one of the major themes of the module content, e.g. the effects of globalisation on VW at Wolfsburg, as experienced and observed by the placement student, in the light of theory and developments worldwide. In this way the learners have a vehicle for integrating their personal and professional experience with the achievement of the following outcomes, namely:

❏ Demonstrate a critical understanding of how companies behave in the target-language-business environment and apply this knowledge and understanding to analysing and discussing authentic case studies.

❏ Demonstrate a thorough understanding of the way in which the business and political context of the target-language country/ies affects the conduct of business in that country and elsewhere.

❏ Demonstrate the ability to analyse specific issues of relevance to the students' specialisms and to apply the outcomes of this analysis to a range of problem-solving activities concerned with the social, political and business environment of the target-language country.

The second of the final-year language modules, the International Consultancy Project (ICP), takes this approach one step further by providing the students with an opportunity to apply the linguistic and cross-cultural competence and expertise gained during their previous academic study and the work placement abroad in a real-life situation by undertaking a group consultancy project for a local/regional company or organisation. The underpinning rationale for the International Consultancy Project is to integrate the student into the local/regional economy by providing a service which local businesses will find valuable. It is hoped that, by undertaking such a project, students will be able make the appropriate connections between their studies and the world of work, thereby further enhancing their employability skills. In preparing for this project, a survey was undertaken with local SMEs in order to ascertain whether they would welcome this type of initiative and the response was universally positive.

In terms of the specific employability skills that the ICP aims to develop and enhance the module specification states that on completion of the module students should be able to:

1 Analyse, synthesise and make decisions regarding complex open-ended situations and formulate appropriate strategies to deal with them.
2 Analyse and compare, if applicable, cross-cultural differences in the business environment and to communicate those differences appropriately.
3 Work effectively as a member of a group in order to fulfil the project brief.
4 Evaluate and reflect on their own performance with regard to:
   • defining objectives and determining strategies
   • communication skills
   • teamwork
   • time management
   • language skills
   • intercultural communication
   • creative thinking.

Evaluation

Our experience has been that our students, on returning from a period of 18 months spent abroad, have begun to develop into mature and confident learners; they are able to identify their own employability outcomes which they have applied on the course as well as during their placement period. These include team/groupwork, leadership, negotiation, and working under pressure. The experience of studying and

> our students are well-prepared and culturally competent in the business environment… the students bring cultural diversity to the workplace and share fresh ideas and practices

working abroad, combined with the in-depth study undertaken in the final year of the course, means that our students are extremely successful in obtaining first destination employment in a field of their choice.

Comments from our placement companies, including Iberia, Ernst & Young, and Desert Rose among others, confirm that our students are well-prepared and culturally competent in the business environment. They further acknowledge that the students bring cultural diversity to the workplace and share fresh ideas and practices.

The effectiveness of our approach is also reflected in the opinion of our students, cf. the comments below from a 2002 graduate on BA (Hons) International Business and German:

I chose to study at Sheffield Hallam because of the course combination of International Business and German was the best I could find at any university. I wanted to combine studying with learning on the job, and to improve my German by living in Germany. Living, studying and working in Germany was my most enjoyable time. I had time to travel around Europe on the weekends and meet lots of different people. At the end of it all I feel I have a very sound grounding in international business both from learning the theory and seeing business in action during my internship at DaimlerChrysler. Additionally, I am now fluent in German and my degree qualification appears to be very attractive to top graduate recruiters.

In addition, our external examiners testify to the soundness of our curriculum:

Guides provided for each module ensure students are aware of assessment procedures and marking criteria used. The practice of stating learning outcomes and marking criteria is in my view excellent. (2004)

The portfolio is obviously underpinned by a well-resourced learning centre and the language learning/portfolio guide which staff have produced to enable learners to produce an effective portfolio is the best of its kind which I have seen across the sector. (2001)

Many of the skills that are practised by the students in their classes are good communication ones that can be usefully transferred to other areas of learning. (2003)

Externally we have been successful regional winners of the National Languages for Export Awards awarded by UK Trade & Investment (November 2003) and have been included as one of the excellent courses in SHU's successful bid to become a Centre for

Excellence in Teaching and Learning (CETL) (Embedding, Enhancing and Integrating Employability).

There are nevertheless aspects that are under review as part of our internal annual evaluations. Currently these are the International Consultancy Project and the portfolio element. The intention is to establish whether the initial aims set for them are still valid and how they impact on resources and staff time. The changing nature of the students we are recruiting through widening participation also has implications, especially with regards to the preparation phase. A student who is the first in his or her family to enter HE is likely to feel a considerable amount of trepidation about studying and working abroad, having just made the transition to university. Special care and attention will be needed to develop the required levels of self-belief. In this context we may also have to revisit the 18-month study and work placement requirement and build more flexibility into the degree structure by providing a range of different pathways, allowing, for example, for shorter amounts of time spent abroad. The overall aim, however, is to continue to provide a flexible structure within a tight resource envelope, while safeguarding the essential elements that develop student employability. This will not be an easy undertaking.

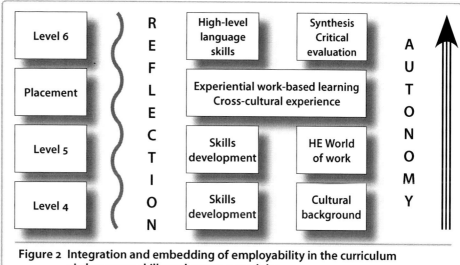

Figure 2 Integration and embedding of employability in the curriculum via language skills and content modules

Discussion

Underlying principles

While this paper takes the language routes at Sheffield Hallam University as a concrete example, the features and principles that are contained within them can be transferred to other subject areas. See Figure 2 for illustration. This is not to say that all of them will fit every degree structure. Each course team needs to identify what best fits their particular context. The languages team at Sheffield Hallam University initially started out with a fairly general list of desirable skills, competences, attributes and attitudes a successful graduate should have and display, namely:

- subject knowledge and expertise in one or two languages and one non-language area
- subject-specific and transferable skills, e.g. in areas such as communication, teamwork, problem-solving, working across cultures
- self-belief in their abilities
- a reflective practitioner who can identify their own strengths and weaknesses, who can influence their career path by identifying relevant employment opportunities and the necessary self-development.

The descriptors listed for a language graduate can easily be changed to fit other degrees by simply changing the subject area. A pedagogically sound curriculum will almost always support the development of employability. In this sense, a coherent curriculum with appropriate teaching, learning and assessment strategies goes a long way to support the development of employability.

Learning outcomes, time and practice

Although time-consuming, a curriculum audit of the learning outcomes contributing to a programme of study helps to eliminate duplication and fill gaps regarding the student learning experience. Furthermore, for students to be able to engage actively in the learning process, it is essential that the resulting learning outcomes are communicated clearly and assessment criteria explained.

,here also has to be awareness that the development of skills and competences takes time and practice. This means that appropriate mechanisms for progression are necessary for students to move to higher levels of skill, confidence, knowledge, etc. While our language students have the added dimension of residence abroad, the stages that take students through any sandwich degree will need to include:

❑ A preparation phase, during which students can practise and receive feedback on their academic work and get ready for their work placement

❑ Experiential work-related learning

❑ Final-year study bringing together academic and work-related learning to underpin a successful transition to the world of work.

The stages in this process need to be carefully graded and the levels of support inversely related to the students' growing autonomy.

Integrating mechanism

In the case of our language routes it is the language skills and language content modules that contain the mechanisms which, through the use of portfolios and real-world activities, link the language and non-language areas together and provide a platform for developing autonomy and reflection. Our experience has been that unless linkages and connections are made students will see their (modular) degrees as a collection of unrelated entities and will not transfer what they have learnt from one context to another. Furthermore, unless the development of skills, knowledge and competences is assessed and formally accredited, it will not be considered an important aspect in the students' mind and effective engagement is less likely to happen.

References

Footitt, H. 2005. *The National Languages Strategy in Higher Education.* Department for Education and Science http://www.dfes.gov.uk/

Harvey, L. 2003. *Transition from higher education to work.* Higher Education Academy Resources, EMP012, http://www.heacademy.ac.uk/

Little, D. 2003. *Learner autonomy and second/foreign language learning.* Subject Centre for Languages, Linguistics and Area Studies, Learning and Teaching Support Network http://www.llas.ac.uk/

The Nuffield Languages Inquiry, 2000. *Languages: the next generation.* London: The Nuffield Foundation

Yorke, M. 2003. *The Undergraduate Curriculum and Employability.* Higher Education Academy Resources, EMP013, http://www.heacademy.ac.uk/

GUDRUN MYERS is Head of Languages at Sheffield Hallam University

The leisure professional using online learning and employer-involvement to develop reflection and employability skills

12

John Buswell and Angela Tomkins

This case study illustrates a recent initiative in a level-one module which involves leisure and sports employers engaging with students in online discussions concerning professionalism and employability in the workplace.

The Leisure Professional (LR103) is a compulsory module on the Leisure and Sports Management degree programme at the University of Gloucestershire. The primary focus of the module is to introduce learners to the 'idea' of professionalism in leisure and sports management contexts and to apply this knowledge to the process of Personal Development Planning (PDP) by developing students' skills in reflection and their meta-cognition.

The module addresses the nature of work in contemporary environments and introduces the idea of professional work practices. It considers personal empowerment and the steps that can be taken towards maximising employment potential during a university career.

Context

The module is an important and integral part of the degree programme for a variety of reasons. It is considered pivotal to all other modules on the degree programme, including a 48-week period of paid work experience. It represents an early stage in the development of students' employability skills and their attitudes to professional development. It also reflects the characteristics of an increasingly dynamic and competitive industry in which consumers' motives are becoming more complex and their requirements more discerning and demanding.

Organisations continually strive for a competitive advantage, and there is more emphasis on the way the service process and consumer experience are managed and delivered. Leisure is a people-based industry, which requires staff that understand the needs of both colleagues and customers and who can work in teams, contribute to problem-solving and enhance continuous improvement.

The teaching team, in designing the Leisure and Sport Management programme and individual modules, have taken into consideration trends in an industry which increasingly require staff to be:

- reflective and reflexive thinkers
- capable of independent judgement and initiative, empowered decision-makers
- able to work within an ethos of teamwork and interdependence
- able to offer specific vocational skills but also know how to learn and adapt to changing circumstances
- able to identify their strengths and weaknesses, and know how to plan and manage their personal and career development.

The latter point provides a key element of both the module and this case study. It highlights an explicit link between the skill of reflection and the transferable skill of 'knowledge of the self' in the PDP process. This manifests itself in the ability to demonstrate and justify what has been learnt from others, including employers. The module therefore makes an important contribution to the development of these skills.

Objectives

The aim of the module is to provide a forum or net-work-learning environment in which students can construct the meaning of models of professionalism and can discuss this understanding and knowledge with practitioners in the workplace. Ultimately they are given the opportunity to reflect upon their learning in relation to personal development planning and future career planning.

Rationale

The Leisure and Sport Management programme emphasises the following features:

- A constructivist approach in which the student is encouraged to contextualise learning and to construct a personal meaning for the knowledge and skills acquired.
- The development of critical thinking skills which enable students to respond to the industry challenges outlined above.
- The development of common transferable skills which prepare students for a range of employment opportunities.
- The skill of transferability to enable students to achieve competence in work contexts.
- The knowledge and understanding of how to learn.
- The development of meta-cognitive skills through reflection and Personal Development Planning.
- The development of independent but co-operative learners though selective support and guidance in level one to increased opportunities for independent and self-directed study through levels two and three.

In the context of these features, the LR103 module harnesses opportunities for skills development made available by extra-curricular activities such as voluntary work, involvement in sport-related activities and part-time work. It provides first-year students with an opportunity to develop awareness of the reality of working in leisure by explaining current thinking in relation to the development of a skilled sector workforce. The module also considers the need for professionalism within the sector from the perspectives of both employers and aspiring graduates. One key outcome of the module is the opportunity it provides each student to become more industry-aware, more self-aware and, consequently, more proactive in their approach to career management. This is achieved by using a combination of teaching and learning activities, notably the opportunity for students to 'talk to' locally-based leisure sector employers in an online environment and, as a result of this and their other learning, to develop skills of reflection.

Learning outcomes

The module has four key learning outcomes and also addresses the development of a range of skills. At the outset it outlines the significance of key organisations in the development of a professional workforce for leisure and sports-related industries. It also examines theoretical models associated with the terms 'reflective practitioner' and 'continuous professional development' and, within this context, investigates a range of skills required for effective employment. The module enables the individual learner to apply a growing knowledge of appropriate theory and work-based practice to their own personal development.

An important aspect of the module is that it identifies specific skills which individuals can develop through their engagement with the module. For example, students can develop their information and communication technology skills through involvement in WebCT activity. They can develop their communication (literacy) skills through online discussions with peers, employers and tutors. They can develop their skills in independent learning and working through undertaking the various activities required in the module. Finally, they can begin to develop specific vocational skills through increasing their awareness of themselves and the industries they aspire to work in. They do this by creating a Personal Development Plan – the ideal opportunity to engage in the practice of reflection and to engage in the skill of deep learning.

Description

Approach to teaching, learning and assessment

Successful teaching is a construction site in which students build on what they already know. Teaching requires much relevant activity from students, interaction with others, and self-monitoring

to check everything is proceeding according to plan.
(Biggs, 2003: 75)

The module is designed around a series of lectures, seminar tasks and the use of a learning and personal development CD-ROM which contains a Personal Development Planning section. All these materials are presented in a WebCT version of the module as well as the more traditional paper-based module guide. For students to meet the requirements of the module they must develop their skills in reflection using a combination of 'hands-on' activities available on WebCT and by undertaking readings which are available in a module reader. Students are asked to ensure that they have undertaken the readings and WebCT-based activities in preparation for seminar-based discussions before the appropriate sessions. These readings and activities are clearly prescribed in the Readings and Independent Study Tasks section of the module guide (also available online in the WebCT version of LR103). The value of this 'blended learning' approach is that it combines traditional methods with new technologies, in this case by using the online learning technology available.

The module provides a discussion forum tool to enable students to communicate with employers online and it also maintains face-to-face contact with tutors and employers. This blended-learning approach is highlighted by Mazoue (1994: 104) who states that:

> [effective] *online teaching has two principal advantages over traditional classroom-based learning. It enables students to spend more time on tasks and it provides more opportunities for collaborative interaction, both of which research has shown are correlated with higher student achievement… the flexible, open-ended availability of online course materials provides students with an expanded range of instructional opportunities for acquiring, exchanging and meaningfully reflecting on the significance of information.*

The module engages the students on a continuum of 'mediated' and 'unmediated' learning processes. Mediated learning has three key characteristics:

1 The purpose of the learning is clear to the learner (learning objectives carefully planned).
2 A good mediator (in this case, the module staff

and workplace representatives) will help to draw out the learner's existing knowledge and use their existing frames of reference on which to build new knowledge into the current learning situation. This embraces the constructivist approach referred to earlier, in which students are encouraged to construct their own meaning around the knowledge they are acquiring and examining.

3 It helps learners to consider the most appropriate forms of learning for them. This begins to develop the students' knowledge and understanding of their own abilities and how they learn and adapt to new situations.(Moon 2005).

The module sets out to connect students with the outside world through the perceptions and experiences of employers and through the online discussions between student and employer. This experience also begins to encourage students to reflect on their expe-

> This embraces the constructivist approach …in which students are encouraged to construct their own meaning around the knowledge they are acquiring and examining

riences. Laurillard (2002: 20) draws the distinction between 'learning percepts' (natural environments) and 'learning precepts' (environments constructed for learning) and how teaching should go beyond imparting decontextualised knowledge to help students achieve situated cognition (based on personal experience and reflections on it). The module embraces both approaches and recognises Bowden and Marton's view that 'all learning is in context' (1998: 140) and also addresses the increasing need for both disciplinary knowledge and transdisciplinary knowledge. The latter acknowledges the increasingly complex demands of the modern world which require skills and capabilities which cross boundaries of knowledge and are more concerned with the process of learning (Jackson and Ward, 2004). It therefore also highlights the importance of reflective practice.

> *Reflective practice emphasises the use of reflection in professional or other complex activities as a means of coping with ill-structured situations.*
> (Schon, 1983; 1987)

– such as understanding industry practice and personal

development planning which is supported, in the case of this module, by employer engagement.

Early stages of the module

Introducing the idea of professionalism in the leisure and sport industry

The early stages of the module concentrate on three major issues. The first issue is associated with acquiring knowledge about employability and the development of a professional workforce for the leisure industry and its related sectors. Typical lecture topics include:

- Approaches to developing a skilled workforce for the leisure industry
- The 'idea' of a profession
- The contribution of key organisations to the development of the leisure profession
- Learning from experience and the significance of the term 'the reflective practitioner'
- An introduction to using WebCT (practical workshop).

Typical independent study tasks (based on prescribed readings) associated with the above topics are:

- Identify the various types of training and education currently being undertaken in the UK in relation to the leisure industry. Draw a simple chart which depicts this framework.
- What is the role of the sector skills councils?
- What is the Institute of Leisure and Amenity Management (ILAM) professional qualification scheme and how does it differ from your degree programme?
- Would you consider joining ILAM as a student member? Make two lists of bullet points in the online discussion area to record your views as to why you might consider joining ILAM and why you might consider not joining ILAM at this stage of your career.

The second issue addressed in the earliest stages of the module involves inviting students to think about professionalism in relation to their own experiences and to encourage them to use the WebCT discussion forum to express their opinions.

A typical introductory activity in week one of the module is:

Think of someone you have met in your life whom

you would consider to be a 'professional' (this could be a teacher, a doctor, a sports coach etc). State the occupation of this person. You must not identify them by name. In your notes, record three distinct characteristics/observations you have made about this person.

In week two students are asked to build on their view of professionalism and their personal experience by completing the following task:

Taking into consideration the views you posted to WebCT in week one and also the associated readings, how would you now define a professional? Post one example of good professional practice and one example of bad professional practice which you have experienced in the leisure and sports industry.

The third issue involves encouraging students to reflect on their readings and to record these comments. For example, a typical activity is:

Reflect on what you have read on LR103 in the past two weeks. On consideration of your readings and your first-hand experiences of the industry, what do you think are the key expectations of employers in the leisure industry? Do you think these expectations are realistic? Your online posting should identify key expectations and be no more than 50 words in length.

As students approach the mid-point of the module they have become more familiar with basic skills in reflective writing and the use of WebCT. Their knowledge of the professionalism and skills required for work is growing, and they are in a more informed and confident position to engage in discussion with employers. At this point students are reminded of the first assessment task which asks them to:

Discuss the key features of 'professionalism' in relation to employment in the leisure industry. Your answer must reflect your understanding of the skills, knowledge and qualifications required in the sector as well as the role of professional bodies in the development of a suitably skilled workforce.

Assignment 1

A key requirement of the assessment is that students demonstrate a thorough understanding of the meaning and application of professionalism and the reflective practitioner in the context of employment in the leisure-related industries. They are also expected to draw upon relevant literature and to illustrate their views by reflecting upon comments made in the online discussion forum by employers about these aspects of working life.

Mid-stage of the module

Online link up with employers and tutors

During weeks four to seven of the module, students are introduced to a number of local employers who provide a brief classroom-based presentation on the nature of their work. Every attempt is made to provide a variety of working contexts by providing employer representation from both public and private leisure and sports providers in and around Gloucestershire. This is a very popular aspect of the module with students and employers alike. Employers attend a dedicated training session at the university to enable them to use WebCT effectively for the purposes of the module.

In the following weeks small groups of students have the opportunity to post questions directly to employers who represent a range of work contexts using the online forum. Students are given the following instruction, and an element of monitoring by tutors is included to ensure that the questions sent to employers are appropriate:

Think about what assignment one is asking you to do. As a group, make a list of the key points you will need to address when answering this question. Each group must post at least three concise ideas about what they think should be included in the essay. LR103 tutors will monitor your comments and will provide feedback on this activity to the group. When this activity has been completed and you have received your tutor feedback you may then, and only then, contact employers for their views. It is expected that employers' views be reflected in your essays and these must be adequately referenced.

Students are given suggested questions to get them started on this process, for example: Where do you work and what is your role? What does 'professionalism' mean in the context of your work? What are the basic qualifications required to work in your sector? What skills do you look for when recruiting staff?

The following student questions and employer comments taken from the WebCT discussion area are rep-

resentative of the current information available using this method and show its potential.

Indicative student questions:

- ❏ With regard to employment, what would you consider to be the most important qualifications that an individual would need to work in your sector?
- ❏ When you are in the process of recruiting and selecting candidates what would you consider to be the most important key skills that an individual would need to have to develop and progress within the sector?

Indicative employer responses included:

●*That is a tough question as there is no one panacea to being a sports or health professional. However, in my view, in order to function in this field in a professional manner I would use/expect a combination of theoretical/knowledge based skills, practical ability and personal skills. I would expect a degree in an appropriate area and extra qualifications to back it up e.g. leadership awards/coaching/voluntary work, evidence of using knowledge gained in either written/pictorial/reference style, and most definitely build on communication skills, prioritising, time management and partnership working.*●

●*Do not be afraid to be innovative/creative and make suggestions.*●

●*You need to be a bit of a chameleon in terms of keeping abreast of changes at national down to local level initiatives/local politics.*●

●*ILAM/ISRM/NASD and sector skills qualifications have been beneficial when I have needed to enhance my CPD. The problem is that they (the courses) are expensive and quite generic at the moment. This will change when ISRM/ILAM/NASD join up to become one agency.*●

●*When employing someone I would look for the essential criteria (usually appropriate degree), coaching and leadership.*●

Final stage of the module

Introducing Personal Development Planning and its relationship to employability

During weeks eight to 12 of the module, the focus changes to the individual student. The group is introduced to the notions of self-awareness and opportunities for self-development. Students are asked to identify those skills and qualities required for employment in the leisure and sports sectors. Special emphasis is placed upon what these issues mean to the individual in relation to their personal development planning and, most significantly, their personal action planning for the following academic year. WebCT provides a series of materials that enable students to consider their current skills and abilities against those issues previously discussed in the module. The employers' comments provide a particularly rich source of information as do a range of resources, particularly a recent research project commissioned by the Higher Education Academy Subject Network for Hospitality, Leisure Sport and Tourism entitled: *Best Of Both Worlds: An exploration of key skills required for graduate work in the leisure and sports industry and links to PDP* (Tomkins, 2004).

Indicative activities in this part of the module ask students to consider various aspects of their personal development at this stage of their undergraduate career and to share these views with their peer group in the WebCT discussion area. These activities created an astonishingly positive response to the process of PDP!

Define and give a brief analysis of the term 'Personal Development Planning' and indicate its significance to you and your career aspirations

Assignment 2

Examples of activities include:
'*PDP – is it worth the effort?*' *Consider the Personal Development Planning section of the Learning and Personal Development materials available on the WebCT version of LR103. In the discussion area post one carefully considered opinion about what you think could be valuable about undertaking PDP. Respond to at least one other student who has made a comment. Your sentence should begin with the words, 'PDP is worth it because…'*

Links to career opportunities – think back to week four when you met employers and were asked to think about a possible career opportunity for yourself. Write a brief paragraph which explains how your views of the skills required for working in the industry may have been clarified/challenged over the duration of the module. Identify which skills you already have and which you need to develop.

Post your comments in the discussion area.

The key requirements of this assessment are that students reflect upon models of PDP which have been made available to them on the module. They should be able to explain component parts of PDP in relation to their own proposed career direction and to apply basic models and theories of reflective practice to their written work.

Evaluation and discussion

Feedback from students

- Students like it – they like the 'blended' approach to teaching and learning and particularly like talking to 'real' employers.
- Meets a need in supporting students with different learning styles – e.g. shy students are quite happy to ask questions in this environment rather than in a large lecture hall.
- Students enjoy reading online comments made by other students – it improves their confidence.
- Students like to be able to retrieve information instantaneously.
- They like pre-posted lecture notes/slides – this has not had an adverse effect on lecture attendance.
- Students have to reflect employer comments in their assignments and therefore need to engage with the activities associated with the module.
- Staff who have engaged in the e-moderators' course (associated with Staff Development for the module) can see numerous applications to their work in other modules.
- Gives tutors greater 'control' over individual student input on particular tasks – input is very 'visible' in this medium!

Feedback from employers

- Employers enjoyed the initial face-to-face meetings with students as part of the blended approach to learning and teaching.
- Employers see the value of this module and its methods and wish to be further involved.
- Some employers would have liked the discussions to have been available in an asynchronous form although this view was not shared by everyone. Those working in the public sector would have preferred a synchronous approach to discussions because of their organisations' approach to web

conferencing.

- ❏ Employers would have preferred students to have asked a wider range of questions and to have avoided repetitive questions.

Impact on students' skills development and employability

It is clear that this module is providing enhanced opportunities for level-one students to engage with employers using contemporary information technologies. Not only does the approach enable greater flexibility in teaching and learning methods but it also introduces a sense of 'reality' about workplace practice. This approach has much to commend it in the eyes of students who are put in an informed position to think about how they might 'measure up' for work in the industry from an employer perspective. This has the potential to make PDP more meaningful than just another academic exercise and to encourage the skill of reflection through discussion. The proposed introduction of peer support, by more senior students who have completed extensive periods of work experience, further enhances the students' understanding of what skills are required for success in the workplace.

Conclusion

New developments on the module

Planning is currently underway to move the module on in the following ways:

- ❏ Development of an enhanced online resource base, to be built by students themselves.
- ❏ A wider employer base to reflect the opportunities for employment in the industry; there is much interest, particularly from the public sector. These employers indicated that they increasingly use video conferencing which could be further explored. An asynchronous facility for online discussion could be maintained for those employers who stated that they preferred this method.
- ❏ Further activities to encourage skills in reflection in the context of work-based practice, particularly peer support from post-placement students who will provide online professional practice profiles (assessed in the post-placement module and inserted into LR 103).
- ❏ Designing new activities within the module which

manage the learning experience in the classroom to enable students to ask more focused questions.

References and URLs

Biggs, J. 2003. *Teaching for Quality Learning in Universities.* Maidenhead: Open University Press

Bowden, J. & Marton, F. 1998. *The University of Learning: Beyond Quality and Competence.* London: Routledge Falmer

Laurillard, D. 2002. *Rethinking University Teaching: a framework for the effective use of learning technologies.* Abingdon: Routledge Falmer

Mazoue, J. G. 1999. The Essentials of Effective Online Instruction. *Campus-Wide Information Systems,* **16** (3), 104–111

Moon, J. 2005. *A Handbook of Reflective and Experiential Learning Theory and Practice.* Abingdon: Routledge Falmer

Schon, D. 1983. *The Reflective Practitioner.* San Francisco: Jossey-Bass

Schon, D. 1987. *Educating Reflective Practitioners.* San Francisco: Jossey-Bass

Tomkins, A. 2004. 'Best Of Both Worlds': An exploration of key skills required for graduate work in the leisure and sports industry and links to PDP. *LINK 11 – Learning from Experience* **11-12**. Available at: www.hlst.heacademy.ac.uk/

JOHN BUSWELL is Principal Lecturer in the Department of Leisure, Tourism and Hospitality Management at the University of Gloucestershire and Director of the phase 5 FDTL (Fund for the Development of Teaching and Learning) project 'Meta: From PDP to CPD'. He is also Liaison Officer for Leisure for the Higher Education Academy Subject Centre for Hospitality, Leisure, Sport and Tourism. He is a member of the Open University Validation Committee and chair of the Professional Development Board of the Institute of Leisure and Amenity Management.

ANGELA TOMKINS is Senior Lecturer in the Department of Leisure, Tourism and Hospitality Management at the University of Gloucestershire. She is a member of the Gloucestershire FDTL team and leads the university's involvement in the Sheffield Hallam-led FDTL project, ELATE. Her teaching interests lie in professional development in leisure, tourism and hospitality management.

13 Enhancing student employability: a New Zealand case study of cooperative education in sport

Jenny Fleming and Lesley Ferkins

The purpose of this paper is to demonstrate how employability is embedded and made explicit within two tertiary-degree programmes in sport and recreation in New Zealand, through the use of cooperative education strategies.

Cooperative education has been defined by the National Commission for Cooperative Education (2004), as:

a structured educational strategy integrating classroom studies with learning through productive work experiences in a field related to a students' academic or career goals.

Work and learning are integrated through the development of partnerships between the tertiary institution, the student and a sport or recreation organisation. This case study demonstrates how cooperative education facilitates student learning and increases the opportunity for meaningful employment at the conclusion of the three years of degree study.

Rationale

The study of sport at the tertiary level has responded to the expansion of employment opportunities in the sport and recreation sector. The two programmes used in the case study have been identified as those that exemplify good practice in the preparation of students for employment in sport and recreation. However, the models that they illustrate are consistent with many operating in the sport sector globally (Fleming and Ferkins, 2005). Through sharing good practice, we hope to demonstrate the efficacy of such programmes and encourage other tertiary providers to include cooperative education as a learning strategy for their students.

Context

New Zealand is a 'proud' sporting nation with a considerable history and tradition associated with its achievement and participation in sport (Collins, 2000). A small nation of 4m people on the world stage, the impact of sport on our society and economic system is a phenomenon that is experienced by individuals and organisations alike. New Zealand, for example, has a trading and political presence in the global community due in no small part to its sporting brands such as All Black rugby, Olympic Games and World Championship achievements and the successes of Team New Zealand's America's Cup Yachting Syndicates. Domestically, the growing business of sport within New Zealand contributes significantly to the domestic economy. An assessment in 1998 determined that the sport sector output, per day, was $4,800m, while direct and indirect employment contributed to 31,000 jobs (Frater, Miller and Harris, 1998). New Zealand also has one of the highest participation rates globally in sport and physical activity. Almost all New Zealand adults (98%, approximately, 2.67m) enjoy some sport or active leisure over the year and on a weekly basis, 68% of the population over five-years-old are considered to be active (engage in a minimum of 2.5 hours of activity per week) (van Aalst, Kazakov and McLean, 2005).

The important place of sport in New Zealand society and the growing number of employment opportunities in the sector have been recognised by tertiary education in New Zealand. A growing number of sport and related programmes, which incorporate study in sport science, sport management and sport coaching from certificate to degree level through to postgraduate qualifications, have been established over the last ten years. In comparison to the early 1990s, most universities, institutes of technology and polytechnics in New Zealand now offer one or more sport qualifications.

The industry that supports graduates with such qualifications is also in an early stage of evolution (Hindson, 1999). As the professionalisation of sport takes hold in New Zealand, there are increasing opportunities for paid employment in sport related discipline areas. The sport industry in New Zealand in the 21st century, although still public sector driven, is now a mix of commercial interest, government involvement and participation by non-profit organisations.

Description

Auckland University of Technology (AUT) and Unitec situated in Auckland, New Zealand both offer sub-degree, degree and postgraduate programmes that focus on applied and vocational learning. This case study will focus on cooperative education components of two degree programmes in sport within these institutions.

Cooperative education in Bachelor of Sport and Recreation (BSR) at AUT

The BSR is a three-year programme that was first developed in 1997 to prepare students for careers in the areas of sports science, sport-and-recreation management, coaching, fitness, physical education or outdoor education. There are currently 100 students enrolled in the third year of this degree. During their final year all BSR students must complete 600 hours of cooperative education, where work and learning are integrated through the development of partnerships between the university, the student and a sport or recreation organisation. The cooperative education component constitutes half of the students' total workload for the academic year.

Cooperative education papers* (Cooperative one and Cooperative two) are structured so that the student spends the equivalent of two days a week during the two semesters of the academic year within one organisation. During Cooperative one, the students complete 200 hours of workplace activities and 100 hours is allocated as academic time for students to reflect on and critically analyse their experiences as

> New Zealand has a trading and political presence in the global community due in no small part to its sporting brands

well as to design a project that is beneficial to their organisation. During Cooperative two the students are required to complete 150 hours in the workplace and the remaining 150 hours allow time for the students to complete, evaluate and present their industry-related project.

Recent research (Fleming and Eames, 2004) has shown that the structure of the BSR cooperative programme was appropriate for student learning and that there was sufficient time in the workplace to build relationships and develop trust. In addition, the flexible structure was able to accommodate the demands related to the seasonal nature of the sport industry. A key feature of cooperative education is that the students will integrate their learning between the classroom and the workplace. In the non-continuous or part-time structure of the BSR cooperative, the students still undertake academic courses within the university. The knowledge and capabilities students learn in the workplace can then be applied directly back in to the classroom and vice versa. A student exposed to the realities of the industry may then have a greater motivation for classroom learning (Burchell, Hodges and Rainsbury, 2000; Weisz, 2000).

Cooperative education in Bachelor of Sport (B.Sport) at Unitec

The B.Sport with majors in management and coaching is a three-year, full-time qualification offered at Unitec, West Auckland, New Zealand. The programme was first offered in 1999 and has prepared students

---

* This term is used in New Zealand instead of the more widely used 'module'.

for a wide variety of roles in 'sport' that include ski instruction, strength and conditioning coaching, school-sport coordination, physical education teaching (following one-year postgraduate study), fitness instruction, sport management and marketing roles in national and regional sport organisations, commercial-product management, event management and facility management and marketing.

B.Sport students choose their major focus at the beginning of their second year of study and are required to undertake 80 hours of 'practicum' work experience in their second year. This compulsory course plays a vital role in preparing students for an elective cooperative experience in the third year, should they select this course, or offers an insight into the type of role they may choose upon completion of their degree. During the third year optional course, students spend approximately 120 to 140 hours within an organisation, with the remainder of the 180 hours spent on academic activities such as assessments and in-class seminars. Students can choose to undertake the course within one semester (14 weeks) or across two. About 25 students opt for it each year. This creates greater flexibility to accommodate industry-organisation needs as well as offering the opportunity for longitudinal immersion for the student within the work environment.

Seminars scheduled throughout the course focus on maximising learning from the experience by making connections with other coursework undertaken concurrently or completed throughout the three years of academic study. The cooperative course constitutes one of ten courses the students usually complete in their final year of study.

Placement process

The students in both programmes are required to find and negotiate their own cooperative placement. This is a deliberate strategy tied to the development of job seeking and communication skills for the students. In the BSR, preparation for this process begins during the students' second year when they are required to undertake two different practicum experiences of 40 hours each. In the B.Sport degree students are required to undertake one practicum of 80 hours.

This provides the students with an introduction to the sport and recreation industry and a chance to identify potential cooperative placement opportunities for the following year. Another strategy used to identify suitable organisations includes students listening to presentations by industry organisations seeking students. These presentations often broaden the students' perspective of the sport-and-recreation industry by highlighting a range of different contexts in which they may undertake their learning experience. Other

> The knowledge and capabilities students are learning in the workplace can then be applied directly back in to the classroom and vice versa

strategies available to students include reviewing advertisements placed on noticeboards and attending the final cooperative presentations by graduating students. After the students have selected their favoured options, they then individually approach the industry contacts. Through imitating the job seeking process, students are able to develop capabilities that can be utilised when seeking employment in the future.

Students can undertake work-integrated learning opportunities in a broad range of settings in commercial, government and non-profit organisations. Industry placements include national, regional or local sports organisations, community-recreation facilities, private and public sector health and fitness clubs, outdoor recreation or tourism operators, schools (physical education and sports departments), regional sports trusts, sport performance and sport science organisations, sports-marketing and event-management companies (see Figure 1).

It has been established that matching and managing expectations from both the student and industry perspective is critical for optimising the success of the cooperative experience (Coll and Eames, 2000). A key strategy we use is the development of the student learning contract. This agreement outlines details of the cooperative requirements, a description of the negotiated work activities and general details relating to supervision and feedback. In addition, the students develop specific learning objectives that relate to their own professional and academic development. Other strategies to help achieve a successful experi-

Type of industry organisation	Organisation example	Placement example
Sport Clubs	Golf Club	Coaching Role
	Squash & Tennis Club	Market Research Role
Regional Sport Organisations Marketing	Auckland Tennis Association	International Tournament
	Auckland Rugby Football Union	Fitness Training Assistant
National Sport Organisations	New Zealand Rugby League	Coaching Development Role
	New Zealand Hockey	Member Database Review
Regional Sports Trusts	Sport North Harbour	Event Management
	Sport Auckland	Physical Activity Promotion
National and Local Government	Auckland Regional Council	Bike Lane Promotion
	North Shore City Council	Leisure Services Assistant
Schools	Secondary School	Sport Co-ordination
	Primary School	Soccer Coaching Role
Public Recreation Centres	YMCA Recreation Centre	Programme Co-ordination
	Leisure Centre	Pool Promotion
Commercial Sport & Fitness Centres	Les Mills Fitness Centre	Personal Training
	Millennium Institute of Sport & Health	Sport Science Support
Sport Consultancies	IMG	Ironman Event Assistance
	Sport Management Consultancies	Sponsorship Coordination
Sporting Goods Companies	Nike Head Office	Athlete Sponsorship Support
	Rebel Sports	Marketing Assistance
Sport Sponsors	Orca	Sponsorship Market Research
	Puma New Zealand	Sponsorship Evaluation
Sport Media	Sky Sport	Outside Broadcast Production
	Local Newspapers	Event Coverage
Outdoor Recreation or Tourism	Outdoor Discoveries	Outdoor Education Instruction
	Fergs Kayaks	Adventure Tourism Role

Figure 1 Examples of sport and recreation placements in the Auckland region

ence include a three-way meeting set up between the organisation, the university and the student where the learning contract is signed, as well as written guidelines and handbooks for the industry supervisor and other staff within the organisation.

Supervision

Effective supervision and mentoring is a critical part of the learning experience and has been shown to result in greater educational and career success for cooperative students (Ricks and Van Gyn, 1997). The students are supported during their cooperative placement by an academic supervisor from the tertiary institution who provides regular one-on-one mentoring. The communication between student and academic supervisor is generally face-to-face. However some

students are now located at a distance from the institution and therefore email and website communication is used as an alternative.

An important part of the supervision process includes communication with the industry supervisor and site visits. Generally the academic supervisor will visit the workplace at least twice during the academic year. It is important to establish a sound framework for supervision as many students are involved in small sport organisations with poorly defined management structures. This is often a result of the reliance on volunteers, who have minimal management training (Shilbury and Deane, 2001). Involvement in a cooperative education partnership assists staff within the industry to develop an understanding of the nature and concepts of the programmes currently available in our tertiary institutions. This enables potential employers to be more familiar with the skills and attributes that our graduates are equipped with.

The links developed with industry supervisors and staff within the organisations have had the added benefit of providing feedback on the relevance and currency of course content. This has enabled our tertiary programmes to keep pace with the rapidly changing nature of the sport industry.

Learning outcomes

The cooperative experience allows students to learn through a variety of experiences that result in changes in their actions and behaviours and enhances employability. The key aim of cooperative education is to apply and integrate theoretical concepts to the work environment. More specifically, it provides opportunities to:

❑ Analyse the role of the organisation and its relationships within the industry.
❑ Enable students to work in a professional manner and in a team environment.
❑ Enable students to critically reflect on their own practice.
❑ Develop generic skills such as communication, time management, planning, critical analysis, reflective thinking, initiative and creativity.
❑ Develop problem-solving, research, project-design and management skills relevant to the industry.

In a study undertaken within the BSR it has been shown that students developed a range of practical and technical skills relevant to their specific work activities. Through their experiences, students develop a sense of what will be useful to them in their chosen career path. BSR students highlighted the importance of the development of soft skills and felt that:

they are the things that you can carry over into anything, they are the things that make you better in the workplace. (Fleming and Eames, 2004: 4)

Students gained confidence, improved oral and written communication skills, as well as developing capabilities related to reflective thinking, critical analysis, initiative, teamwork, and problem-solving. In particular, improving time management was highlighted as a critical learning outcome.

A study of job advertisements that were placed in New Zealand print media during a three-month period identified competencies required to gain a posi-tion in sport and recreation. Soft skills such as communication, customer service, motivation, passion and enthusiasm, as well as practical work experience, were highlighted as being important requirements for employability (Wiersma and Bradbury, 2004). The inclusion of the cooperative education experience within our degree programmes facilitates the learning opportunities for our students to develop these capabilities that are not taught within the classroom.

As employment opportunities in some areas of sport, such as sport performance and exercise science, are limited, transferable skills are essential for creating expanded opportunities in related vocations. In addition there is considerable diversity within the sport and recreation industry such that a full range of skills cannot be covered in any one degree structure. A graduate with specific knowledge may have an advantage with some employers but more often this knowledge is better learned in the work context where it will be used.

A critical part of the learning experience for the students from both programmes is the design and implementation of a project that is considered beneficial to the organisation. Students may design and implement physical activity or training programmes within a school or the community. Some projects may include market research, customer satisfaction surveys or programme evaluations. Other projects include reliability and validity studies for equipment or fitness testing protocols with athletes or members of the community.

The project provides the opportunity for students to apply a range of technical skills and knowledge that have been learnt during their studies, yet also to develop a wide range of new capabilities. Undertaking the project facilitates personal development by providing an opportunity for the students to take responsibility, which develops confidence and the use of initiative. BSR students have commented that by undertaking the project they have learnt:

the importance of planning, the need to be organised, to set goals and objectives and to allow time because they often had to rely on others. (Fleming and Eames, 2004: 4)

The involvement in a 'real-life' project is a valuable strategy that enhances student learning and prepares them for the demands that they may encounter in the workplace. As many of the projects involve people, the students are able to develop, through their own experience, an understanding of the principles necessary to undertake projects in an ethical manner in the sport and recreation industry (Fleming and Walton, 2004).

The skills and capabilities that are developed through the cooperative learning strategy in our programmes are underpinned by findings from research in other discipline areas (Eames, 2003; Rainsbury et al, 2002). Jones and Linn (2004) summarise the following capabilities as being important for employability in any discipline area: academic skills – that is, the ability to learn, think critically and communicate effectively; personal skills, such as self-confidence; positive attitude to learning; initiative; ability to plan and manage time; and teamwork.

Assessment of learning

Cooperative education is not just 'work experience'. Academic credit is given for the learning that results from the experience. Students in both programmes are required to keep a reflective journal throughout the whole period to reflect on and critically analyse their activities. In the BSR, for example, learning is assessed in the form of a reflective essay which allows the student to summarise their progress in terms of achieving their learning outcomes and comment on critical incidents. Personal learning can be unforeseen and unpredictable and is maximised by reflection on experiences. Therefore, it is important that there is flexibility in assessment of the individual learning outcomes identified by the student in the learning contract, so that the learning derived from the experience is not constrained.

In the BSR the first reflective essay is submitted halfway through Cooperative one. A second reflective assessment forms part of the final report and the students are expected to reflect on and critically analyse their whole cooperative experience. In the B.Sport, the reflective journal is formally assessed at the end of the experience.

A key assessment of student learning occurs through the project proposal and subsequent project report. This strategy of project-based assessment links the real-life application with academic theory.

Communication skills are developed and assessed through the process of formal report writing and the presentation of the student projects to industry and academic staff.

In an attempt to prepare the students for employment, a component of the assessment includes an

> Personal learning can be unforeseen and unpredictable and is maximised by reflection on experiences

analysis of the organisation and its relationship with the sport and recreation industry. This encourages students to further contextualise their work with an in-depth understanding of the structure, operation and culture of the organisation. Other assessment tools which provide feedback on student performance include industry supervisor evaluations and student self-evaluations. These often identify personal and professional strengths that are valued by future employers. In addition, they highlight areas for further growth.

Employment and career pathways

Cooperative education aims to help students understand aspects of the real world by exposure to authentic work that is related to their career aims (Coll and Eames, 2004). Career pathways in sport are often not well-defined (Hayes and Gunson, 1999). The placement experience is therefore a vital stepping-stone to career guidance and future full-time employment. The cooperative experience exposes the students to a wider variety of options that they may not have considered previously. Students are able to discover the type of work they are passionate about and this can be used either to confirm or eliminate career options.

Careers in sport in New Zealand until recently have centred around physical education teaching or fitness instruction. However, as an outcome of their cooperative-education experience, students may instead find themselves prepared for a wider range of positions than were available ten years ago. Many positions in sport and recreation or postgraduate training courses will not even consider applicants unless they have experience to add to their qualification. Therefore, the cooperative experience they have gained provides a valuable component to their CV.

Many sport and recreation organisations use our cooperative education programmes to identify potential employees. As employees, students who have undertaken a cooperative experience as part of their degree have been shown to have a better understanding of the demands of the industry, are more willing to volunteer for new roles and learn new skills that lead to advancement and success (Calway and Murphy, 2000). Employers recognise that there is considerable cost (financial and emotional) associated with managing an appointment that does not work for either the employer or employee.

In addition, research has shown that cooperative students in many discipline areas are more likely to be hired than graduates who have not undertaken a cooperative experience (Braunstein, 1999; Ricks and Van Gynn, 1997). Cooperative graduates usually remain longer in their first job and tend to progress faster. Tertiary qualifications in sport are relatively new and therefore employers are often unaware of the knowledge and skills graduates are equipped with. Therefore, employers' involvement in the cooperative partnership gives them a 'feel' for the quality they should expect from new graduate employees.

Conclusion

This case study has established the benefits of work-integrated learning for the employability of students in the sport and recreation industry. Overall, from our experience, which is supported by research in other disciplines, students who have undertaken cooperative education have a competitive edge in the employment marketplace (Hayward and Horvath, 2000). In addition, during the cooperative experience, students develop the desirable capabilities, beliefs and attitudes that make them valuable employees. This case study has highlighted the structure and processes necessary to achieve successful outcomes for the student, tertiary institution and the sport and recreation organisation.

References and URLs

Braunstein, L.A. 1999. Employer benefits of, and attitudes toward postsecondary cooperative education. *Journal of Cooperative Education* **36** (1), 7–22

Burchell, N. Hodges, D. and Rainsbury, L. 2000. What competencies do business graduates require? Perspectives of New Zealand Stakeholders. *Journal of Cooperative Education* **37** (1), 10–21

Calway, B. A. and Murphy, G.A. 2000. Career progression of cooperative education graduates. *Journal of Cooperative Education* **35** (2/3), 68–76

Coll, R. K. and Eames, C. 2000. The role of the placement coordinator: An alternative model. *Asia-Pacific Journal of Cooperative Education* **1** (1), 9–14

Coll, R. K. and Eames, C. 2004. Current issues in cooperative education. In R. K. Coll and C. Eames (eds.) *International Handbook for Cooperative Education*. Boston, MA: World Association for Cooperative Education, pp 270–282

Collins, C. (ed.) 2000. *Sport in New Zealand Society*. Palmerston North: Dunmore Press

Eames, C. W. 2003. *Learning through cooperative education work placements in science and technology*. Unpublished PhD thesis, University of Waikato. Hamilton, New Zealand.

Ferkins, L. 2002. Sporting best practice: An industry view of work placements. *Asia-Pacific Journal of Cooperative Education* **3** (2), 29–34

Fleming, J. and Eames, C. 2004. The time course of learning: Student views on the structure of their placements. In C. Eames (ed.) *Proceedings of the 5th Asia Pacific Cooperative Education Conference*. Auckland, New Zealand

Fleming, J. and Ferkins, L. 2005. Cooperative education in sport: Building our knowledgebase. *Journal of Hospitality, Leisure, Sport & Tourism Education* **4** (1), 41–47

Fleming, J. and Walton, J. 2004. Sport and recreation cooperative projects: A medium for teaching and learning ethical principles. *Asia-Pacific Journal of Cooperative Education* **5** (1), 45–49

Frater, P., Miller, J. and Harris, F. 1998. *The growing business of sport and leisure: The economic impact of sport and leisure in New Zealand, an update to 1996.* Wellington: Hillary Commission

Hayes, L. and Gunson, L. 1999. The structure of sport and its management in New Zealand. In Trenberth, L. and Collins C. (eds.) *Sport business management in New Zealand.* Palmerston North, New Zealand: Dunmore Press, pp 39–52

Hayward, C. and Horvath, P. 2000. The effect of cooperative education on occupational beliefs. *Journal of Cooperative Education* **35** (1), 7–14

Hindson, A. 1999. The evolution of sport management in New Zealand. In L. Trenberth and C. Collins (eds.) *Sport business management in New Zealand.* Palmerston North, New Zealand: Dunmore Press, pp 25–38

Jones, P. D. and Linn, P. L. 2004. Cooperative education in liberal arts. In R.K. Coll and C. Eames (eds.) *International Handbook for Cooperative Education.* Boston, MA: World Association for Cooperative Education, pp 123–139

National Commission for Cooperative Education 2004. Retrieved 14/05/04 from http://www.co-op.edu/mdel.html

Rainsbury, E. Hodges, D. Burchell, N. and Lay, M. 2002. Ranking workplace competencies: Student and graduate perceptions. *Asia-Pacific Journal of Cooperative Education* **3** (2), 8–18

Ricks, F. and Van Gyn, G. 1997. Mentoring relationships as learning opportunities. *Journal of Cooperative Education* **32** (3), 41–55

Shilbury, D. and Deane, J. 2001. *Sport management in Australia: An organisational overview,* 2nd ed. Victoria, Australia: Strategic Sport Management

van Aalst, I. Kazakov, D. and McLean, G. 2005. *SPARC facts.* Wellington: Sport and Recreation New Zealand

Weisz, M. 2000. Developing a measure of student attributes. *Journal of Cooperative Education* **35** (2/3), 33–40

Wiersma, C. and Bradbury, T. 2004. Academia and Industry: Ever the twain shall meet? *Australasian Parks and Leisure,* Spring 2004, 35–36

JENNY FLEMING is a Senior Lecturer at Auckland University of Technology, New Zealand. Jenny is the coordinator for Cooperative Education in the Bachelor of Sport & Recreation and Bachelor of Dance degrees. She is currently Deputy Chairman of the New Zealand Association for Cooperative Education and is on the editorial board for the *Asia-Pacific Journal of Cooperative Education.*

LESLEY FERKINS is Senior Lecturer in sport management and Programme Director in the School of Sport at Unitec New Zealand. Lesley also coordinates the practicum courses within the Bachelor of Sport and is published in cooperative education. Her work appears with co-author Jenny Fleming in the *International Handbook for Co-operative Education,* the *Journal of Hospitality, Leisure, Sport and Tourism Education* and the *Asia-Pacific Journal of Cooperative Education.*

14 Establishing virtual working within the business curriculum

Mary Malcolm

This case study describes the redesign of a suite of undergraduate business and management courses to feature virtual working. It demonstrates how it promoted communication and teamwork enhancing both employability focus and portfolio differentiation.

In 2002, during the course of a substantial reorganisation of its membership and activities, the Dundee Business School (DBS) at the University of Abertay Dundee (UAD) comprehensively redesigned its provision of undergraduate business education. The primary aim was to refresh its curriculum in the context of changing requirements posed both by labour markets and within the HE sector.

One feature of the programmes that emerged through the review and redesign process to form the business portfolio (first operated in 2004/05) was the inclusion throughout those programmes of virtual-group working. Skills associated with this theme were embedded in modules core to all programmes within the portfolio (a total of four programmes, one of which incorporates eight pathway variants).

This paper explains the process by which virtual working was developed, and articulates one element within a comprehensive generic skills framework, closely associated in particular with skills related to communication and teamwork, as an enhancement both of employability focus and portfolio differentiation. It also identifies structural and contextual challenges to the successful implementation of skills programmes likely to be common to design teams operating within modular schemes, rationalising provision through portfolio redesign.

The paper outlines the structure and development of the virtual working theme, from online communication to extended collaboration, and sketches the initial achievement in leveraging opportunities offered by skill integration and the transfer to an online environment. These were opportunities to develop knowledge building and critical thinking skills in an environment significantly different from that of the classroom.

Finally, the paper identifies design and operational issues relating to the initial implementation and lists challenges for further development.

Making the case for virtual working in the curriculum

In the design team, we had several objectives in identifying virtual working as a particular curriculum focus and selecting it from a broad range of subject and skill options. These objectives reflect conditions in which other programme teams working in the same area may undertake curriculum review and development of generalist undergraduate Business and Management programmes.

From the outset, we recognised fundamental changes in business models and practice, wrought by the interlinked forces of globalisation and the changing economics of information. We understood that to respond fully to and effect these changes within our business portfolio we would have to do more than develop the content-based syllabus. We would also need to review the development of skills within the portfolio. In doing this, we would need to recognise changes in the nature of work both for organisations and for the individual and the economic and moral imperatives to develop a workforce with a substantial grounding in working and learning practices sufficiently robust to withstand and to inform ongoing change. Achieving all this would require changed priorities within the curriculum, beyond the manipulation and/or expansion of content. The redesigned portfolio would need a substantive and structurally significant skills focus.

Furthermore, we well understood that for claims of relevance to employability that resonate with potential students' own career objectives in choosing to study business to be sustainable, they must be supported by learners, graduates and their employers. Such claims cannot rest solely on an assumption that a business-related degree must, by virtue of its subject matter, contribute significantly to employment prospects and performance. Neither can they rely substantially on the adoption in programme delivery of a generally businesslike approach, incorporating the use of business resources and formats, and sustaining the application of theory to practice throughout. Central objectives of the curriculum design process were, therefore, to specify and substantiate claims to an employability-relevant curriculum, and to identify employability skills clearly, as a significant curriculum element, to stakeholders.

This determination to articulate and implement employability with clarity and precision entailed a further condition: the skills selected would have to be amenable to close incorporation with subject development throughout a busy and potentially overcrowded curriculum. There is a vast range of both subjects and skills that can be justified for curriculum inclusion on the basis of broad and substantial evidence of their importance to business and to organisational life. Certainly there was ample evidence available to indicate that virtual working constituted a valid component of the new programmes, serving a stated portfolio aim of preparing graduates for 'productive participation in a networked and knowledge-based economy', in the 'multifaceted virtual culture of the network enterprise.' (Castells, 2000: 214). Justifying the selection and prioritisation of certain skills in a curriculum already pressed to include other foundation and contemporary subjects and skills is, for curriculum developers in business and management, perhaps the most challenging task.

Thus, the programme team sought to identify among the employability-related skills available and justifiable for inclusion in the portfolio, those that, if effectively integrated into the curriculum, would:

1 Represent curriculum innovation within the sector so that, while the DBS portfolio might resemble those of other business curricula (not least for reasons of market expectation), the power and persuasiveness of the school's offerings would reside, in part, in the various ways in which employability was articulated within that curriculum.

2 Be amenable to integration not only into the diverse syllabus content that forms the basis of general undergraduate syllabus in business and

> Central objectives… an employability-relevant curriculum …to identify employability skills clearly, as a significant curriculum element, to stakeholders

management, but also with the focus on academic skills development identified as a significant requirement of the undergraduate business curriculum, and with other employability-related skills.

The skills associated with virtual working met all of the objectives set for the selection of employability-related skills within the new curriculum. They were of contemporary relevance, consistent with and supportive of other proposed content and skill components within the curriculum, and they could be articulated to and by stakeholders as a coherent component of portfolio differentiation. They offered a clear opportunity to go beyond the expression of employability as a curriculum value, and to position and develop specific employability skills within the curriculum.

Determining the focus

With the decision made to incorporate virtual working into the new curriculum, two critical decisions emerged to be made in order to guide our implementation of virtual working as an employability skill and as a curriculum element. Exactly how should we articulate its relevance to employability? And how would we introduce it throughout programmes?

Virtual teamwork or digital literacy?

Two primary (though far from mutually exclusive) foci presented themselves at the outset for the treatment of virtual working; a communicative focus on the skills and techniques of online interaction, and a digital literacy focus on the informational aspect of virtual working.

We selected the former as offering a particularly good fit with what we anticipated to be a consistent portfolio focus on the development of teamworking skills such as group decision-making and the preparation and delivery of team presentations. It also offered a focus in curriculum content on changing business and organisational models in which collaboration assumes an increasingly significant role:

> more than people and applications working together – [crossing] the entire business chain to include processes, architecture and communication. (Filho, 2001)

Enhancing group working with virtual working skills generated a portfolio outcome promising graduates able to 'perform effectively as a team member, in formal and informal, face-to-face and online contexts', embracing aspects of collaboration such as:

> willingness to engage in change processes ...to monitor critically their own knowledge and performance ...communicate, including the arguments and perspectives of others... perform effectively as a team member ... plan, manage and take responsibility for completion of tasks [in a] task-based group. (UAD, 2004: 8–13)

Additionally, we felt it important that the context for virtual working should be relevant both to a range of careers and to the full range of potential employers at different stages of progress in their deployment of virtual working. Focusing on teamwork would support the development of collaborative skills more generally. Digital information literacy, while an important aspect of employability and in no way excluded from the emerging virtual working concept, could – we decided – play a supporting role in the area of virtual working, because of overlap with the already well-established portfolio focus on the development of academic and business-related information handling skills.

Skill or task focus?

With the decision to prioritise teamworking aspects of virtual working, and to leverage online groupwork to develop a broad range of knowledge- and learning-related skills, a further decision remained as to how we would operationalise skill development. Here, once again, two broad choices presented themselves. The first was to focus on sub-skills associated with virtual-group working, to organise and to accumulate these to imply or practise a composite performance; the second was to simulate that composite performance repeatedly as a requirement and to analyse and develop performance progressively within it.

The decision to focus on sub-skills, developed in staged practice environments, lay partly in contextual factors associated with modularity and programme interlock, as discussed below. But it was a decision also informed by a commitment to providing graduates, at each stage of their programme of study (and allowing for exit points at each of the four stages in a Scottish honours programme), not only with the knowledge, skills and aptitudes employers sought and would value, but also with:

> an articulate understanding of the value and the detail of their learning experience, such that they are able to identify for themselves and for future employers, their potential to contribute to organisational development and transformation. (UAD, 2004: 7)

This ability to formulate with conviction and some precision the basis of their claim to employment and career advancement we generally agreed to be critical to graduate competitiveness. But such an approach would also, we hoped, support learner persistence. It would offer carefully graduated levels of challenge, and a series of 'cues and clues' as to the nature of the challenge at each stage supported by confidence in successful achievement of prior challenges (Yorke and Knight, 2004). It would also allow us to maintain firm links between specific skills directly associated with online group working and a range of other closely related and underpinning skills developed at the same stage of study, in areas such as information literacy, IT, group process and project management.

The review context

Contextual challenges also emerged. It had been recognised early in the review process that the development of a revised undergraduate business portfolio

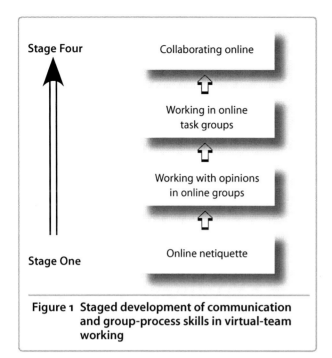

Figure 1 Staged development of communication and group-process skills in virtual-team working

Stage Four

Collaborating online

Working in online task groups

Working with opinions in online groups

Online netiquette

Stage One

by a much smaller academic staff. Thus, introducing generic skills required particularly careful attention to the status of individual modules as core or optional, on various programmes, and in some cases with heterogeneous module populations.

The design process was therefore a protracted one, in which each of the skills-focused teams, subject groupings and programme teams developed their ideas in more or less close harmony (occasionally disharmony) with the broadly parallel progress of the others. And in implementation, the information-sharing requirement, particularly in relation to assessment, exceeded anything required previously of module tutors. Task types, grade weightings and assessment criteria had to be aligned if skill development was to be assured and to keep pace with skill requirements.

From communication to collaboration

The outcome of this process was a structured programme of skill development and assessment, one element of which was the staged development of communication and group process skills associated with virtual teamworking (see Figure 1). At each stage, the virtual working skills were as follows:

Stage one: communicating online

In the stage-one Business programme operating across the portfolio, students learn foundation IT and communication skills. One module contextualises basic IT skills for business (as well as familiarising students with WebCT), and they learn communication skills in a series of modules across a range of subject areas, reinforcing the centrality of communication across disciplines and business functions. Thus, for example, in the stage-one Accounting module, students are asked to consider how a reader-centred approach to memo writing might inform the structure and phrasing of a covering memo summarising a lengthier explanation of a financial situation, targeted at non-specialists. In the parallel Law module, they tackle the task of formulating for an organisation's legal advisors a problem that requires attention, and in their first Economics module they focus on the communicative power of visual aids, designing a single PowerPoint slide that meets elicited principles of good communication practice.

– contemporary in 'feel' and content, and reflecting the academic strengths and interests of an academic staff profile changed by both normal turnover and a voluntary severance scheme – would not be achieved through marginal changes to the school's existing provision. Comprehensive review and ambitious renewal of its existing provision would be necessary to restate the remodelled school's commitment to attractive and successful undergraduate programmes, and its engagement with national agendas and priorities for economic development and growth.

In order to ensure that the skill development programme – of which virtual-group working constituted one element – was coherently presented, the design of the skills programme could not be driven by sporadic innovation and preference; nor could its implementation rely on variable uptake at module level. In implementation, particular skills and sub-skills that were the focus of particular modules would have to be practised, developed and assessed across modules and levels in such a way that the confidence of students in their intellectual and skill development would be maintained.

Key objectives of the review as a whole included reducing the module proliferation that had occurred through the independent design of individual programmes and leveraging module utility to create an expanded portfolio of titles that could be delivered similar approach is taken to the development of shared principles of online communication – at this stage in email. Rather than presenting learners with a particular and restrictive view of 'correct' netiquette, their experience as email recipients is used to elicit preferences that form the basis for agreed principles of communication. The development of a particular email register or format is avoided, and learners are instead encouraged to view email simply as a channel through which various degrees of formality and detail can be expressed, with appropriate reference to communicative purpose and audience, rather than to any presupposed bias or generally agreed email format or style. This approach, consistent across online and offline communication, avoids focus on format, concentrating instead on communicative impact, estab-

> encouraged to view email simply as a channel through which various degrees of formality and detail can be expressed

lishing from the outset the importance of planning for and reflecting on communication as interaction. The teaching approach adopted in all instances is that of discussion and practice, allowing students to formulate shared (and divergent) views of communicative effect and priority before being asked to produce particular items.

Stage two: co-operating online

Whereas the focus at stage one has been primarily on the effective presentation of information, at stage two the focus shifts to the more contentious area of formulating and receiving opinion.

Once again, virtual working skills are supported by other skills under development in offline contexts – particularly in the following areas:

❑ Identifying and evaluating alternative solutions
❑ Reaching group consensus
❑ Drafting and revising pair-generated documentation.

Thus, learners are engaged in the challenge of understanding and formulating relevant differences in stated positions, developing the contributions of others, and seeking common ground among a range of positions. In their online work, the requirements are,

at this stage, particularly carefully constrained. To allow time for learners to experience and explore the basis of group collaboration, they focus at this stage solely on recognising and responding constructively to (in development and/or disagreement with) the stated positions of others in an online environment. Presented with two sharply divergent positions on an organisational issue (not academic viewpoints), they are invited both to express and account for their own opinions and to comment on and develop those of others in a small group (maximum six members) over a period of a couple of weeks. They are not required, in this context, to reach a consensus; their contribution to the debate is evaluated on the basis of their interaction with the group and its opinions. The teaching approach at this stage moves to a task-debrief pattern, with a limited set of principles being established prior to the task. The challenge for learners is to develop their individual skills in an online small-group context, and only when they have experienced the impact of their own and others' interactions are they likely to be able to formulate for themselves and others the significance and the relative effectiveness of a range of possible approaches and techniques.

Stage three: co-ordinating online

It is here that learners confront the process challenges of online group decision-making, as they are required to complete a group task, with a specified outcome and deadline, once again in small groups. Here the focus shifts decisively from individual to group performance, in alignment with parallel developments throughout this stage in the curriculum, with students required to develop and deliver group projects as presentations and reports, and to undertake extended and multi-stage projects based on emergent requirements, on an individual basis. Once again, as at stage two, only in the attempt does the challenge become clear. Therefore, in this case an unassessed practice iteration of a group task is undertaken, and its outcomes and shortcomings are explored in plenary session, before the assessed task is undertaken.

Stage four: collaborating online

At honours stage, the skills of virtual working are more closely aligned than earlier with the academic requirements of programmes. Whereas at earlier stages there was a clear focus on business-related (rather than academically directed) activity, at stage four that distinction is less firmly upheld. While the task set has a business focus, the collaboration in which learners engage to complete it feeds into their development of an individual coursework task submission. The criteria for assessment of this collaboration are necessarily distinct from those for the individual report that develops from that collaborative effort. For example, the requirements related to a Direct Markcting case study include the following (in addition to originality and participation criteria):

❑ Suggestions for the group to discuss in response to the challenges set.
❑ Contribution to the discussion of suggestions made by others in the group, through comment, suggestion of a different perspective, an added factor, a problem.
❑ Useful connections between the challenges posed and direct marketing theory.
❑ Development of the ideas contributed by others in the group, taking their ideas further.
❑ Critical comment on the ideas of others that is constructive and seeks to move their ideas forward.

The task set is multi-stage, raises multiple issues, and is of extended duration (six weeks, rather than two or three at earlier stages). In the offline environment, learners at this stage undertake extended research tasks, their response to which is expected to be structurally – as well as substantially – informed by their independent research. In this online environment they are encouraged to seek out alternative opinions and approaches, to contribute to group learning and understanding of the task at hand, and to develop and deploy the ideas of peers.

Evaluation – leveraging opportunities

We are evaluating the first implementation of virtual working, and of the generic skills programme as a whole. Early indications are that levels of student satisfaction with their online activity and their overall confidence in the value of the experience for their career prospects are very high.

A guiding principle for us was that – in positioning and articulating individual skills – we would pay close attention not only to the delivery of each specific skill component, but also to the integration of the various skills that comprised the programme as a whole. Otherwise there was a danger that we could create either isolated skills modules, or scattered and equally isolated skills elements within largely unrelated subject (module) contexts. In either case, we would leave each skill area within the portfolio unsupported by, and unsupportive of, both surrounding content and other skill areas, undermining any claim to the

> students at stage four appear to be clear about where they might use the skills they have developed, and are able to relate those skills closely to the effectiveness of online group working

articulation of a consistent employability focus. This interlinking of skills appears to have been achieved and to be recognised by students as constituting a significant and coherent employability skill set.

What is less clear is how well the link between the various virtual working sub-skills and the overall theme of virtual working was sustained. Without careful design and attention to the 'big picture' at each stage, this focus on sub-skills might obscure entirely from learner view the relevance of their work to the overarching theme of virtual-group working. This was a challenge addressed through task design at each programme stage (see below), with a requirement that tasks at stages one to three, in particular, were business-focused rather than academically formulated. However, students at stage four appear to be clear about the business context in which they, as graduates, might use the skills they have developed, and are able to relate those skills closely to the effectiveness of online group working at earlier stages.

The focus on online groupwork within virtual working provided opportunities to develop a range of other skills and attitudes associated with an individual's effective contribution to an organisation and its development. In transferring a proportion of learner interaction to an online environment, and to a group-working context in particular, certain features of institutional learning – and of face-to-face delivery in particular – that might be considered to constitute barriers to simulating the dynamics of organisational life, could be overcome. Brown and Duguid analyse a description of an effective project group as follows:

in getting the job done, the people involved ignored divisions of rank and role to forge a single group around their shared task, with overlapping knowledge, relatively blurred boundaries, and a common working identity. (2000: 127)

How are we to recreate such an experience either within a classroom or in out-of-class groupwork necessarily evaluated primarily as product rather than process?

Focusing on group working as an aspect of virtual working, we found we could promote the development of collaborative techniques and approaches in learners precisely because of the 'distance' from the standard classroom configuration where that work takes place. Online, teachers have an opportunity to withdraw from centre stage – a withdrawal which some teachers, as well their students, may need support in adjusting to (Palloff and Pratt, 2001: 21–22). Thus it is possible to design a team context rather closer in certain significant respects to that of the organisational environment than it is possible to create, or at least sustain, in a synchronous face-to-face teacher-managed classroom – a context in which the dynamics of teamwork can be explored and enacted.

More broadly, by altering standard patterns of face-to-face interaction, virtual-group working, appropriately designed and managed, can allow focus on developing an understanding of aspects of organisational knowledge sharing and knowledge building generally. There are opportunities, for example, to examine the difference between idea contribution and ownership: who 'owns' a group-developed idea? How and why should appropriate credit for its initiation and/or emergence as a viable idea be given? How do individuals get their ideas accepted by a group, and what are the impediments to achieving this? How are pooled ideas to be evaluated and, where necessary, selected, rejected, refined and reworked without damage to group effectiveness? How do individual and collective responsibility operate in extended projects and process? The dynamics of online groupwork – asynchronous, text-based and archiveable – permit an attention to aspects of knowledge generation that

is difficult to sustain convincingly in an offline delivery format in which individual contribution is largely independently provided and individually evaluated. Thus it is possible to develop, in addition to skills directly associated with online group working, those skills associated more generally with contemporary organisational life and development, identified by Salmon as:

self-direction together with a willingness to support others, the ability to work in multi-skilled teams (which are likely to operate without regular meetings), to cooperate rather than compete, to handle information (rather than know everything) and to become critical thinkers. (2000: 91)

But there is also emerging evidence in the e-learning literature of the value of online working as a means of developing broader-based critical thinking skills in learners. The 'no significant difference' debate continues around e-learning as a more or less wholesale replacement for face-to-face delivery of higher education, and the results of online working initiatives remain mixed as far as the demonstration of 'higher order' skills is concerned (see, for example, Oliver, 2001). Nonetheless, recent literature fairly consistently identifies academic advantages to well-designed and firmly managed online working (e.g. Painter, Coffin and Hewings, 2003).

An asynchronous online environment promotes uninterrupted contribution by all group members, based on adequate and individually-determined time for reflection, synthesis and composition. It allows the informal rehearsal of ideas, as well as their peer review and development. Even the very availability for viewing by others of peer-generated ideas indicates for online group working a valuable dual focus both on career-focused employability skills associated with knowledge building and organisational learning, and on more immediate academic skill requirements (Garrison and Anderson, 2003: 26).

We also found that operational challenges included not, as might have been expected, too much tutor time spent in managing these tasks (this was carefully minimised in task design), but too much time on the assessment required at stage two: in particular, in evaluating individual student contributions made in a considerable number of fragmented and dispersed postings.

Further challenges remain. Can we develop in this

virtual-working environment skills that are difficult to implement within a modular scheme? Could we, for example, develop an equitable and sustainable approach to practising skills associated with the formal management of others? Could we use the online environment to create groups in which students are required to adopted specific function perspectives? And, once the initial implementation has been fully evaluated and further refined, can we operationalise the skills programme as a whole as Personal Development Planning?

MARY MALCOLM is I W Stewart Professor of Lifelong Learning and Head of Dundee Business School, University of Abertay Dundee. Following a decade in the Middle East, in education and as managing partner of a number of small businesses, Mary led the Division of Marketing, Communication, and Operations before becoming Head of School in 2004.

References

Brown, J. S. & Duguid, P. 2000. *The Social Life of Information.* Boston Ma: Harvard Business School Press

Castells, M. 2000. *The Rise of the Network Society (The Information Age: Economy, Society and Culture* Vol. 1). Oxford: Blackwell

Gartner, 2001. *Rethinking Collaboration, Business Challenges and Opportunities* by W. A. De A. Filho (http://www.gartner.com)

Garrison, D. R. & Anderson, T. 2003. *E-learning in the 21st century: A framework for research and practice.* London: Routledge Falmer

Oliver, R. 2001. Exploring the development of critical thinking skills through a Web-supported problem-based learning environment. In Stephenson, J. (ed.) 2001, *Teaching and Learning Online: Pedagogies for new technologies.* London: Kogan Page

Painter, C. Coffin, C. & Hewings, A. 2003. Impacts of directed tutorial activities in computer conferencing: A case study. *Distance Education* **24** (2) 159–74

Palloff, R. M. and Pratt, K. 2001. *Lessons from the cyberspace classroom: The realities of online teaching.* San Francisco: Jossey Bass

Salmon, G. 2000. *E-moderating: The key to teaching and learning online.* London: Kogan Page

UAD, 2004. *The Business portfolio: New programme approval document* (internal document). Dundee: University of Abertay

Yorke, M. & Knight, P. 2004. Self-theories; Some implications for teaching and learning in higher education. *Studies in Higher Education* **29** (1) 25–38

15 Placements and employability in sport and leisure management

Marc Keech

This case study is based on the placement process established by the Chelsea School at the University of Brighton for the BA (Hons) Sport and Leisure Management (SLM) degree. The case study outlines the practices that underpin the placement process and evaluates the extent to which students benefit from the variety of activities undertaken. Inherent are two principles that are examples of good practice: first, the building of experience with employers and businesses into courses through partnerships; and second, embedding employability within the curriculum and making it explicit within the learning experience.

Recent years have seen sports-related degree programmes become one of the most popular areas of higher education (HE) in the UK. Three quarters (74%) of institutions offer sports-related courses, with a further seven per cent planning to do so in the near future. Sport and recreation has a workforce of 621,000 people in paid employment, working in 231,000 businesses and organisations, spread across the public, private and voluntary sectors throughout the UK. It has growth forecasts and the potential to expand to a workforce of 750,000 in paid employment by 2008. In addition, almost 15% of the population are volunteers in sport, representing an estimated contribution of £14.1 billion to the economy (LIRC, 2003; 14).

Work-related learning in HE Sport and Leisure degree programmes

Increasingly, HE institutions (HEIS) are questioned about their effectiveness in preparing students for the competitive jobs market in this industry. Research has shown that sport and recreation employers feel that many graduates do not have the skills to take up employment following graduation (Ravenscroft et al, 2002). Many HEIS are now taking up the challenge of providing sports degree courses which combine academic rigour with vocational relevance. A number of students on sports-related degree programmes are studying sport because of an interest in the subject area, but some may have no ambition to work in the sector. In order to best serve students seeking work in the sector, and those who are already in work and wish to access higher education, HEIS need to consider providing vocational pathways within their provision (Gittus, 2002). This vocational provision can benefit students by making them more employable, benefit the sector by providing potential employees who have higher level analytical and technical skills, and benefit HEIS by assisting widening access strategies and improving first destination statistics.

If industry is to benefit from the large number of sports graduates, there needs to be a better match of supply and demand to ensure that regional and national skills gaps are met. Employers have indicated that they are looking for employees with vocational, and specialist technical and communication skills. Working on behalf of employers, it is planned that Skills Active UK will, in the future, work with partners in HE and FE who wish to provide vocational education and training and continue with the developments outlined here. Nolan (2002) provided a wide range of examples of how the University of Brighton enhanced his placement at Reading Football Club. Working with the stadium manager at the Madjeski Stadium, Nolan recognised that not only did he acquire a range of customer service skills, such as dealing with irate fans, but also that his placement offered a range of project management opportunities.

There are six important concerns regarding the different forms of work experience.

1 Work experience should be meaningful, relevant to future career development, effective as a learning tool in aiding personal development planning and in enhancing career prospects. If non-traditional forms of work experience are to be maximised for their learning opportunities, then students need some kind of structure and support so they can reflect on and articulate the learning.

2 It should be intentional and planned. Students should be able to reflect on it and identify what has been learned.

3 There is pressure to formally assess and accredit work experience that is integrated into undergraduate programmes. Assessment also provides evidence of learning, which may be demanded by higher education institutions and employers. Evidence suggests that students prefer nationally recognised accreditation of work experience to local schemes. Unfortunately, there has been little progress, despite several attempts, towards a national scheme. There is little hard evidence that employers are interested in accreditation of work experience. The emphasis in institutions is now shifting towards documenting work experience through progress files, which are likely to fulfil the certification and accreditation role in a rather more inclusive and consistent manner.

4 To ensure work experience is a good quality experience, employers, academics and students must all be committed to it and fully aware of the implications. The quality of work experience is greatly enhanced by prior induction and briefing, facilitation of ongoing reflection by the student, debriefing, and identification of outcomes.

5 Students should be encouraged to develop a varied work experience portfolio, such as a mixture of course-embedded placements and part-time working.

6 Finally, the ongoing processes of reflection on and articulation of learning from work experience are pivotal to employability development. When recruiting, employers are interested in the ability to identify and communicate what has been learned from work experience (Universities UK and CSU, 2002: 36–37).

Objectives

Placements are the most promising vehicle to bridge the gap between academic knowledge and industrial practice. The challenge is to sustain a placement system that assesses the skills and abilities of the students in the context of their knowledge and understanding in order to permit students to diversify, while at the same time producing graduates with evidence of their abilities.

The placement process has been continually refined since 1997 with two key aims that shape specific objectives. These are to develop evidence of employability amongst students and graduates, and to examine the usefulness of knowledge, understanding, skills and abilities learned on placement in current employment. Of particular importance has been the extent to which graduates are able to develop a reflective approach to their employment, heighten awareness of their own skills for themselves and others and their ability to embed critical thought into workplace practice. The process aims to adhere to the intended objectives for placements set out in the National Council for Work Experience's (NCWE) Placement Tutor Handbook. These are to:

- ❏ Link theory and practice by providing practical experience of work to reinforce and complement the academic components of the course of study.
- ❏ Obtain source material for a project or dissertation which forms part of the academic assessment of the placement period.
- ❏ Learn new technical skills.
- ❏ Reinforce and complement existing skills.
- ❏ Develop and exercise thinking in a practical context.
- ❏ Encourage self-development through critical reflection.
- ❏ Enter into, and identify with, a professional role.
- ❏ Acquire knowledge, key skills and competences relevant to the subject discipline, workplace and the later stages of the course of study.

(NCWE, 2003: 8)

Description

This section of the case study describes the specific practices that underpin the placement process for the degree.

Placement preparation

The placement process begins in year one, and from the outset students are told that it is their responsibility to access a placement that meets their expectations. Among a number of relevant level-one modules that provide underpinning knowledge and skills, Introduction to Sport and Leisure Management, a ten-credit module, has been designed specifically to provide generic understanding of the fundamental principles by which the majority of sport and leisure organisations operate. Using knowledge acquired on other modules, students begin to identify the particular areas of the industry and the specific job roles

> a talented athlete developing a unique programme of activities that enabled successful completion of the placement without disruption to the employer or the athlete's training and performance

that they might be interested in. Having completed the academic year, students are charged with further research into their likely choices for placement.

The placement takes place at level two of the degree programme. Students returning for level two are immediately offered two introductory workshops in order to begin their preparation for the year. The first explains in detail the how the placement operates. In support each student receives a placement handbook. The document contains a number of sections:

- The value of work experience
- The module descriptors for the three level-two placement modules
- A number of sections on preparing for placement
- A number of sections to support students while on placement
- All relevant documentation/pro-formas
- The placement learning diary
- University policies which affect placements – e.g. health and safety, equal opportunities, harassment etc.
- A placements complaints policy.

In semester one, students arrange their placements. If students wish to do a local (within Sussex) placement, they go through a process of application and interview. There are 15 to 20 local organisations that regularly host students, all of whom supply applica-

tion forms or supply details of how they would like to receive covering letters and CVs. Employers have the discretion to interview as many or as few students as they wish, depending on the quality of applications. The careers officer responsible for liaising with the course supports the application and preparation process in various ways. Students make individual or small group appointments in their own time to, for example, improve CVs or prepare for interviews.

In addition, the course tutor and the careers officer have co-authored a supporting document called *Headstart* (Hudson and Keech, 2005), initially written for the Sport and Exercise Science degree programmes. *Headstart* also now serves the degree programmes in Sport Journalism and the Sociology of Sport and Leisure and can be used throughout the final two years of all degrees. Students receive *Headstart* along with the placement handbook.

Some students wish to undertake placements with new organisations. Once this is arranged, the tutor will meet a representative of the organisation to ensure they can support fully the student's requirements while on placement. Students are encouraged to maintain contact with their hosts once the placements are arranged and look for possible opportunities that will help on the placement. Some students gain qualifications paid for by the employers, but this is dependent on the nature of the host. It is hoped that this can be further encouraged in future years, as employers view additional qualifications as being highly important.

Building and cementing relationships with employers

It is essential that contact is maintained with employers throughout the year and not just during the period of the placement. There is nothing new about this practice. Simply put, maintaining relationships with employers is based on the fundamental principles of working in partnership, a practice now embedded within industrial practice in sport and leisure. The key principles, which have cemented the relationships with local employers, are:

- co-existence
- cooperation

- coordination
- collaboration
- co-ownership

(http://www.lgpartnerships.com 2006)

The many practical outcomes are too numerous to mention here so an example is given for each principle:

Co-existence is a rational solution to ensuring each placement meets the individual student's needs. Employers are empowered to make decisions with the students to ensure that clarity is brought to who does what and with whom. In one instance, this resulted in a talented athlete developing a unique programme of activities that enabled successful completion of the placement without disruption to the employer or the athlete's training and performance.

Cooperation is often a prerequisite of further degrees of partnership, cementing a relationship with an employer. Therefore, within the placement handbook and in documentation given to employers, there is early recognition of the prospective mutual benefits and opportunities to work together in order to demonstrate the productivity of an effective placement.

Coordination is an acceptance by the parties of the need to make some changes to improve practice and make better use of their own resources. This often results in changes to working relationships or, in one case where the placement complaints procedure was enacted, making changes to what the student had to do in order to successfully complete their placement.

Collaboration involves an agreement by the parties to work together on strategies or projects, where each contributes to achieve a shared goal. This has been especially relevant to new placements in, for example, schools, where non-teaching sport-related placements are increasingly common. The key here has been to explain to employers how to develop the student placement and it has required ongoing support and communication. The following year, the employer is able to be more independent.

Co-ownership means that the parties commit themselves wholly to achieving a common vision, making significant changes in what they do and how they do it. Through employer forums, changes have been made to documentation, procedures and practice.

Employers therefore need to know what co_ good practice on their side. This is explained, (with many local examples of good practice) whenever a new organisation becomes involved and prior to the student accepting the placement.

Undertaking the placement

The whole of semester two is given over to the placement process and is assessed through three 20-credit modules. Initially students complete a module called Reflective Practice in Sport and Leisure. Initially designed as a ten-credit module, the success of the subject matter in preparing students for placement, especially with regard to improving students' awareness of how they learn, has led to the module being revised and expanded. Further information can be found at http://www.hlst.heacademy.ac.uk/resources/cases/case81.html.

This module is useful in ensuring that students prepare properly for their placement and includes sessions on how to complete the two 20-credit modules that are assessed for their actual placement. These two modules are called Personal and Professional Development for Sport and Leisure Industries and Project Management for Sport and Leisure Industries. For the former, students identify how to obtain evidence for their portfolios, the types of evidence required and how to critically reflect upon their personal and professional development. A key element of this assessment is the learning diary. The learning diary is just one of a series of tools and support structures embedded in the placement process. For the latter, they are shown how to write the learning outcomes for their management report and how to deal with potential problems on the placement that may impinge on the project. More information can be found at http://www.hlst.heacademy.ac.uk/resources/cases/case82.html.

At the end of the Reflective Practice module, students submit their first piece of assessment – a portfolio that details all their preparatory activities and understanding of reflective practice. Finally, the group discusses how to ensure that all students have equal access to resources while on placement in order to ensure equitable treatment. This discussion only finishes once all students understand their 'group-identified' esponsibilities in preparing for the placement. These principles are agreed between the tutor and the group. Also, before the placement, students undertake the Chartered Institute of Environmental Health's (CIEH) Basic Health and Safety Award. Students receive this full-day tuition at a hugely subsidised cost, as the school is an accredited centre for the CIEH. This certificated award is part of the added value that the placement provides for the students and represents the university's duty of care to its students.

Placement support, monitoring and guidance

While the students are preparing for placement, the tutor visits the hosts and takes them through the placement process. Many are regular providers and have now completed at least two to five cycles of the

> Hosts then sign a copy of the agreement… to ensure that students are treated equitably and empowered to undertake tasks that are representative of their position on the degree

assessment and support procedures introduced since the arrival of the present tutor. Others are new and are sent information before the meeting. Hosts then sign a copy of the agreement to say that they understand their responsibilities. This is designed to ensure that students are treated equitably and empowered to undertake tasks that are representative of their position on the degree. Furthermore, such an agreement ensures that students are not seen as 'an extra pair of hands' by the host. Students complete 300 hours of contact time in the workplace and this must be 'signed off' by the host. Students receive a phone call in week two in which they are asked about initial progress. Employers also receive a call and are asked for their early impressions. Employers and students then have to agree the structure for their project management report, and have this agreed by the tutor prior to the commencement of the project.

Throughout the placement, informal and formal feedback takes place between student and host. This is formally recorded in four meetings between student and host. At the final meeting, overall feedback

is given. Between weeks four and seven all students receive a visit from the tutor. They are notified of the visit in the week two phone call. The visit contains two sections. First, a discussion takes place with student, host and tutor. Student and host both have opportunities to discuss the process so far. Second, the tutor and the student go through the portfolio as it stands, review areas for further work and look at possible projects for the management report. At the end of this meeting students are informed of areas they need to address and hosts are asked to provide opportunities, if required, for students to obtain further materials. Throughout the process, the tutor is on hand to offer advice, guidance and emergency visits to all parties.

Two-thirds of the way through the process, students return to the university for a study day. Students work through a series of exercises designed to enable them to reflect on their own progress, and that of others. Students submit their work at the end of semester two. Employers provide formal feedback to students at the end of the placement. Students all complete comprehensive feedback sheets, the results of which are contained in the annual evaluation of the process. Students receive their feedback on their return in year three. Employers also complete evaluation forms, which form an integral element of the final placement report. The report feeds into the Course, Subject Area and School's Annual Academic Health Report.

Assessment of the placement

There are numerous issues regarding the assessment of placements. For Poikela (2004), there are three key issues to address if reflective practice is to be competently assessed and embedded within a curriculum. Tacit knowledge exists especially in those skills and attitudes which should be made visible in the processes of knowing and assessing. This problem raises important questions for studying assessment. First, it is essential to define the observation units of assessment – which are the criteria needed for measuring learners' knowledge at the moment of assessing – and for predicting their professional development. Second, the criteria have to be compiled in an optimal way, so that there are not too many or too few units of observation. Assessors with different backgrounds need to understand the criteria in a similar way. Third, a scientific basis for context-based assessment has to be created for understanding and improving the assessment practices (Poikela, 2004: 273–74).

The assessment on the placement of the Personal and Professional Development for Sport and Leisure Industries module requires industrial and technical knowledge, as well as the ability to examine the student's ability to reflect upon their practice. The tutor has for some years been accredited as a workplace assessor. This has enabled insight into the competencies that students exhibit. In addition, the students are aware of the need to articulate the nature of their learning within the broader environment in which they have operated. Students produce reflective portfolios based on four key elements: organisational understanding; working with others; working on their own; and acquiring and responding to feedback. Guidance for the types of evidence included in each section is indicative and students are wholly responsible for the final content. Each section is underpinned by a piece of reflective writing that ascertains exactly what the student has learnt.

The assessment of the Project Management for Sport and Leisure Industries module requires students to produce a report evaluating work that they have conducted while on placement. Students are assessed against their own learning outcomes and also through a generic assessment grid to ensure consistency of grading. External examiners have praised the process and the assessment methods, noting the 'high quality of the student experience'.

Post-placement follow-up

The placement forms the basis for the applied nature of a ten-credit third-year module entitled Managing Change in Sport and Leisure. This module will be further revised into a new 20-credit form in 2006. To ensure continuity, this module is also led by the placement tutor. The aim of this module is to extend the placement process further through the examination of shared experiences using a thematic approach and a thorough and detailed individual analysis of aspects of the student placement. The latter involves using both knowledge and skills to tackle a clearly

defined area for potential improvement identified within their host organisation, and an analysis of the environmental forces which are likely to shape the host's future development. The impact of change is a consistent theme throughout the module. Students exchange information about their experiences in the various sectors of the leisure industry and detail the projects undertaken, gaining insight into the commonalities and differences between the organisations experienced through action learning sets. Themes of organisational structure, change and culture are used to examine how services are delivered in individual cases in order to highlight the impact that these factors can have upon organisations. Students undertake an in-depth environmental analysis of their host organisation and select a defined area in conjunction with the tutor for detailed analysis.

The work for this module is assessed through a 'live' examination. Students make a 30-minute presentation in the largest lecture hall available. This is video-recorded and their peers act as the audience and

> using both knowledge and skills to tackle a defined area for improvement within their host organisation and an analysis of the environmental forces which are likely to shape the host's future development

inquisitors. The structure of the seminar is entirely down to each individual. Each student receives an individual grade based on the criteria in a generic assessment grid. Students must also work to ensure that they generate audience involvement, for example, through exercises and/or Q & A sessions. The final grade is awarded based on individual work. The comments from peers and self-evaluation are used as a formative, reflective exercise and offer guidance for future development.

Students from the past five years generally agree that this module's learning outcomes were fully met and that the module developed the critical analytical skills which are appropriate at level three. Students appreciated the theoretical applications they were required to make. A number of students noted that the presentation was a positive element of the module content, particularly in giving them confidence and experience for the future. Most students found the

Table 1 Sample of student responses indicating key learning experiences on placement (2005 cohort)

What if anything did you learn about yourself?	Has the experience contributed anything to your understanding of the leisure industry? (Note any major areas if yes).	Have you developed any skills you did not have before? (Please list main ones if yes).
That I have good literacy and IT skills Confident in doing multi-tasks Enjoy marketing and the commercial industry.	Yes How difficult sports development can be. It's not straightforward.	Yes My writing skills have improved Communication skills – verbal.
That I need to improve my time management skills.	The importance of volunteers.	Computer skills Communication skills.
I can be organised if I have to. I know a lot more about the sport and leisure Industry than I thought I did.	Yes. Outreach work is a very important scheme and every borough should have one.	Yes, sessions with old people Managing staff.
Willing to develop my own personal knowledge and therefore was enthusiastic in completing challenging tasks during my placement.	Yes, I now understand the importance of trust status to maintaining local leisure provision.	Computer skills. Time management.
I enjoy working with children – do have patience! Enjoy practical side of sports development. Enjoy working disability clubs I found it very rewarding.	Helped me build a picture of how sports development helps and provides many services to the community. Does not just improve inclusion, provides children with skills, prevents crime, improves health.	I have developed my communication skills, especially when working with professionals. Gained skills on how to work with disabled people.
Before my placement I had no idea that I had the skills to teach, but on my …placement I had the opportunity to tutor and really enjoyed it as well as being good at it.	I now understand that the leisure industry doesn't just concentrate or stay in the leisure field but assists in other areas too.	Tutoring. Communication. Managing and organising.
During placement, I learned that I have good communication and organisational skills and that I should have more confidence in my ability and be more willing to put forward ideas.	Yes. I have mainly learnt how leisure trusts function and the differences between public and private leisure facilities.	Yes. Mainly writing marketing plans.
I learnt that I am able to work in an office environment, enjoy it and develop new skills at the same time.	Yes. It gave me an understanding of how wide the leisure industry is.	The importance of communication with a variety of partners and event sponsors.
How effective communication and management can produce a good team ethos.	It has added and developed my existing knowledge with regards to health and safety management.	Critical reflection and action learning.
My ability to work with and cooperate with people on a professional level.	Yes. - Knowledge of operations and procedures within leisure centres.	Yes. Working with children.

assessment 'challenging', 'daunting', 'nerve wracking' and 'scary'. Afterwards, students thought the experience had been 'rewarding... a useful learning experience', 'very helpful for the future' and a 'good way to make students gain confidence'. Students saw that the informal peer- and self-review enabled them to learn from their mistakes. All students saw the detailed assessment criteria as 'very useful' and a number of them added that, in addition to the learning they experienced, the presentation developed 'a transferable skill we will need in the future'.

The student experience

Each year, extensive evaluation of the placement takes place. The responses of over 140 students over a six-year period indicate that the experience has been extremely valuable to almost all of the students. Students often mentioned self-discipline/new skills and abilities, good social skills and increased confidence as key facets of their learning experience. Many students realised that they were now capable of 'doing things' with regard to employment. Some students thought that they still suffer in terms of confidence and would have liked a longer placement in order to improve this. Unfortunately, a longer placement is not possible, mainly due to the logistical constraints of operating a three-year degree. Table 1 provides some indicative responses from students regarding their learning experience. It also indicates that, as students consider the development of their skills, they also realise the knowledge that they have acquired. Hence, it is important that their 'context-based competence' is assessed through strong and robust criteria.

Evaluation and discussion

Allan Edwards (1999: 75–6) has argued that:

There are two kinds of theory in sport management. First, there are theories about sport management. Second, there is the knowing-in-action that derives when sport managers draw on their knowledge (including theories about sport management) and reflect-in-action... By reflecting on their practice and on formal professional development activities, sport managers continually refine, revise, and renew their personal practical knowledge, which contains their theories about sport management.

Obviously, sport management knowledge is, in

a sense, personal knowledge since the knowing-in-action of sport management practice is created within the individual. However, the action takes place on the basis of a shared understanding of what is appropriate sport management practice... So far, we know so little about sport managers' processes of reflection in- action that it is not possible to say whether there is any shared understanding in the profession... What is now required is more research into the nature of practitioners' theories (implicit and explicit) about sport management. We also need to know more about how sport managers develop and revise their theories.

Through research conducted with former graduates now working in the areas of sport management and development, evidence is beginning to emerge about how sport managers achieve what Edwards wants to know (Keech, Bartlett and Harris, 2005). It is evident that if the processes put in place in HEIS are to have any effect, graduates must continue to adopt the processes learned in HEIS and adapt to the changing work environment in which they operate. This approach, if successful, can be termed 'context-based competence', which can be defined as the extent to which an individual employee is able to use their learned knowledge, understanding, skills and abilities in order to make correct decisions within their current working environment.

An optional final-year module was developed in response to students expressing a wish to further their industrial knowledge. According to Ravenscroft and Gilchrist (2004: 56), the following features are at the heart of the social-entrepreneur model:

❑ Meets community needs.
❑ Gives people a voice/ ownership in designing their project.
❑ Fosters partnerships with the local community.
❑ Provides initial training, plus ongoing supervision and support.
❑ Provides opportunities for reflection.
❑ There are opportunities to celebrate the work.
❑ Participants engage in ongoing assessment and evaluation.

Community-university partnership work at the University of Brighton in 2003/04 led to the creation of the Eastbourne Sports Council Policy Action Group. This Group was formed of final-year Leisure and Sport Management undergraduates who opted

Table 2: Meeting best practice criteria

Best practice criteria	Evidence from this case study
Learning objectives are set (by the HEI, employer and student), within an agreed structure or framework, i.e. a Learning Agreement or Learning Contract.	Learning objectives are set within the course and each module. Employers and students agree objectives for the placement in job descriptions and agreed expectations prior to placement. All three parties agree objectives for the project management report.
The student is taught by the HEI to identify and recognise potential learning outcomes, including key skills development and subject related skills.	Through preparatory and post-placement modules and with the support of the employer whilst on placement.
Supervision is by an employer supervisor who understands the objectives, benefits and learning outcomes of work experience.	Regular supervisors add value to the process. The placement tutor mentors new supervisors.
Academic supervision and visits take place at an agreed frequency.	Regular contact by phone, email and visits.
Regular feedback is given.	By host supervisors in pre-planned meetings.
An appraisal is given during and at the end of the work experience by the employer/supervisor.	Through regular meetings and in final evaluation recorded and put into student assessment.
A project is undertaken, and report is written.	Through the Project Management module.
Learning, development and achievements are articulated by the student in written form.	Through the Personal and Professional Development module.
A presentation is given of results, achievements and personal development.	Through both modules named above, through formative work with hosts and summative assessment in post-placement module at level 3.
Guidance is provided to integrate this learning into longer term career planning.	Integrated through PDP and career planning at level three.
An assessment is made of skills development (by HEI, employer and student).	Carried out and recorded in annual monitoring report.
The student integrates the learning into a career management plan.	Integrated through PDP and career planning at level threee.
Recognition, credit or a certificate is awarded.	80 credits of the degree related directly to the placement. Additional qualifications before, during and after placements are obtained. Some students gain employment with host organisations.

for a module on Volunteer Management as part of their degree programme. Most had been through the placement process. The placement tutor also led the module. The students were divided into specially designed teams to undertake a series of tasks for the local Sports Council. Through the application of the pedagogic basis outlined above, the students were able to develop their knowledge of cultural and sporting activity and policy priorities in the local area as well as gain key transferable skills which enhanced their employability. Community outcomes of their work included a conference for local leisure officers on sport development, a youth participation event (Eastbourne Skipping Festival in association with local primary schools and the British Heart Foundation) and the creation of an updated sports club directory.

When asked what they had learnt, some common themes emerged amongst the students' responses:

Students developed new understandings:
Sustainable development, empathy and respect for others, technological innovations.

Skills development:
Technical and workforce skills, collaboration and communication skills, leadership skills, entrepreneurial and business skills.

Empowerment:
Increased confidence, increased self-esteem, increased motivation to succeed.

Contribution to the social good:
Meets community needs, promotes a lifelong commitment to civic engagement and social responsibility, seeds the next generation of social entrepreneurs.

Clearly, further research is required, but there is a suggestion that through operating in and understanding a policy context students were able to develop and refine not only basic skills but also deeper, more complex knowledge of their skills. This has been of great benefit when applying for jobs (Keech, Bartlett and Harris, 2005).

Conclusion

According to the NCWE, the following items represent criteria for good practice in experiential learning, based on the experience of practitioners and the contributions of the writers in the compendium of best practice. Table 2 demonstrates how this placement process meets these criteria.

One of the best indications of the sustainability of this placement process is that former graduates now working locally have become placement supervisors, thereby adding credence to the process and providing live examples of the overall success of the degree programme to current students. It is critical to remember that the evidence generated through this case study is the product of a number of years work. Placements are labour intensive; and institutional recognition of this fact is critical to the future success of the programme.

References and URLs

Dearing, R. 1997. *Report of the National Committee of Inquiry into Higher Education: 'Higher Education in the Learning Society'*. London: HMSO

Edwards, A. 1999. Reflective Practice in Sport Management. *Sport Management Review*, 1999, **2**, 67–81

Gittus, B. 2002. Vocational Pathways in Sports Education: the Contribution of HE/FE Partnerships. *LINK*, **6**, http://www.hlst.heacademy.ac.uk/resources/

Hudson, H. & Keech, M. 2005. *'Headstart' A Planning Guide for degree programmes in Sport and Leisure Management, Sport Journalism and the Sociology of Sport and Leisure*. Eastbourne: University of Brighton

Jordan, F. 2001. The Place of Placements in Leisure Management degree programmes. In Garrett, R. Holmes, K. & Nichols, G. 2001. *The Vocational Relevance of Leisure Management Courses*, Conference Proceedings, Learning and Teaching Support Network for Hospitality, Leisure, Sport and Tourism, Oxford Brookes University

LIRC, 2003. *Sports Volunteering in England in 2002*. London: Sport England

Keech, M. Bartlett, H. & Harris, K. 2005. One step ahead: The Value of Sport and Leisure Management Placements to Graduates Working in Sport. Paper presented at the University Placements Conference, Falmer, University of Brighton, September 15, 2005

Moon, J. 2004. *A Handbook of Reflective and Experiential Learning*. London: Routledge Falmer

NCWE, 2003. *The Placement Tutor's Handbook: A Guide to Higher Education Institutions on Arranging Placements and a Compendium of Current Best Practice in the UK*. London: NCWE

Nolan, G. 2002. Learning on the Job. *Stadium and Arena Management*, December 2002, p. 31

Poikela, E. 2004 Developing criteria for knowing and learning at work: towards context-based assessment. *The Journal of Workplace Learning*, **16** (5) pp. 267–274

Ravenscroft, N. and Gilchrist, P. 2004. *Developing a Learning Agenda for the Cultural Industries in the South East of England*. Report prepared for the South East England Cultural Consortium

Ravenscroft, N. Harvey, S. Hayes, S. and Rogers, G. 2002. *Sector Area Review: Sport and Recreation*. Eastbourne: University of Brighton

Taylor, P. 2001. Vocational Relevance in Postgraduate degree programmes. In Garrett, R. Holmes, K. & Nichols, G. 2001. *The Vocational Relevance of Leisure Management Courses*. Conference Proceedings, Learning and Teaching Support Network for Hospitality, Leisure, Sport and Tourism, Oxford Brookes University

TNS 2003. *Audit of Sports Provision in the Higher Education Sector*. Report prepared for Sport England by Clare Lambley

Universities UK and CSU, 2002. *Enhancing employability, Recognising Diversity: Making links between higher education and the world of work*. London, Universities UK

MARC KEECH is a Senior Lecturer at the University of Brighton, where he is Course Leader for the BA (Hons) in Sport and Leisure Management and Course Leader for the MA in Sport Development. His research interests include sport policy and development in Britain, the political history of sport and sport in South Africa.

Enhancing travel, tourism and hospitality management graduates' employability

16

Bridget Major

This case study is about providing career information to enhance the employability on graduation of undergraduate BA (Hons) Travel and Tourism Management students and Tourism and Hospitality Management students at Newcastle Business School (NBS), Northumbria University.

My colleagues and I wanted to embed employability in our courses and in doing so work productively with employers. I set about preparing Blackboard web pages to fill what I saw as an employability skills gap in our undergraduate curriculum in management.

Objectives

Our main aim was to provide our students with information, advice and guidance about possible graduate careers within the travel and tourism industries and the potential opportunities available to them.

Rationale

We knew that specialist information on career opportunities within the travel, tourism and hospitality industries was not readily available in any form for our students. Although diligent students could try to collate it, the limited extent of their knowledge and experience would make this a difficult and lengthy task. Further, we wanted a collation from an impartial perspective, not directed at any one sector or organisation. The information would be provided from a stance relevant to graduates at the outset of their careers.

We saw there was an employability skills gap in our undergraduate curriculum at the Newcastle Business School and that it could be filled through the develop-

ment of and the provision of information on opportunities available in specific job markets. Such work was beyond the remit of the Business School Placement Office and the Careers Service, although some synergy was likely. The Placement Office facilitates the one-year work placement for students following year two. The Careers Service provides sector information on the travel and tourism industry. *Prospects* (see www.prospects.ac.uk) is the UK's official graduate-careers website which provides links to specific job sectors.

Academics cannot be expected to maintain detailed current knowledge and information on a wide range of industry organisations. Even if they have a background in industry their sources and information rapidly become out of date.

As stated in the One North East (2003) report:
High quality, work-related curriculum development activity goes beyond the involvement of the traditional course team. It can involve representatives from employers groups, sector skills councils and professional bodies as well as learners themselves.

Context

The work involved raising students' awareness of the existing job market and scope within the travel and tourism industry. This industry is the largest employer in the world and is made up of a variety of very diverse sectors. The enormous quantity of information is complicated by the dynamic nature of the industry and rapid changes in its organisational structure.

Our students have difficulties in accessing and gaining advice and guidance on their careers and, indeed, even on deciding in which sector they would most like to start. There are a few print publications available. For example, the Institute of Travel and Tourism publishes *Careers in Travel and Tourism*. However, this is mainly an overview of sectors, is not specifically aimed at graduates and does not have all the benefits of information online.

I was helped by a grant from the Tyne and Wear sub-regional partnership for a project called Work-Related Learning from Modern Apprentice to Graduate and Beyond. This had some influence on my methodology and objectives. The project's definition of work-related learning is 'learning through activities that are based on, or derive from, the context of work or the workplace' (One North East, 2003). My Blackboard pages initiative was deemed to fit in with the aims of this project.

I should explain why I became so closely involved. I knew that I held a wealth of relevant information, including contact details and links for students to potential employers and career paths. Aside from making the odd comment in lectures or giving advice on work placements, I had no means of formally imparting it to students. It seemed a missed opportunity. Surely my academic role could be enhanced by enabling students to take advantage of the best available opportunities or at least to explore diligently the options open to them. There is, of course, tangible satisfaction in assisting a graduate to take these very important first career steps. I felt I had the skills and knowledge to take the initiative.

1 I had worked in tour operating at a senior level for over ten years. Although my contacts were very out of date, I had the essential operating knowledge of the industry.

2 My dual teaching focus was on Travel Industry Management and Operations and on Hospitality Management. To do my job, I had to know about current industry affairs, often in a state of flux, with continual changes in organisational structure.

3 I happen to be the only higher education member of the Association of British Travel Agents (ABTA) Education and Skills Committee – on which there are representatives from across the industry. I meet there with People First, the new Sector Skills Council for hospitality, the licensed trade and gaming.

4 I regularly attend and speak at international travel industry conferences such as the Institute of Travel and Tourism and ABTA.

5 My responsibilities include the NBS Travel and Tourism guest lecture programme, which draws on high-profile industry professionals.

6 To stay current, I subscribe to and read the industry trade press such as *Travel Weekly*, *Travel Trade Gazette* and online newswires such as *The Travel Mole* (www.travelmole.com) and *E-tid: Electronic Travel Industry Digest* (www.e-tid.co.uk) and quality daily travel sections.

7 My interest and involvement in work-placement activities for travel and tourism management students is relevant too, as is my genuine love for and interest in the travel and tourism industries.

The initiative was in line with the objectives of several different organisations. The partnership of North East Universities behind the Work-Related-Learning Project is led by Northumbria University and partnered by Newcastle and Sunderland. It had already shown strong commitment to developing work-related learning and 'graduates into employment' initiatives, though the partners said they felt the initiatives lacked coherence, flexibility and transparency (One North East, 2003). The Northern Economic Research Unit also commented that universities had no explicit strategies for developing work-related learning or, engaging with local employers.

So my initiative was in line with the Work-Related-Learning project in developing a coherent package of work-related learning opportunities aimed at traditional students undertaking work-related activity as part of their study. It was also in line with the proposed development of an Employment and Career module for level five students at NBS. The White Paper, *The Future of Higher Education*, supported work-related learning initiatives and I knew that partnerships between higher education and employers were on the increase. I applied for and was awarded a grant.

Approach and methodology

A condition of the grant scheme was that the proposal had to relate to a programme and/or a full module at the university. At the time, I was on a working party developing an employability module for Newcastle Business School (NBS) entitled Preparing for Graduate Employment, a ten-point core module for all full-time level-five students in the school. This module was to be run in the first semester when students were also seeking work placements for the following year. The module's aims were to develop students' knowledge of available career paths and to improve their skills in career-related activities, particularly in preparing employment applications. Specialist knowledge from practitioners in the university's Careers Service, the NBS Placement Office and graduate employers underpinned development of the module. After one year we know that the module has been a success: the learning outcomes have been achieved and it has met with general acclaim from our large and diverse student population.

I asked for the grant, first, to buy out my time for developing the initiative. As it happened, I spent it on attending two key travel-industry conventions, where I was able to make important contacts for students, which I later developed. I also asked for money for a consultant.

At the same time as this project was evolving, at my instigation, NBS became partners of Springboard (www.Springboard.org.uk), a wholly owned training subsidiary of Springboard Charitable Trust, the mission of which is:

> to educate people about career and job opportunities in hospitality, leisure, and travel and tourism to meet the industry's staffing needs and aspirations of potential recruits.

Springboard promotes careers within the industry and works with many far-reaching partners across all industry sectors. NBS became a Springboard partner after sponsoring the GCSE double-award Resource Pack which is distributed to secondary schools and FE colleges that deliver travel, tourism and hospitality courses throughout the UK. Springboard also produces *Careerscope*, a publication offering an informative and lively overview of possible employers and career paths across the industry. It helps students to grasp the breadth and scope of the industry even if this may not have become apparent during their earlier courses. Springboard was able to provide me with key contacts and resources that were incorporated into the project.

Tools: how to impart the information

I had to decide how the information was to be relayed to and accessed by students. Electronic methods would enable me to update and add to whatever I had posted earlier. Resources were limited. I was the only person working on the initiative. I considered putting the information on the University of Northumbria website, so that students from other institutions might be able to access the material. However, writing and putting up web pages on this site would have involved forming a team. Instead, I thought my initiative could be a pilot for other courses across the business school.

A basic advantage for me lay in fact that the travel and tourism industry is a discrete and measurable entity, despite being spread across several sectors. To develop a similar resource for finance or business studies students, for example, might demand an even wider range of data covering a multitude of different organisations. The boundaries and definitions might become so blurred that the objectives would not be achievable, at least not if they were to adopt the model described here.

The Blackboard system is a web-based-server software platform adopted by many academic institutions. It enables academics to customise and manage programmes, modules and information of all kinds for students. It is ideal for someone like me because I am not technologically minded. I find it provides the ideal platform from which to impart information on possible career paths for students. I can operate the system by myself and can easily add the updates and additions. Example web pages are in the Figure 1.

I started with an information retrieval exercise, before a sifting, followed by some qualitative research in selected areas. I uploaded the data onto the Blackboard site in categories. My approach was to start broad and narrow down to industry specifics. I wanted students to grasp the scope of the industry, not just within the framework of the main sectors of Tour Operator, Travel Agent, Principal (e.g. hotel, airline) or Public Sector (e.g. destination, government) but also in terms of the multitude of suppliers attached to these sectors, such as distributors, technology providers, financiers, marketing and PR consultants, media-related opportunities and so on. These suppliers have expanded hugely, partly as a result of technological

What is *Your Career*?

This site has been developed in order to give you a starting point from which to commence your career in the Travel, Tourism and Hospitality industries. The diversity of areas within the industries is enormous, as is the scope of differing roles and organisations. The information provided here is to assist you in your initial research and navigate you through some of your options.

Who is *Your Career* for?

Although aimed primarily at final-year Travel, Tourism and Hospitality students, the information contained here will also be of assistance to first and second year students in making decisions about their placement year or starting to think about what they will do after graduation.

What about a gap year?

If you are taking a year out after graduation, it is strongly suggested that you make some enquiries and contacts before you go. You may not have any idea which area of the industry it is that you wish to work in, but this site is only available to Northumbria students and you will not have access to it when you return from Woga Woga. Also, you may have contacts available to you now – e.g. from work placement; tell them what your plans are and ask if it is OK to get back in touch with them on your return. It is a fact of life that you are more employable when in a role of some kind, be it a student or in employment; that is not to say that a gap year is not a good experience, it is just that it can be hard to 'pick up' on your return.

Where do I start?

Finding out the options open to you is your starting point. There is a huge amount of information on careers, jobs etc available and sifting through it will help you realise what it is that you don't want to do and present some ideas of opportunities which you may find appealing and hadn't previously thought of.

Northumbria University's career service is your first stop. You may already have been in touch with them as a result of your year two career and employability module or work placement research. Many graduates say that they wish they had made full use of this service while studying at University and many also wish that they had made use of their services earlier than they did.

The careers service is of course generic and not specific to travel, tourism or hospitality but what is important is that you get a feel for what opportunities other industries are offering so that you can make comparisons. Tourism is a relatively new industry and career paths are really only just starting to evolve; it is important that you see the bigger picture. The careers service also offers a Graduates section. Full details are available on the Northumbria University website.

Prospects is the UK's official graduate

Figure 1 Selected Blackboard pages from the *Your Career* website

developments and partly as consumer interest and the uptake of holidays have increased with an expansion of media opportunities.

My site is called *Your Career* (see Figure 1). It briefly states its rationale and provides discussion about the concept of a 'gap year', a current rite of passage for many students. I wanted to develop links wherever possible between the Career Service and academics, to demonstrate the interrelationship of these two bodies' aims. I wanted students to appreciate the synergies between their learning and their future careers. None of this was easy to put into practice: I found that, other than programme leaders informing students of talks and services provided by the Careers Service and presentations by potential employers, there is little overlap. At least there were many opportunities for development.

Following my introduction, which I hope is couched in student-friendly language, the Blackboard pages provides links to *Prospects* and to the university's career website, which many students at levels four and five may not have yet visited.

Graduate recruitment schemes

Next, my Blackboard pages had to deal with graduate recruitment (see 4). The travel and tourism industries are still youthful compared with many blue chip companies, FMCG organisations and service industries. Their product is still quite new, but has become large-scale and diverse over the last 50 years or so. The very low profit margins allow little scope for important employment elements such as training, career development and progression structures. Out of the big four vertically integrated operators engaged in owning and supplying three out of four of the sectoral elements I mentioned previously (travel agent, airline and tour operator), only three operators have a graduate-recruitment scheme and one of these (First Choice Holidays) is not exclusively for graduates. Airtours/Going Places, the fourth of the 'big four', has recently faced such massive financial uncertainties that a graduate recruitment scheme has been low in its priorities. Unfortunately, this is indicative of the industry's general state and attitude; training is a low budget priority.

The competition that graduates face in getting a

careers website and here you will find useful information and advice; there is also a job vacancies site with positions in leisure and tourism. See the electronic link below.

Graduate recruitment schemes

Of the 'big four' operators only Thomas Cook and TUI offer formal 'graduate recruitment programmes'. These are essentially fasttrack placements which provide opportunities to learn across the key areas of the business. Salaries are good and training is excellent. Competition for places is fierce… Last year Thomas Cook had 600 applicants for 12 places; an NBS graduate was lucky enough to get one. TUI have over 19,000 employees in the UK – and 16 placements were offered in 2004.

The application and interview process is rigorous; you will need to display some special skills to be selected for interview, and be predicted to get a 2:1 degree. If you are selected for interview, you will be put through a variety of tests; competency interview, group exercise, presentation and psychometric testing. Please don't let this put you off! These opportunities are for people like you – so seize them; there could be no better start to your career.

First Choice however offer what is called a 'Product Executive Development Scheme', which is aimed at graduate-calibre candidates. They normally advertise this on the First Choice website around May/June time…so keep your eyes open.

If you are having a gap year, find out about application deadlines for the following year before you go…

Recruitment agencies

There are many – and many are specialists in certain areas. They are a good way of seeing what is available on the job market and can give you some ideas. However, remember that their responsibilities to their clients are onerous and although they may be able to assist you initially, if you are for instance, geographically immobile or have ideas well above your station or experience, you will get nowhere.

The suggestion is that you have a look through the websites and select an agent or so that you feel offers the type of position that you may be after and then register with them. Newcastle Business School has a good personal reputation with most of these agents, so please represent us in a manner that we can be proud of!

Some of the websites have some excellent tips on job applications, interview skills etc, especially Argyle recruitment, so it would be well worth your while in brushing up on these… Argyle tend to have jobs at the top end of the spectrum, but it is worth having a look to see what you can aspire to!

Work-placement experience – remember this is central and crucial to employers; it demonstrates your experience and the fact that you are employable! So, make the most of it…

---

placement is fierce. TUI, of which Thomson Holidays is part, had over 19,000 UK employees in 2004 but offered only 16 graduate placements that year, Thomas Cook had 600 applicants for its 12 places (an NBS graduate student gained one of these). I obtained details of the criteria for these schemes during face-to-face interviews with senior human-resource staff in these companies. They stressed that relevant skills had to be stated in applicants' curriculum vitae (a prediction of a 2:1 degree is essential), and they told me about the selection procedures, which include a competency interview, a group exercise, a presentation and psychometric testing. I found it refreshing to hear such a professional approach being adopted by the mainstream operators. Successful applicants benefit immensely from these 'fast-track' schemes and the variety of tasks and experiences entailed.

Recruitment agencies

There is a plethora of recruitment agencies, far more than those now on my Blackboard site (which are ones I know well and think reputable). They vary in specialism and indeed some of them – for example, Argyle Recruitment and Simpson Recruitment – cater for more senior appointments than graduate level. On my Blackboard pages, I encourage students to visit these sites to gain some idea of positions that they may aspire to after suitable industry management experience.

I expected that salaries for managers might attract students' attention. Senior managers in the travel industry are actually paid 8.3% better than those in other industries, but junior managers are paid 14.4% less than other sectors (Croner Reward, 2004).

Some sites offer excellent tips on job applications, interview skills etc. In fact, a wealth of information is available to students. Making them actually read it, absorb it and put it into action is a far more difficult task. I decided not to include such advice on the *Your Career* site. All level-five students have access to the Employability Module (in any case, where such information is posted on Blackboard).

Finally I stress on my Blackboard pages the importance of the placement year. Unless students have a

Trade journals

Throughout your time at university, you have been encouraged to use trade journals. These are also an invaluable source of job opportunities.

The Travel Mole and *e-tid* are the two on-line newsletters which will also keep you up-to date with what is happening in the industry; you will be expected to know this in interviews. Both of these are free to register with and have job sections.

Travel Weekly and *Travel Trade Gazette* are the main trade papers – and have jobs advertised weekly. *TTG* is only available in hard format.

Springboard

Springboard UK is a charitable trust which promotes careers in hospitality, leisure, travel and tourism. It offers free advice for over 14,000 people each year – at all levels, school through to mature workers. They have a specialist careers service and a lot of very good information, advice and links on their web site. Springboard also produce *Careerscope* a periodical with a lot of information in particular on working in the hotel industry, graduate schemes, jobs etc. There are links to this from their web site.

You are strongly encouraged to use Springboard – for all your careers, jobs or even placement queries; that is what they are there for – and they are independent specialists. Newcastle Business School is a Springboard partner – your enquiry will be welcome.

Travel industry portal

WWW.surf2travel.com is a travel portal with information and links which extend right across the industry; operators, agents, airports, airlines, hotels, ancillary products etc are all there with links attached. You should have a good look through it as it will give you an idea of the breadth of the industry and may trigger off some possibilities that you had not considered before.

The hospitality industry

The hospitality industry is in many ways, more developed for potential careers for graduates than the travel industry. The profile of the industry is also very much on the up – as a result of good media focus (restaurants, celebrity chefs etc) and the minimum wage which has resulted in it becoming a more desirable career choice. Many of the big chains have excellent graduate-recruitment schemes which provide really good opportunities and training; wherever you go from there, your experience will always be valued. The best approach is to have a look at the different web sites and then make enquiries. There are obviously opportunities to work throughout the regions and indeed the world.

Figure 1 More Blackboard pages from the *Your Career* website

year's worthwhile work experience they are of little use to the industry upon graduation.

Trade journals

Students are encouraged throughout their academic practice on the NBS Travel and Tourism Management degree to keep up-to-date with industry affairs and to integrate and relate these with academic references. Suffice to say, the trade press acknowledges that a large percentage of their readership flick straight to the appointments section, such is the nature of the industry. Students, however, can benefit by keeping up-to-date with what is available and also by once again considering the scope of the industry.

I have on more than one occasion recommended a level-five student to apply for a position as a possible work placement – while obviously confessing to the potential employer that this was the *raison d'etre* for the application. The application has been rewarded with a year's contract in a very worthwhile organisation. Upon successful completion of the year, as in so many cases, some students have been offered the chance to return to employment with the organisation upon graduation. In fact, a current student has just been offered a position upon graduation with the organisation where he is currently undertaking his placement year – within two weeks of starting the job!

There are two key online newsletters within the travel and tourism industry – both are free to subscribers. Potential employees need to be informed about current industry affairs, searches of issues relevant to organisations, recent events, takeovers etc, all of which are regularly reported. *E-tid* is a sister company to Argyle Recruitment. It has a very regularly updated list of opportunities within the industry and has started a career-profile section covering the career development of well-known senior executives within the industry. This section provides motivation for potential employees, not least because NBS has many graduates now holding senior industry positions.

Other sections

My Blackboard pages contain information on or links to trade associations, useful websites and portals, key

The links below will take you to listings of the main UK hotel brands and a little bit about them and also a Who's Who of the UK restaurant sector. Print them out – so that you will always have them and then look whatever interests you up on the individual web sites. You will find full details about graduate schemes available. If your degree was not in Hospitality Management, you will find that in many cases, your Travel and Tourism Management degree as a related degree is acceptable for entry into hotel-graduate-training schemes.

The world is literally your oyster…

A career in business travel

Career opportunities in Business Travel for graduates abound. The way the travel industry is moving means that the demand for good business travel houses is still very much there for the foreseeable future. The skills required and the complexities involved in putting together clients requirements are such that graduates are in demand. Salaries are much more competitive too! This is an area of business that you should definitely consider – organisations like Carlson Wagon Lit Travel and ATP International have ex-Northumbria graduates working in very senior positions indeed. The link below will take you to the GTMC – Guild of Travel Management Companies which will provide you with further information on working in this sector.

Airlines

Many of the airlines, like Hotels will have either graduate schemes or graduate level jobs available. It is worth cruising through some of the web sites to see what is on offer. BAA, British Airports Authority is also worth looking at if this line of work interests you and it is well worth just approaching the Human Resources Department of specific airports. Start with BA's site – they have an area dedicated to career opportunities.

The Flight Centre

The Flight Centre has made it for the third year running into the top 15 of the *Sunday Times* 100 Best Companies to work for. They are 10 years old, have currently (04/05) 72 shops and employ 550 staff. The salaries are unusually competitive and staff turnover is much lower than average.

Expedia

Expedia were 99th in the Sunday Times Best companies to work for, with a reputation for excelling at career growth.

The tourism sector

Some of the resources above will have opportunities available in the tourism sector advertised, such as *Travel Weekly*. You are more likely however to find local opportunities in local sources, such as newspapers, Regional Development Agency Web sites etc.

Visit Britain (see link below) have a Human Resources recruitment web site.

Leisure Opportunities is published weekly and has a large amount of jobs in the leisure sector advertised within the regions, these include tourism and sports positions.

hotel organisations and restaurants, the sites of which contain information on how to develop a career within the relevant company. I included some limited information on opportunities in the public sector and the leisure industries. I am adding the airline industry and more about many of the topics I have already posted.

Evaluation

For this resource to be effective, I need to learn how to use Blackboard to enhance the site's presentation and use. My pages could be moved to a more eye-catching place. At the end of the year, Blackboard looks cluttered with a year's worth of modules for the programme, instructions and announcements.

I need to tell students that my site exists. At first I used the Blackboard email facility, which was not working properly. I now know the solution is to contact students by using their Microsoft Outlook email addresses. Students' visits to my pages can be tracked with Blackboard and I shall analyse the data a second time round, when my pages are relaunched to new students and those returning from the work-placement year. So far, the only feedback that I have received has been from students who told me they found find the pages useful and informative and wished they had had access to them earlier in the year.

I know the pages are not complete and I view them as a project in progress, but where should I draw the line in a near limitless supply of information? I am well aware of deficiencies in my own knowledge; a team would probably be more effective, with knowledge of public-sector (tourism and destination) opportunities as well as private sector and industry. And, of course, the pages will need updating as links become obsolete or change.

Discussion

The government target of increasing participation in higher education towards 50% of those aged 18 to 30 by the end of the decade has had an impact across all sectors of higher education. Enhancing students' employability has to be integral if student participation is driven up. Business schools and departments have only slowly adapted by embedding employability in the curriculum and working more closely with industry and employers.

I was aware of these issues because I spent many years in industry prior to becoming an academic and was fortunate enough to be given an excellent start to a satisfying and successful career. Ideally, today's graduates should have the same opportunities. Given the current throughput of students, however, travel, tourism and hospitality management are much more competitive fields than they used to be.

I want to add value to the learning experience of BA (Hons) Travel and Tourism Management undergraduate students by providing them with specialist knowledge and information relating to possible career paths. The resource I developed is basically informative but as yet there is little else available. It complements the NBS undergraduate programmes on Travel, Tourism and Hospitality in that students can start to transfer their academic knowledge and skills to develop their future careers by considering options available to them.

I believe my Blackboard pages can be of real value to undergraduate travel and tourism students, but a much more fully developed version can perhaps be implemented.

References

Croner Reward, 2004. *Travel Industry Rewards* 5th ed. London: Croners

HEFCE, 2002. *Strategic Plan 2003–2008*. London: HEFCE

Institute of Travel and Tourism, 2003. *Careers in Travel and Tourism. Opportunities in the world's greatest industry.* London: ITT

One North East (ONE), 2003. *Work Related Learning 'From Modern Apprenticeships to Graduation and Beyond'. Interim Report*

DfES, 2003. *The Future of Higher Education. Government White Paper.* January 2003. Norwich: HMSO

BRIDGET MAJOR is a Principal Lecturer at Newcastle Business School, Northumbria University. Prior to becoming a lecturer she spent many years working at a senior level in the Travel Industry – thus her research specialism and work on travel and tourism management higher education and career development for graduates.

Enhancing enterprise, entrepreneurship and employability through PDP

17

Karen Bill and Will Bowen-Jones

This case study reflects on the University of Worcester's (UoW) School of Sport and Exercise Science customised programme of Personal Development Planning (PDP). This vehicle for the development of student employability skills builds upon an established PDP programme at the university.

It is generally acknowledged that higher education should produce graduates who are equipped to operate in a highly competitive, complex and dynamic workplace. One of the five stated ambitions of UoW is 'to produce highly employable, innovative, professional alumni' (Green, 2003).

If students are to reflect on their experiences and gather evidence of their personal and skills development, then these learning opportunities have to be recognised by the students and embedded in all aspects of the curriculum and student life. The way forward necessarily involves an integrated approach within the whole university life of students – within the academic curriculum, student union activities, work experience and careers advice, as well as the PDP framework. Tomkins (2004) supported this view, concluding that work experience (including community or live project work), practical modules and Personal Development Planning (PDP) were important vehicles in supporting the key skills development of students.

Rationale

In September 2001 the Student Qualities Profile (SQP) was launched within the Undergraduate Modular Scheme at UoW (Peters, 2001). The rationale behind the SQP was that it should support students in the development of their skills and, at the same time, act as the focus for student planning, reflection, develop-

ment and recording of achievement as they progressed through their undergraduate studies.

The identified student qualities include subject-specific skills, transferable skills, and personal attributes developed through undergraduate study. The inclusion of personal attributes (not easily categorised as 'skills') is a key aspect, incorporating as it does personal development, an important part of educational growth as an undergraduate. The SQP elements were identified (through research with employer organisations, universities and others interested in undergraduate education) as fundamental to graduate qualities and what makes graduates valuable to society. For SQP to be successful it was important that students understood that many of the skills they would develop in their studies were transferable both within and beyond academic study.

The SQP has the full support of the Worcester Students Union, supporting the SQP by providing training in transferable skills, opportunities to volunteer or participate in or organise sporting and non-sporting activities, and offering paid employment. It also provides a certificate, *Degree+*, for skills developed by students within the Student Union, which can be added to the SQP. Thus the SQP, used to its full potential, will enable students to leave Worcester, not only more independent and confident, but also more employable.

The challenge facing academic and pastoral tutors is how to encourage students to engage with the process of developing their qualities profile. Students just embarking on a university programme tend to feel that preparing for employment is too far away to be of immediate concern, and that other issues are of higher priority, e.g. learning to cope away from home for the first time, developing a new social life, or coming to terms with the demands of academic work.

Objectives

Two years after its introduction (2003), student feedback suggested that engagement with the SQP was limited. The academic modules were assessed and contributed to the final degree classification, while the SQP, in contrast, was seen to be rather bureaucratic and not assessed, and so ultimately had no impact on degree classification. The primary reason for lack of student engagement was the lack of assessment, rendering it not directly relevant. Nevertheless, after fur-

> The primary reason for lack of student engagement was the lack of assessment, rendering it as not directly relevant

ther consultation with the Careers Service and Student Union, the school decided that the rationale behind the SQP was fundamentally sound and decided to:

1 Customise the SQP for the school.
2 Incorporate this customised version into the subject programmes and the personal tutor system.
3 Pilot the new system with the 2003–04 student cohorts.

Description

The customised version of the SQP developed into the School Personal Development Planning (PDP) system. It has now run with two cohorts of students. The role of the tutor in delivering PDP is seen as pivotal, based on the premise that, since PDP is a very individual process, the personal tutor is the ideal person to promote discussion and reflection, as well as guide students towards consideration of their future career plans. All students within the school are allocated a tutor. Tutors report that attendance at personal tutorials during the two pilot years has been generally good

(around 90% for first years), though this has shown signs of slipping to below 60% for second years.

The customised PDP system currently includes six skills:

1 planning and time management
2 responsibility and independence
3 interactive and group skills
4 problem-solving
5 reflection
6 communication and presentation skills.

These have been mapped onto a matrix which details the competences, abilities, capabilities and proficiencies of each skill (see Figure 1).

Year one

During induction week the new first year received a presentation explaining the rationale behind the PDP process and its practical implementation within the personal tutor system. Many of the intake were in fact already familiar with the concept as they had experience of recording their achievement from secondary school. In the first week of the first semester all students met their tutor and a written record of the meeting was kept by both student and tutor. In essence the purpose of the meeting was to establish contact, enable the tutor to find out more about the individual student and discuss the purpose of PDP.

Students were encouraged to meet with their tutor whenever necessary, and were expected to book a second tutorial in the first week of the second semester. Grades achieved during semester one would then be discussed along with the completion of a skills development sheet (see Figure 2), which identifies current strengths and priorities for development. The first section was completed by the student who was then encouraged to reflect on their experiences (including non-academic development) and to identify evidence that demonstrated skills development.

Year two

The second year of the PDP system included a focus on support for careers education. The aims of the School's Careers Strategy are:

1 To promote awareness amongst UOW undergraduates and diplomates of the importance of enhancing their academic profile.

Quality	D The competence to…	C The ability to…	B The capability to…	A The proficiency to…
Planning and time management	Meet imposed deadlines.	Plan own time within established deadlines.	Set and achieve targets over an extended period.	Select, apply and defend the most appropriate time management study.
Responsibility and independence	Meet imposed obligations.	Be trusted and relied upon, though reliant on judgement of 'experts'.	Make own judgements and take responsibility for self.	Take responsibility for self and others.
Interactive and group skills	Comprehend and respond to direct communication. Perform supervised work in a group.	Assess own and other's strengths and weaknesses. Work in a group and assimilate own results into group projects.	Able to negotiate and persuade. Structure teamwork, including negotiation of roles and responsibilities.	Apply appropriate communication techniques. Coordinate group activity and carry forward an effective strategy.
Problem-solving	Recognise and comprehend basic texts and data.	Undertake problem-solving with initial direction.	Apply an appropriate strategy to a specific problem.	Evaluate and improve problem-solving strategies independently.
Reflection	Recognise external criteria.	Identify own strengths and weaknesses.	Self-evaluate to focus on personal development needs.	Continually apply reflective practice for personal development purposes.
Communication and presentation skills	Comprehend and make statements of opinion. Present given information visually.	Analyse and produce a structured statement. Apply a range of visual communication techniques.	Give a convincing oral presentation and field questions. Evaluate and present effective visual communication.	Design and coordinate appropriate presentations. Design appropriate visual communication techniques.

Figure 1 Matrix of PDP skills for sports graduates at UoW

2 To build on the importance of the PDP/key skills/ common skills in acquiring relevant skills and qualities attractive to employers.

3 To promote the opportunities available for UoW undergraduates and diplomates to enhance their experience and knowledge base.

This is in line with the QAA *Code of Practice on Careers Education, Information and Guidance* which seeks to ensure that institutions are:

meeting students' expectations in respect of their

Student:		
Personal tutor:		
Academic year: Semester: 1 2		**Which semester for me: 1 2 3 4 5 6**
SELF-ASSESSMENT SECTION: TO BE COMPLETED BY THE STUDENT		
Planning and time management:		Please circle D C B A
Responsibility and independence:		Please circle D C B A
Interactive and group skills:		Please circle D C B A
Problem-solving skills:		Please circle D C B A
Reflection:		Please circle D C B A
Communication and presentation skills:		Please circle D C B A
(DISCUSSION SECTION: TO BE COMPLETED AT PERSONAL TUTORIAL)		
What strengths and areas of development have been identified?		
What other issues were raised?		
Date of next personal tutorial:		
Student initials:	**Tutor initials:**	**Date:**
Copy one: Student sends to registry	**Copy two: Tutor**	**Copy three: Student**

Figure 2 Tutorial record sheet

preparedness for their future career, and that they [institutions] are producing graduates [and diplomates] equipped to meet the demands of the employment market of today and tomorrow. (QAA, 2003)

The Careers Strategy is implemented through PDP:

1 Through the personal tutor system – tutors have advice packs on helping students to 'fill in the gaps', identifying opportunities for developing skills both within the academic setting and outside it.

2 Employability/entrepreneurship skills are made explicit to students within the modules, and are highlighted within learning activities that can be used to enhance these skills.

Year three

At the start of the first semester, each year group attends presentations aimed at enhancing their employability prospects and experience of the curriculum. The emphasis for the third years is on PDP tutorials, the benefits of BASES membership, 'BizCom' competitions and enterprise awareness events such as 'Enterprise

Fest'. The focus of the third and final year PDP tutorial is the production of a personal statement, which is aimed at providing the students with a summative and comprehensive account, aided by a checklist, which the students can use as a basis for job applications or to continue their studies at postgraduate level. The personal statement is an opportunity for students to provide evidence of employability skills gained during their time in higher education and to differentiate themselves for the job market. Early evidence from tutors suggests that though many students find this very challenging, a high percentage are using their statements as a supporting document for entry into the employment market.

Evaluation

Engagement with PDP

Students have reported most difficulty in finding evidence for the development of problem-solving skills during the course of their studies. Tutors have tried to prompt and encourage students to reflect on specific learning tasks undertaken during lectures. It remains an area where students do not feel confident that they are making progress. A significant number of students also find it difficult to recognise the development of generic skills while following the curriculum. Indeed some students tend to compartmentalise skills and focus on the specific learning outcomes of each module. It appears that when PDP is used with undergraduates on non-professional programmes, specificity is difficult to establish. However, in contrast, those students who aspire to PGCE or other recognised career pathways quickly learn the value of developing skills, which they know will be either desirable or essential.

Assessment of PDP

Staff acknowledge that the non-assessed nature of PDP needs to be tackled. It is worth noting that on many vocational programmes, such as the PGCE Secondary Course, students are required to keep a portfolio (a reflective record of their development as a student teacher) in which they are required to write a series of reflective commentaries detailing their progress. These are submitted and marked (pass or fail) on three separate occasions. Since this is a fundamental requirement of the course, engagement with the process is altogether more immediate and the focus is maintained to the end of the course.

Both staff and students recognise the value of the school's customised version of the SQP and, in particular, the process of engaging with PDP (through the personal tutor system). Nevertheless, we still question whether this learning should be more formally accredited. Further development and a deeper level of engagement will only be possible when the value of the learning is acknowledged.

Other developments

Curriculum development

One of the desired outcomes of higher education is the preparation of graduates to participate fully in the world of work, so higher education needs to recognise and address the significance and incidence of self-employment in the development of employability aspects of the curriculum. The significant graduate interest in business start-up has to be cultivated and assisted in order to reach fruition. More opportunities and support are necessary to establish graduates' small businesses. One such example at UOW is a recent successful funding application to the Mercia Institute of Enterprise for £10,000 to develop technology enhanced enterprise education (TE3, 2004).

Essentially the project is about 'supporting entrepreneurship' by designing and delivering two new modules both at undergraduate and postgraduate level within the Sports Studies curriculum. The aim is to develop interactive online learning materials using WebCT, and to hold a day-long 'Sport Fest' event, similar to that of an 'Enterprise Fest'. (See Figure 3)

The undergraduate module entitled Enterprise and Innovation in Sport has been validated and delivered. One of the pieces of assessed work was the production of a brief business plan and the making of a business pitch to a panel of investors. The criteria attempted, where practicable, to reflect the assessment used in the first stage entry of the BizCom awards as outlined in Figure 3. The BizCom awards encourage students

though many students find this very challenging, a high percentage are using their statements as a supporting document for entry into the employment market

to think about setting up their own business by developing and testing either an idea for a business or a social enterprise venture. This joined-up curriculum approach with regional initiatives has proved successful with a group of year-three sports graduates using the module and assessment as a platform to enter the competition. They won first prize!

The school is always looking for opportunities for curriculum enhancement in relation to employability. A recent initiative has been the appointment of an academic member of staff to the post of work placement coordinator to further links between employers and the school.

A project which came out of discussions at the Sport Employers Group (Figure 3) and was identified through the School Careers Strategy, has received funding. Its aims are to produce a multimedia DVD of selected local sport employers reporting on their personal experience. This will be used to increase the career skills awareness of sport students and to disseminate information given by employers concerning vocational opportunities available in sport. There are also plans to include the new module, Enterprise and Innovation in Sport, in the BSC (Hons) in Outdoor Adventure Leadership and Management degree that is currently being validated.

Links with business and employers

In order to support and enhance curriculum development, the school recently initiated the development of a Sport Employers Group in order to develop a cluster of sport-related employers willing to champion relevant workforce development and to engage with the skills, employment and productivity agenda in the sports industries. One of its main functions is to act as an advisory group to 'enhance and enrich student employability within the school'.

The school has also created a Business Enterprise Group whose mission is to develop a more commercially driven culture within the school which has at its core values of 'courage, commitment, contribution and creativity.' One of the roles of this group is to provide a forum for the key academic areas of the school and to focus on the Knowledge Transfer and Innovation agenda. This will enable the coherent development of intra-organisational and administrative infrastructures to facilitate knowledge transfer and innovation amongst staff and students. It is hoped that this will facilitate a more entrepreneurial culture amongst sports graduates to develop strong employability, enterprise and creative skills in order to prepare them to operate effectively in the knowledge economy.

In the future, it might be necessary to redefine skills for learning and employment and make them more explicit, so that they become interwoven into learning and teaching philosophy and strategies. This would necessitate giving students, for example, the opportunity to develop and gain a better understanding of self-employment in public and private sector business, knowledge of the business start-up process or employment in the SME sector.

The aim of the school is that our students will act as 'change champions'. Important developments such as business planning competitions (BizCom), awareness events like 'Enterprise Fest' and commercialisation workshops are incorporated into the academic programmes through working alongside internal groups such as alumni, the UOW business partnerships office, student services and careers. Figure 3 demonstrates the framework used to incorporate such entrepreneurial activities into the curriculum.

High-level plan					
	Year 1 *Awareness*	Year 2 *Interest*		Year 3 *Decision*	Graduation *Action*
ECP	Enterprise Fest (delegate) Taster workshop in idea development	Enterprise Fest (delegate) 15-credit vocational enterprise module	Enterprise Summer School	Enterprise Fest (exhibitor) BizCom Graduate Enterprise	Enterprise Fest (speaker) EFS InvoRed
WIN	Junior member of development team	The Ideas Generator		Individuals and teams building business proposals	Mentoring CPD Student placement

Figure 3 Plan for Entrepreneurial Skills (Corcoran, 2005)

Proposed future action

1 Ensure that all elements of the drivers and support for skills development at school level (for example, the learning-and-teaching strategy, careers strategy, sport-employer networks, and the students union) are making a valid, coordinated and transparent contribution towards the PDP of students.

2 Review the matrix of PDP skills for sports graduates. It might be that we need to consider developing 'creativity' as a skill.

3 Identify and make more explicit, through module outlines and during lectures, the links between learning outcomes, learning tasks and the development of generic skills and attributes.

4 Endeavour to replicate a PGCE subject/professional mentor system for students.

5 Establish more opportunities for the students to gather evidence of personal development.

6 Continue and extend our external engagement with key stakeholders/ employers.

7 Undertake a curriculum audit to identify and ensure the embedding of employability skills within the curriculum in order that they are made explicit to students within the learning experience.

References and URLs

Corcoran, Andrew, 2005. Internal presentation to the 'Knowledge Transfer, Innovation and Enterprise Committee'. University of Worcester

Green, David, 2003. *Strategic Plan 2004–08*. Worcester: University of Worcester

Peters, J. 2001. *The Student Qualities Profile*. Worcester: University College Worcester

QAA, 2003. *Code of Practice for the Assurance of Academic Quality and Standards in Higher Education: Career Education, Information and Guidance*. London: Quality Assurance Agency

TE3. 2004. http://www.te3.bham.ac.uk/

Tomkins, A. 2004. Best of both worlds: An exploration of key skills required for graduate work in the leisure and sport industry and links to Personal Development Planning. *LINK* 11. Available from: http://www.hlst.heacademy.ac.uk/

BizCom, Mercia Institute of Enterprise. http://www2.warwick.ac.uk/mercia/bizcom/

KAREN BILL is Principal Lecturer at the University of Worcester and her main leadership role is Development and Innovation within the School of Sport and Exercise Science. She teaches sports enterprise and has recently published an NCGE working paper on the development of entrepreneurship education within uk sport.

WILL BOWEN-JONES is Senior Lecturer at the University of Worcester. His main leadership role is Chair of the Learning and Teaching Advisory Group within the School of Sport and Exercise Science. He has just co-written a chapter for a forthcoming book on *PE and Education through Sport in the European Union*.

18

Enhancing student employability through a team exercise on a visitor-attraction management module

Debra Enzenbacher

This case study highlights a team exercise that forms one mode of assessment for a first-year undergraduate module on an honours tourism management programme. It shows how the employability skills of students can be enhanced by building direct contact with tourism employers into modules and the wider curriculum. The content and delivery of the Managing Visitor Attractions module at Bath Spa University (BSU) demonstrates how this assessment item links to the learning objectives and the aims of the programme in general.

The coursework for this Geography module is designed to help students gain valuable experience and confidence by dealing with tourism managers in their business setting and learning about the many challenges facing them. In short, this module makes employability-related learning more explicit within the curriculum. The team exercise provides an opportunity for students to enjoy meeting tourism managers while relating what is learned through reading in class and their work in a field setting.

Objectives

The Managing Visitor Attractions module at BSU is designed to provide subject knowledge drawn from lecture and seminar material, case study fieldwork, assigned readings from a required text (Swarbrooke, 2002) and other published or unpublished sources, e.g. journals, industry documents, visitor data. The learning objectives of the module include the development of students' appreciation of the scale and scope of the visitor attractions sector of the tourism industry both in the UK and abroad. On successful completion of the module students should also be able to grasp how visitor attractions are managed, appreciate the role of visitor management in providing a satisfying visitor experience at attractions, identify and describe some of the major developments that have occurred in the attractions sector and understand the importance of effective marketing, quality and high service stand-

ards to the visitor attractions sector.

The learning, teaching and assessment methods that are embedded in the programme's curriculum have an impact on student employability. Building employability skills into modules and the programme overall meets several objectives:

1 Students are able to demonstrate their current level of skills acquisition.
2 Teaching staff are able to assess students' current skills sets, so that feedback and additional tasks may be designed to develop them further.
3 Students interact with tourism professionals in their work setting and thereby understand better the industry context and establish valuable contacts.
4 Students broaden the skill base on which challenging, lucrative and interesting tourism jobs depend.
5 Students are better prepared to compete for jobs and undertake a tourism career.

Rationale

The Tourism Management BSc (Hons) programme at Bath Spa University is committed to enhancing student employability. This is achieved through careful curriculum design including relevant fieldwork, Personal Development Planning which entails a work placement in year two, and the involvement of industry in student learning where appropriate. The programme encourages direct contact with tourism businesses and employers during each phase of student learning. This valuable contact provides a foundation for their understanding of the work environment. It goes beyond the curriculum by allowing students to see the management context in industry.

Students often benefit from a range of industry links made on tourism management degree programmes. Typically these links include liaising with tourism industry professionals when designing a tourism management curriculum, hosting guest speakers in class, teaching materials that reflect knowledge and insights gained from industry consultancy work and hosting departmental research symposia, conferences, workshops or other gatherings that allow students to meet and interact with tourism professionals.

Our programme aims to develop a broad range of skills that are desirable to employers. Given the broad range they cover, various attempts have been made to categorise skills. For purposes of discussion, key skills include among others:

❑ oral and written communication including presentations
❑ numeracy and data handling
❑ the command of computers and information technology (IT)
❑ reading ability
❑ listening
❑ time management
❑ observation
❑ problem solving
❑ critical analysis
❑ individual and teamwork.

It takes time to develop skills that make students more employable. While a programme approach is needed to foster student employability, individual modules may set specific tasks that enhance the pace at which skills development occurs. This case study highlights student fieldwork in the attractions sector, thus illustrating how benefits may be gained from direct tourism industry contact and experience, at the module level.

Context

There are roughly 2m people employed in tourism-related jobs in the UK. According to a recent report by the Tourism Skills Network South West (2003), the tourism industry employs more than 40,000 peo-ple in the West of England and generates £1.4bn per year for the local economy. The Network, which was established in 2001 through a South West of England Regional Development Agency initiative, promotes the productivity of tourism establishments in the region. They commissioned a survey of local tourism businesses and the findings identified a skills gap that needs to be addressed if the industry is to remain prosperous. The skills that are in short supply include disability awareness, customer care, information technology (IT), supervisory/management, sales, first aid and health and safety. Tourism graduates are encouraged to develop the skills sought by industry in order to fill the gaps. The report noted that the problem may be exacerbated by the competition from other job sectors whose candidates have transferable skills. How universities prepare tourism graduates to enter the workplace therefore remains an important factor in this equation.

Given the growing number of university graduates in the UK, the development of a wide-ranging skill set is essential to gaining employment in the tourism industry's competitive job market. Subject knowledge may not be the main prerequisite for employment in the tourism industry as relevant knowledge may often be acquired in the workplace. Employers value not only work experience, but problem-solving abilities and insight into the many complex issues facing organisations. It is therefore important to incorporate industry experience in the tourism management curriculum in ever more creative, interesting and useful ways.

The study of tourism management is interdisciplinary in nature. As a result, tourism management programmes are offered in different departments within universities. Some are located within a business school, while others are organised through a department of geography, economics or leisure studies, to name but a few. The location of the programme within a university has a significant effect on the approach taken to the study of the subject. This has implications for the skills that are developed on a given programme and opportunities to link the curriculum with industry. At Bath Spa University, the BSC (Hons) in Tourism Management is offered as a specialised award within the Geography Department of the School of Science and the Environment. A geographical approach might consider tourists, destinations, host populations and the tourism industry in a spatial and temporal context placing emphasis on field visits. Geography departments are well known for valuing field studies highly. Consequently, fieldwork is often granted considerable resources, which suits the subject well. The value of field visits to academic and practical learning should not be underestimated. They help reinforce what is learned in the classroom and, through reading, allow students to observe with their own eyes and make valuable connections as a result.

Our undergraduate Tourism Management programme employs a modular scheme, with compulsory and optional modules offered through the Departments of Geography, Business and Management, Professional and Academic Development, Food Studies, Environmental Management and Sociology. The academic year is divided into two 15-week semesters and students are required to take three modules per semester. While a majority of the programme's curriculum is delivered by the Department of Geography, including all Tourism modules, many are offered by the Business and Management Department in the School of Social Sciences. The modular structure is outlined below.

Students on the Tourism Management programme learn in the first semester of year one about the different sectors of the tourism industry, including transport, accommodation, catering, attractions, retail travel, tour operations, tourism organisations and financial services on the module, Tourism: an introduction. They also learn about the business environment on a Business and Management module. In this way, when they are asked to relate their academic learning to industry on the Managing Visitor Attractions module in semester two, they have a solid grasp of the industry's structure and how each sector fits into the tourism puzzle. The key issues students explore when studying attractions (e.g. customer service, disability awareness, access issues, principles of human resource management, marketing tactics, pricing strategies) are often transferable to other sectors of the tourism industry and to business in general. The Business and Management module, Introduction to the Management and Functions of an Organisation, which is the fourth required module in year one, further familiarises them with workplace principles. The students then choose one option module each semester in their first year.

The Professional and Academic Development module is compulsory in year two and is designed to develop further skills that enhance employability such as personal development planning. The module is contextualised to reflect the broad range of student interests. Choices include: Leisure and Tourism; Entrepreneurship; Retail, Business and Finance; Creative Industries; Public Administration; Advertising, PR and Marketing; Science and Environment; Health and Society; and Education and Postgraduate Studies. For example, Tourism Management students with an interest in an events management career might take the Advertising, PR and Marketing PAD module. On this module, students arrange a work placement with a suitable agency which provides direct experience in industry along with further valuable contacts to prospective employers. Other required modules include Tourism Research Methods which also entails fieldwork, and Tourism Policy and Planning which employs a field visit to learn about tourism development plans at the county level. Students therefore have three option modules to select in year two.

In year three, Tourism Dissertation is the only required module and it runs over both semesters. That means students can choose two option modules each semester in their final year. This works well since, by this time, they tend to be much more focused in terms of their academic and career interests and may specialise to some extent. Given our modular scheme, students may follow a variety of 'pathways' from year one onward. Among the option modules are Tourism and New Social Forms, Tourism Field Course (visiting the Amalfi coast of Italy), Recreation Management and the Natural Environment, Enterprise Project and Business Plan, Management Tools and Techniques, Food Law and Consumer Protection, Geodemographics, e-Business, Marketing Management, Employment Law and Landscape Heritage.

The programme is endorsed by the Tourism Society and benefits from active collaboration with local, regional and national organisations. Overall, students undertake a mix of practical and academic work on the Tourism Management programme in preparation for careers in the tourism industry. Given our prime location in Bath and proximity to Bristol, many students undertake part-time employment in the tourism industry while enrolled. For example, many jobs are available in the accommodation, catering and attractions sectors and we are approached by local employers for our students as a result. Those who undertake such work and reflect on how the material covered on their modules relates to their industry experience deepen their understanding accordingly.

Description

The Managing Visitor Attractions module builds on student learning by focusing on one sector of the tourism industry. I serve as the module co-ordinator of this class which meets each week for a one-hour lecture and two-hour seminar. The module is assessed through coursework comprising a group seminar presentation and handout (20%) and a 2,000 word essay (40%) and an unseen exam (40%). This case study focuses on the group seminar presentation and handout in order to show how having students establish direct contact with attraction managers helps them gain insight into tourism industry practice that makes them more employable.

Clear and thorough guidance is provided for this team project in the module handbook which is distributed in the week one seminar. In this session, I talk the students through the guidance at length so they can start their coursework. Students form themselves into groups of four and are handed a set of brochures and leaflets featuring local attractions. Each team must identify a local visitor attraction that will serve as a case study. They are to assume the role of consultants and undertake a critical analysis of the management of the attraction they have selected.

The 30-minute team presentation, including five to ten minutes for questions and answers, should include the following content:

a An explanation of the historical development of the attraction and its context in the market.

b Product range and description, current provision, ownership and management structure at the attraction.

c Consideration of the marketing tools employed by the attraction.

d Analysis of operational issues, including quality, staff training and customer service, based on their observations, information contained in publica-

tions and/or gathered from management and/or other staff at the attraction.

e Discussion of any relevant financial information relating to the attraction.

f Presentation of visitor numbers, a visitor profile and/or any other relevant data generated by in-house research, obtained from their interview or contained in reports.

g Identification of the key management challenges facing the attraction.

h Conclusions and recommendations drawn from their analysis of the attraction.

Teams are advised that their analysis might also consider such issues as access, the need for refurbishment, target markets, seasonality, health and safety policies and security. They are encouraged to think about how the key management challenges facing the attraction might be addressed so that it remains competitive.

Peers observe presentations and provide anonymous feedback to each team using a departmental form developed for oral presentation work

The aim is for students to demonstrate insight into how the visitor attraction is managed, what is being done well and how it might be improved compared with what the textbooks and academic literature have to say about what is happening in this sector of the tourism industry. Providing tacit guidance to students to draw upon the literature in conducting their analysis assists them in the process of linking what they are learning in the field to what is covered in the classroom and assigned readings.

The attraction may operate in the public, private or voluntary sector. Their choice needs to be approved by me. No two teams may study the same attraction, nor may they use the attractions we visit as part of the organised field visit for the module. They then contact directly the management of their chosen attraction and request an interview, explaining they are studying the management of visitor attractions and wish to learn more about the subject from industry professionals.

The size of an attraction tends to reflect the number of managers that run it. For example, small-scale attractions often have one general manager whereas large attractions may have a large management team reporting to a managing director, e.g. operations manager, customer services manager, marketing manager, human resources manager, facilities manager, financial manager, sales manager. If there is more than one manager at an attraction, teams may select the one they most wish to interview. Once the interview is agreed, teams advise me of the name and title of the manager concerned as well as the date of the interview. Teams must secure their interview before selecting their presentation slot. One seminar in week seven is devoted to self-directed study to allow students time in lieu to visit the attraction and conduct the interview.

Teams then design appropriate interview questions to put to a manager at their attraction, drawing on information provided in module support materials and a special class briefing on interview techniques in

> There are personal as well as academic benefits to be gained by undertaking this assignment

the week-six seminar. The students are also directed to visit the attraction and experience it before their interview in order to identify any further issues they wish to put questions to management. Once the visit and interview are completed, comparisons are to be made between what is learned in the field and what relevant academic literature has to say about best practice. The exercise aims to provide students with direct industry contact, insight into how visitor attractions are managed and greater knowledge of the visitor attraction product overall. Presentations are made during the seminars in weeks ten and 11.

The presentation should include varied visual elements, although content is more significant. Presenters are given a group mark, although I reserve the right to award different marks when there is a clear disparity in the quality of the contributions. The work is submitted on disk or CD ROM along with a hard-copy version of any material presented via computer or other visual aids, all notecards and a copy of the handout. This includes a complete printout of PowerPoint slides if these are used. The handout for each group's presentation should set out its key themes and content

along with a full list of references, using the module textbook for a start. It should not merely be a reproduction of PowerPoint slides used for the presentation. A handout is then distributed to the class before each presentation is made.

This assignment allows a number of skills to be developed and assessed, including written and oral communication, information gathering, data collection and handling, teamwork, time management, use of PowerPoint or other computer software and referencing. However, it is acknowledged that some aspects of employability may not lend themselves to accurate assessment, especially if they are difficult or costly to measure. Clear marking criteria for the group presentation and handout have been established, so students know what is expected and how the assignment develops their skills set which makes them more employable. Students are assessed on their ability to:

1 Provide balanced, clear and accurate coverage relating to the attraction selected and employ a range of relevant sources, key data to substantiate discussion and full citation of sources using the Harvard style of referencing.
2 Provide a well-timed, suitably paced and audible presentation; establish regular eye contact with the audience; interact with audience members and stimulate discussion using clear supporting visual elements with no spelling, grammatical or typographical errors.
3 Demonstrate clear evidence of teamwork and co-operation.
4 Produce a balanced and well-argued response to any questions or comments made during the discussion following the seminar presentation.
5 Distribute a handout for the presentation that contains key findings, along with supporting data and figures that cite relevant sources and a full bibliography of all sources employed.

Students are advised that the handout should have a logical structure, provide a balanced use of information and relevant supporting statements, draw upon a wide range of appropriate sources, e.g. books, journals, reports, employ complete and accurate referencing in the Harvard style, use proper grammar, spelling and punctuation throughout and be well presented.

A form was developed for use when marking team

presentations. It contains a checklist of the criteria set for the assignment as they appear in the module handbook. This allows me to note which elements of suggested content have been included and whether key points of guidance have been followed. A similar form is used to assess the quality of the handouts. There is room for summary comments at the end of the form.

Peers observe presentations and provide anonymous feedback to each team, using a departmental form developed for oral presentation work. It asks students to identify how the presentation helped them to learn and the extent of its effectiveness. A scale from A (high) to D (low) is provided to rate clarity of aims, quality of explanation provided, balance in terms of depth and breadth, relevance, and the extent to which the work is logical, informed and interesting. Further ratings are sought on structure, audibility, pace, sources, quality of handouts and visual materials, ability to stimulate discussion and whether teams field questions well. Students are then asked to suggest improvements and highlight the best features of each presentation. These forms are collected and submitted to the departmental secretary who compiles the data. Peer evaluation results are returned to each team along with the tutor's feedback and their submitted work later in the semester.

Evaluation

This assignment requires students to contact and interview managers in the attractions sector which makes employability-related learning explicit within the curriculum. Students gain direct experience of a tourism product, examine the contents of attraction websites, when available, and negotiate meeting terms. The key skills developed through this coursework include: negotiating teamwork (ensuring all team members pull their weight) and conflict resolution; oral, written and visual communication; computer and IT skills; interview techniques; direct observation of business practices; data capture and handling; critical analysis; time management; and presentation techniques. Other skills may be developed depending on how the project work unfolds. Honing their skills serves students well for future work on the programme and helps prepare them for work in the tourism industry.

Having delivered this module for three consecutive years I consider that most students engage fully with the subject matter, enjoy the work and learn a great deal from the process of approaching a tourism business, meeting an attraction manager and learning first-hand from them about the challenges facing their business. There are personal as well as academic benefits to be gained by undertaking this assignment. These include satisfaction upon completing a group project, gaining confidence, and learning to be resourceful or troubleshoot while in the field. This past year, one student team reported enthusiastically that they were invited to participate in a special costumed event hosted by the attraction on which they focused their project.

Local attractions seem to welcome the opportunity to support our students and learn more about their programme of study. Care is taken to prevent attrac-

> Another advantage of this coursework is that it caters for diverse student interests

tions being approached too often, at least by my class, which hopefully results in more managers consenting to be interviewed.

Another advantage of this coursework is that it caters for diverse student interests. Rather than requiring all students to undertake an evaluation of the same attraction, teams are allowed to select an attraction that interests them, which keeps interest levels high. Given the vast array of attractions in the South West of England, especially Bath and Bristol, students have the choice of purpose-built, heritage and/or natural attractions or special events. This past semester students selected Bristol Zoo, Bath Postal Museum, the American Museum, Old Wardour Castle, the Jane Austen Centre and Avon Valley Railway.

Not only do students gain vital first-hand experience of industry, they learn to employ observation skills in new ways. For example, by noticing marketing materials, the design, layout and safety features of the given attraction and whether it provides access for the disabled, students are trained to see and experience attractions in new ways. This assists them in their work on the module field trip to the Roman Baths.

The task also allows them to consider the visitor experience from a new perspective. Team findings benefit the class by broadening knowledge of attractions in the area. The handouts provide a bank of case study material on which to draw in their exam and coursework essays as appropriate.

Overall, this assignment makes our students more employable, especially after all teams have presented, because they have a clearer sense of the work undertaken by attraction managers, can share useful contacts and learn to relate material from the classroom to actual work settings better. Additional benefits include input into career decision-making and knowledge of available opportunities.

The value of fieldwork on a tourism management programme should not be underestimated. This assignment encourages reflective thinking, provides useful experience in planning and conducting an interview and collecting data and challenges students to focus their energy and ideas early on in the module.

The use of a form to help me assess presentations ensures that all marking criteria are considered for each presentation. It also helps limit the amount of writing needed to provide useful feedback to students. While the peer-evaluation process takes valuable class time to administer, it is deemed to be worthwhile as, in many cases, fellow students offer similar feedback to that of the tutor. The process also helps students reflect on what works well when presenting and what does not work well. They gain experience looking for specific elements of individual and team performance which helps to reinforce how and why marking criteria are set.

It seems fitting to consider feedback provided by students who have taken the Managing Visitor Attractions module. The quotes below are drawn from the module evaluation forms:

- *Fieldwork was excellent. Good to meet managers.*
- *Field trips and groupwork have been helpful in this module. Putting theories into practice has been really helpful for me.*
- *The experience of the fieldwork was brilliant as you were able to speak to a manager up front.*
- *Really enjoyed the module overall. Was delivered extremely well. Favourite module and year one field trip was good.*
- *This module has given me a better understanding of how to manage visitor attractions.*

Discussion

This case study takes a closer look at merely one mode of assessment on a module within a Tourism Management programme that aims to deliver employable graduates. While individual modules and even specific coursework may contribute to student employability, arguably it is the coherence and progression inherent in the programme that may ultimately determine the extent to which graduates develop employable skills.

Careful tourism-management curriculum design allows the linking of assessment of fieldwork to some or all of the learning outcomes on a given module. In this case, the group seminar presentation and handout links to all the learning objectives of the module. Feedback on team presentations is provided by the tutor and peers, based on content, style and delivery and encourages improvement and reflection on the learning aims of the assignment.

Student feedback on this coursework tends to be positive which suggests that they enjoy the work and remain motivated to complete the tasks involved. The extent to which students gain insight into attraction management issues will depend on many factors ,including the role they play within their team, their listening skills, the amount of relevant reading they have done and how much they reflect on what they have learned in the process. What remains important is that we set assignments that allow students opportunities to tie complex ideas together, to observe or grasp an aspect of industry practice and understand it in its management context, as well as in subject-specific terms.

This module prepares students for years two and three by requiring them to work effectively in teams, handle data, design and distribute a useful handout, produce interesting text and visual material and compile it in a presentation, critically analyse what they have learned and observed and undertake fieldwork without having a tutor present.

Refinements to the assignment as well as the module are appropriate and inevitable. For the former, possibilities include decreasing group size and increasing the weighting of the assignment, providing further guidance on work loading within groups and revising the assignment feedback form. Examples in terms of the latter include updating teaching material, changing case studies, discussing relevant newsworthy items in class and changing essay topics or attractions visited. Recent demands on departmental clerical staff may result in the need to adapt the peer-evaluation scheme, e.g. rather than compiling the data, the forms may need to be photocopied and given to students.

Reflecting on current practice and making improvements accordingly allow us to deliver relevant, coherent and useful programmes. It is also vital to keep track of just where we have embedded particular skills within our programmes to ensure adequate coverage and avoid overemphasis.

Curriculum auditing offers a way of testing how and where employability-related learning is incorporated into curricula. It may also point to the need to rethink pedagogic and/or assessment practices. (Yorke and Knight, 2004: 2)

if logical progression through a given programme is to result.

In modular schemes, achieving the right balance for every student creates even greater challenges as no two paths over the three-year programme are necessarily identical. A balance must also be struck between efforts expended to develop rounded skills sets that make graduates employable and imparting the necessary subject-specific knowledge that will hold them in good stead.

This case study has shown how the employability skills of students may be enhanced by building direct contact with employers and businesses into programmes and making the employability-related learning that is embedded in the curriculum more explicit. Sharing practice in this way allows staff from different institutions to compare approaches taken to develop their students' employability skills and adapt useful ideas where appropriate and transferable. It is hoped that these efforts, taken together, will culminate in the production of university graduates who are well-equipped, prepared and eager to embark on careers in the tourism industry in which they are able to manage change with great effect.

References and URLs

Learning and Skills Council at http://www.lsc.gov.uk

Learning and Skills Development Agency at http://www.lsda.org.uk

Higher Education Academy, 2004. *Learning and Employability Series* (6 volumes). York: HE Academy. (http://www.heacademy.ac.uk)

Swarbrooke, J. 2002. *The development and management of visitor attractions*, 2nd ed. Oxford: Butterworth-Heinemann.

Tourism Skills Network South West, 2003. *Tourism Sector Work Force Development Plan* at http://www.tourismskillsnetwork.org.uk/local/WDP.

Yorke, M. and Knight, P.T. 2004. *Embedding employability into the curriculum*. Learning and Employability Series 3. York: HE Academy.

DEBRA ENZENBACHER is a Senior Lecturer in the Geography Department at Bath Spa University where she teaches the module Managing Visitor Attractions as part of the Tourism Management specialised award. Her doctoral research was on Antarctic tourism management and policymaking and she continues to specialise in this area.

19 Students' awareness of the importance of transferable skills for employability

Petia Petrova and Dorota Ujma

In 2001 the University of Bedfordshire (then known as the University of Luton) conducted a survey amongst its tourism undergraduates, looking at students' assessment of the skills, knowledge and personality characteristics that they believed would give them a competitive edge in securing employment in tourism. The results showed that we not only need to develop students' skills, but that we also need to take steps to improve their ability to self-assess and be aware of their own skill levels.

This case study presents the results from the original survey and the subsequent steps taken to improve students' skills awareness and development in order to improve their employability prospects within their intended industry of tourism.

Rationale

As a result of government policy on widening participation in higher education (HE), the number of degree courses in the UK has increased substantially. Government figures show that 40% of young people go to university (HM Treasury, 2004). This trend is replicated in tourism courses. The number of undergraduate tourism courses has increased dramatically – from two in 1972 (Ryan, 1995) to 80 in 2001 (Busby and Fiedel, 2001). In tourism degree courses:

> vocational, career and industry issues stand out as the key elements which are stressed in the material that is given to prospective students. (Airey and Johnson, 1999: 233)

The increase in the number of tourism degrees indicates students' desire to study a vocational course leading to a career in tourism. Tourism students should therefore expect their degrees to deliver exactly that – the opportunity to acquire the skills needed to secure a job in the tourism industry. Furthermore, changes in work patterns and a decrease in job security mean that graduates need to acquire the skills required by employers that enable them to transfer from job to job with ease.

> Expectations are, increasingly, built around mobility and change and the anticipation that an individual may move between companies and sectors at a number of points within a working life. (Baum, 1995: 190/1)

Transferable skills play an important role in the potential employability and mobility of graduates (Stewart and Knowles, 2000) and should therefore be an important part of the tourism courses provided by universities.

Objectives

In this case study, we present our findings of the 2001 survey and the steps undertaken by the university to improve students' awareness of the skill requirements they need to secure a job in tourism, in addition to developing those skills within the curriculum. The survey sought to establish whether undergraduate students were aware of the importance of transferable skills and, specifically, whether they felt they possessed such skills. It was largely based on Purcell and Quinn's (1996) study, and addressed the following issues:

- ❏ Why do students embark upon higher education?
- ❏ The development of skills and perceptions of employer demand.
- ❏ What do students expect to do on graduation?
- ❏ Employment expectations.
- ❏ Are graduates 'prepared' for today's labour market?

This case study focuses on the development of skills

and perceptions of employer demand. The population of the survey included all students enrolled on undergraduate tourism-related courses at Luton in 2001. The university provides undergraduate tourism courses in Travel and Tourism and International Tourism Management.

Context

Reasons for studying tourism

To put the results of the study in context we needed to understand students' reasons for studying tourism and how much those reasons reflected their career aspirations. The students were offered a choice of ten statements based on Pitcher and Purcell (1998) designed to indicate their reasons for studying tourism. The statement that generated the highest number of responses (89%) was 'I was interested in the tourism industry', followed by 'I thought it would lead to a good job in the tourism industry' (71%).

Ninety-one per cent of students were convinced that they had chosen the right course. Reasons given included general satisfaction with the course itself (44%), while 58% of students stated reasons relating to the tourism industry and careers. The importance of the vocational/practical side of a tourism degree was also demonstrated by 37% of the respondents choosing 'I wanted a mixture of practical/academic course'.

Students had chosen to study tourism because of their interest in the subject area and in working in tourism. Yet the career prospects for tourism graduates in the industry are believed to be bleak (Formica, 1996; McKercher et al, 1995; Parsons and Care, 1991; Thomas and Long, 2001). Employers do not believe tourism graduates have the necessary skills to work in the tourism industry (Petrova and Mason, 2005a). There have also been suggestions that that as many as 50% of graduates will not succeed in finding a career in tourism (Evans, 1993).

Core areas of skill development

The 'skills which are required in almost any job' (DfEE as cited in Stewart and Knowles, 2000: 68) are often described as transferable skills. In 1998 the DfEE listed the following as the most important transferable skills:

- basic literacy and numeracy
- the ability to work well with others
- communication skills
- self-motivation
- the ability to organise one's work
- a basic capability to use IT.

The above skills are important to any employer. Kelly and Dorsman (1984, as cited in Ineson and Kempa, 1996: 15) listed the following transferable skills most important to graduate employers, in particular:

- self-motivation
- enthusiasm
- effective communication skills
- problem-solving skills
- ability to work in a team
- effectiveness in meeting deadlines
- interpersonal skills.

> There have also been suggestions that that as many as 50% of graduates will not succeed in finding a career in tourism

The University of Bedfordshire's skill descriptors identify six core areas of skill development in its graduate programmes: communication; application of number; IT; problem-solving; working with others; and improving own learning. These largely reflect the above list. However, there are particular skill needs associated with working in a customer-service environment. The skills requirements specific to the hospitality industry (Mayo, 1997: 97) are as follows:

- service attitude
- flexibility
- enjoying serving people
- management and leadership qualities
- enjoying what they do
- dedication and commitment.

The tourism and hospitality industries (Baum, 1995: 191) consider the following graduate competencies as most important to them:

- management of guest problems with understanding
- effective communication in both written and oral form

- achievement of positive working relationship with employees
- professional appearance and poise
- development of positive customer relations
- motivation of employees to achieve desired performance.

These studies show similarities in the groups of skills requirements and can be grouped (Petrova, 2001) as follows:

- Development of positive customer relations – enjoying serving people, management of guest problems with understanding, service attitude (Mayo, 1997; Baum, 1995)
- Communication – effective communication skills in both oral and written form (Kelly and Dorsman, 1984; Baum, 1995)
- Enthusiasm, dedication and commitment – enjoying what they do, self-motivation (Kelly and Dorsman, 1984; Mayo, 1997)
- Teamworking – achievement of positive working relations (Kelly and Dorsman 1984; Baum, 1995)
- Problem-solving skills (Kelly and Dorsman, 1984)
- Management and leadership qualities – motivation of employees (Baum 1995 and Mayo, 1997)
- Interpersonal skills (Kelly and Dorsman, 1984)
- Effectiveness in meeting deadlines (Kelly and Dorsman, 1984).

The discussion of and comparison between employers' requirements of transferable skills and students' awareness and possession of those skills were conducted on the basis of this grouping.

Findings and discussion

Students' awareness of transferable skills

The first aim of this analysis was to determine students' awareness of which of their skills may prove important and/or beneficial in the labour market. The questions posed did not use the term 'transferable skills'; neither did they give a list of skills. In this way any possible influence on the answers was avoided. The questions referred to skills, knowledge, experience and personality characteristics beneficial in securing employment. Table 1 presents the summary of responses.

Customer service, communication and IT

Communication and IT are two of the skills most commonly required by employers (DfEE, 1998).

Skills	% of total respondents
Customer service skills	23%
Communication skills	23%
IT skills	19%
Language skills	18%
Teamworking skills	9%
Organisational skills	8%
Interpersonal skills	8%
Marketing skills	4%
Management skills	4%
Problem-solving skills	3%
Office skills	3%
Leadership skills	1%
Decision-making skills	1%

Table 1 Skills perceived beneficial in securing employment

Effective communication skills are amongst the most important skills to tourism and hospitality employers (Kelly and Dorsman 1984, Baum 1995). These skills are also regarded as important amongst the University of Bedfordshire's tourism students: 23% and 19% of students cited the importance of communication and IT skills respectively. Development of positive customer relations and service attitude (Mayo 1997, Baum 1995) are also considered very important to tourism and hospitality employers; again this was reflected in student responses at 23%.

While it was encouraging that the students were aware of the importance of the three areas cited, response rates to other skill areas were low, highlighting the necessity of raising awareness of the importance of these skills.

Business

Skills important to working in a business environment provided an even lower number of responses. The five areas that registered minimum response amongst students were decision-making, office, marketing, organisation and problem-solving. Problem-solving is one of the most important skills to graduate employers (Kelly and Dorsman 1984, as cited in Baum, 1995). This indicated that more emphasis on these skills was required.

Interpersonal

Interpersonal skills are also rated highly by employers but generated a low response from the survey.

However, students were asked to list personality characteristics that they thought would be beneficial to them in securing employment, some of which relate to interpersonal skills. Table 2 groups these characteristics into two categories: 'friendly' and 'outgoing'.

These personality characteristics could be perceived by students as an advantage in securing employment as they are aware that their future careers may involve high levels of interaction with customers.

Friendly	Outgoing
Polite	Bubbly
Helpful	Happy
Nice	Sociable
Easy to get along with	Enjoy working with people
Kind	Enjoy meeting people
Approachable	Lively
Understanding	Extrovert
Caring	Positive attitude
Patient	Cheerful
Good listener	Smiley

Table 2: Friendly/outgoing

Students' awareness of the importance of skills and their own skill levels indicate a number of areas for improvement. Nevertheless, it was encouraging to see that 27% cited dedication and commitment to their future tourism careers.

Perceived importance of knowledge in securing a job

The majority of respondents (68%) stated that their specialised knowledge of the tourism industry would prove advantageous to them in securing employment in the industry. Yet such knowledge is regarded by tourism and hospitality employers as being much less important in comparison to other skills (Baum 1995; Li and Kivela 1998; Petrova and Mason 2005b). Further, Evans (1993) stated that employers are 'all supportive of "general intellect, calibre, personality and fit" being the key criteria for graduate selection and not the degree subject itself'. This highlights the importance of raising students' awareness of the fact that in addition to the knowledge they are gaining, their degree courses are developing skills which will enable them to secure employment.

The results discussed above show that students have little awareness of the importance of skills to their employability, and that more needs to be done to increase awareness of the skills they have developed during their degree. In the next section we describe the practical steps to achieve this that have been undertaken within the tourism courses at the University of Bedfordshire.

Approach to teaching and curriculum development

There are two undergraduate tourism courses in the Department of Tourism, Leisure and HRM, based within the Bedfordshire Business School. These are: BA (Hons) International Tourism Management and BA (Hons) Travel and Tourism. Both courses offer a mixture of business and tourism modules.

Most of the business modules are taught at level one. Students are not always keen on these, especially at the very beginning of their studies. They do not always perceive the benefits of studying business and how it relates to tourism, and often find general-business modules more difficult than the tourism options. However, as their studies progress, some comment favourably on activities and assessments in Marketing, Business Environment, Business Analysis and Finance for Business that they have covered in level one.

We recognise the importance of business skills to tourism employers (Petrova and Mason, 2005a) and our tourism courses are based around these skills. Business modules give the students opportunities to enhance their skills with regard to decision-making, problem-solving, marketing and organisational skills. Interestingly, students find it hard to make the link

> students have little awareness of the importance of skills to their employability. More needs to be done to increase awareness of the skills they have developed during their degree

between these groups of skills developed during the business modules and their importance to employability. We have therefore taken steps to improve the ability of our students to reflect on their skills, namely through the Personal Professional and Academic Development in Tourism (PPAD) and Personal Development Planning (PDP) modules which are discussed below.

As students move on to levels two and three, the number of business modules decreases, leaving more space for tourism and leisure options. These can be divided into two groups – practical and theoretical.

Theoretical modules are designed to develop general intellectual skills which have always been associated with higher education. They enrich the students' way of thinking, analysis, discussion and reflection. Research Methods in Tourism, for example, develops research and information-retrieval skills, as well as analytical techniques. It also teaches students how to use different research methods. Sport Tourism introduces theories applicable to this relatively new area of research, so that students can make a link between theory and their own experience. Tourism Behaviour introduces theories behind behavioural issues brought up by tourism. Sociology of Sport and Leisure is currently being introduced.

Recently the curriculum was further enriched with a number of practical tourism modules and initiatives designed to improve students' employability prospects within the tourism industry. Practical modules are very popular amongst our students. These modules include Airport Services Management, eDestinations, Information and Communication Technology (ICT) in Tourism, ICT Management, Work Placements, Conference and Event Management and Air Transport Management.

eDestinations

This is a new hands-on, practical module which trains students in the use of the Tiscover content management system. Students develop a trial website for both a destination marketing organisation and an accommodation supplier in a fictitious destination. It is taught in an unconventional way, as a 'short and thick' module, comprising an intensive approach where students attend four full-day sessions (9.00-17.00), throughout the semester, mirroring a traditional working pattern. Students are then required to work independently on their assessments in order to develop their self-reliance. As it is a module developing IT skills, further assistance from the tutor may be obtained via the virtual learning environment, 'Blackboard' and email.

This module is a result of cooperation between the module coordinator and Tiscover, a leading supplier of destination management systems. Bedfordshire is the first university to deliver this module in the UK. It was previously introduced in Austria where it was branded as Tourism Online Manager. This module equips students with practical knowledge and skills, specifically technical training, how to use content management systems and how to use best practice in the use of new media such as search optimisation, website design and email marketing.

Airport Services Management

This module was introduced several years ago and is based on the ServisAir training programme, delivered by their staff at Luton Airport. Students who achieve good results on the module are offered summer employment with ServisAir at Luton. Some of them get the opportunity to extend the period of their placement to a full year. Students have commented that this module gives them the chance to experience the realities of working in the industry and to compare it to their own expectations and aspirations. As a result, some choose an alternative career path while for others it is an opportunity to confirm that their career plans are suited to them.

Students who complete a full year's work placement show greater confidence and self-esteem. They become more confident of their skills and abilities to perform in a work environment and gain maturity as a result of their experience.

Personal Development Planning

To maximise the benefits of our courses we need to ensure that students have the ability to reflect on the skills they have developed during their studies and work experience. We have used the QAA's Progress File recommendations to adopt a curriculum model that integrates personal development planning (PDP) with career management skills at all levels of the undergraduate portfolio (Ujma and Kumar, 2005).

As previously mentioned, Bedfordshire now has two modules that deal specifically with reflection on skills developed: 'PPAD' at level one and 'PDP' at level two. PPAD concentrates on the development of academic skills of new students, with PDP designed to follow on. Level-two students are encouraged to take their development a step further, to enhance their employability skills through interactive exercises, group activities and individual reflection. These processes often pose problems; to facilitate them we have worked closely with the university's careers service professionals. We believe this has enhanced the quality of our delivery of this module and has improved the ability of our students to reflect on their own skills.

We aim for a holistic approach to our curriculum by combining efforts between all of the modules mentioned. Transferable/key skills are written into each of the modules and play an essential part to the outcomes. In addition, our students have the ability to take work placements to further their skills, work experience and, ultimately, their employability prospects.

Conclusion

There are indications from the literature that tourism graduates face particular industry-based challenges when looking for employment. From our own research we found that skills development and self-awareness needed to be further embedded within our curriculum.

In recent years, we have undertaken a number of measures to develop comprehensive subject-specific support for skills relevant to the tourism industry. The range of modules we provide within our tourism courses develop, or at least provide, students with opportunities to gain a number of skills, both academic and practical. Examples of this are:

❑ ICT in Tourism, eDestinations, ICT Management raise the profile of IT skills.
❑ PDP and PPAD evaluate communications skills.
❑ Work Placements, Conference and Event Management and Air Transport Management aid students' reflection around practical issues and learning 'by doing'.
❑ Further skills are developed through activities such as volunteering and mentoring.

PDP aids students' ability to look at their course and skills development as a whole. It teaches them how to assess and apply their skills in a context. This is made possible by the way the module is set up – it teaches students to reflect on modules we offer as part of our tourism courses. To enable this process, the Tourism PDP coordinators explore the links with other modules within the tourism curriculum, particularly where there is an emphasis on the development of

practical skills and reflection on the overall development of our students. Finally, all through their studies and particularly in the final year of their degree, students are provided with general careers support by the university's careers service.

Most of our students are 'non-traditional', so there is a great need to empower all of them with skills and experience that will help them in their careers, in a competitive and ever-changing market.

References and URLs

Baum, T. 1995. *Managing Human Resources in the European Tourism and Hospitality Industry – a Strategic Approach.* London: Chapman & Hall.

Evans, J. 1993. Current Issues: The Tourism Graduates: A Case of Overproduction. *Tourism Management*, 243–246.

Formica, S. 1996. European Hospitality and Tourism Education: Differences with the American Model and Future Trends. *International Journal Hospitality Management*, **15** (4), 317–323.

H M Treasury 2004. *Skills in the Global Economy.* London: H M Treasury.

Ineson, E. M. and Kempa, R. F. 1996. Selection for Vocational Courses at University: Part I – Perspectives of the Employers of Graduates. *Education and Training*, **38** (6), 14–19.

Li, L. and Kivela, J. J. 1998. Different Perceptions between Hotel Managers and Students Regarding Levels of Competency Demonstrated by Hospitality Degree Graduates. *Australian Journal of Hospitality Management*, **5** (2), 47–54.

Mayo, C. 1997. The Hospitality Industry: Choices, Options and Opportunities for the 21st Century. *Black Collegian*, **27** (2), 96–99.

McKercher, B., Williams, A. and Coghlan, I. 1995. Reports: Careers Progress of Recent Tourism Graduates. *Tourism Management*, **16** (7), 541–549.

Parsons, D. J. and Care, P. 1991. *Developing Managers for Tourism.* London, National Economic Development Office.

Petrova, P. 2001. *Tourism Students Career Expectations and Aspirations: An Examination of Attitudes, Perceptions and Expectations of Current Undergraduate Tourism Students at the University of Luton of Tourism Degrees and Tourism Careers*, Unpublished MSc Thesis, Department of Tourism, Leisure and Sport Management. Luton, University of Bedfordshire.

Petrova, P. and Mason, P. 2005a. Employment Practice in Tourism – Limits and Opportunities to Potential Employees. Paper presented at International Conference.

Petrova, P. and Mason, P. 2005b. Knowledge and Vocationalism in Tourism. Irish Academy of Management 8th Annual Conference. Galway, Ireland.

Purcell, K. and Quinn, J. 1996. Exploring the Education–Employment Equation in Hospitality Management: A Comparison of Graduates and HNDs. *International Journal of Hospitality Management*, **15** (1), 51–68.

Stewart, J. and Knowles, V. 2000. Graduate Recruitment and Selection: Implications for HE, Graduates and Small Business Recruiters. *Career Development International*, **5** (2), 65–80.

Thomas, R. and Long, J. 2001. Tourism and Economic Regeneration: The Role of Skills Development. *International Journal of Tourism Research*, 229–240.

Ujma, D. and Kumar, A. 2005. Where Would We Be without the Careers Service? Knowledge Sharing in the Teaching of Personal Development Planning. www.hlst.heacademy.ac.uk/

PETIA PETROVA is a PDP Research Fellow at the Department of Tourism, Leisure and HRM, involved in redesigning the 'PDP in Tourism' module at the University of Bedfordshire. She is also a PhD candidate researching how employers see the value of tourism degrees and their relevance to the tourism industry.

DOROTA UJMA is Senior Lecturer and Field Chair in Undergraduate Tourism Studies and a Centre for Excellence in Teaching and Learning (CETL Bridges) Fellow at the University of Bedfordshire. Her CETL work focuses on employability issues, links between employers and curriculum and the processes guiding development of tourism career management skills.

UWIC Academy of Athletics
Addressing employability within the total student experience

20

Sean Power

This case study looks at how The University of Wales Institute, Cardiff (UWIC) is addressing the practical issues associated with the delivery of sports-related degrees that, by definition, assume a vocational outcome. This objective has been approached partially through establishing sports academies. This chapter will examine the UWIC Academy of Athletics, which includes a Junior Academy currently involving some 180 children who are coached by students from UWIC Athletics Club, the Senior Academy. All the students involved in this scheme are studying on one of four BSc (Hons) undergraduate programmes from within the School of Sport, PE & Recreation (School of Sport).

Currently there are 15 student coaches and one student Head Coach involved in working in the Junior Academy, all of whom are mentored by the Academy Director. Increasing numbers of these students are now pursuing employment related to their undergraduate programmes and are specifically using their Academy experience to assist them in securing such appointments.

While the coaching and mentoring process within the Academy links directly to specific modules and particular programmes within the school's portfolio, the possibility for embracing the opportunities for student placement and the associated employability consequences is not as yet embedded. Recent programme restructuring that also encompasses other curriculum and sports coaching/sports development issues on a national scale is attempting to take these considerations on board.

Rationale

The 1999 Bologna Declaration emphasised the need for courses to have a relevance to the labour market, for degrees to have a vocational purpose and for higher education to develop transferable skills that are relevant to subsequent employment. As a consequence, in higher education across Europe there has been a move to ensure that the link between sports-related courses and employability is made more effectively.

In 2003 the European Network of Sport Science in Higher Education (ENSSHE) changed its name to the European Network of Sport Science, Education and Employment (ENSSEE). Its mission reflected this change in emphasis. Subsequently, the European Union (EU) has clearly taken on board the growth of sport-related employment across Europe by funding recent ENSSEE projects such as the European Observatoire of Sports Employment (EOSE), the study of the relationship between vocational training and employment in sports in Europe (VOCASPORT), the European Observatory for Sport Education and Employer Network (EUROSEEN), and Building the Social Dialogue in the Sports Sector (BSDSS) (ENSSEE, 2005). European HEIs have been core to development and progress in each of these projects, and project outcomes are likely to have long-term effects on EU policy in relation to the sports industry. As a consequence, it is probable that this will also affect course content and student experience for those undertaking sports degrees of a vocational nature.

Within the UK, particularly since the recommendations of *The Coaching Task Force – Final Report* (2002), the government has also developed policies that are being implemented by the governing bodies of sport, and national and regional sports councils. Therefore, within England (and in equivalent developments in Wales), the growth of posts such as generic and sports-specific development officers, School Sport Co-ordinator partnerships, and the more recent Community Sports Coach posts has a particular resonance. It should be assumed that other developments (such as the UK Coaching Certificate) will continue to provide improved employment opportunities for our graduates, particularly in relation to sport-specific posts such as Coach Development Officers and Performance Coaches.

Those students whose undergraduate experience includes relevant work-based learning schemes which are embedded in the curriculum in the way ESECT suggests, will experience activities similar to the Context case studies and materials (http://www.geog.leeds.ac.uk/courses/other/casestudies/). This will enable the academic curriculum to be developed in ways which enhance not only the students' knowledge and understanding of their subject, but also their employability.

Curriculum change has continued unabated over the past several years. In fact higher education has been asked to respond to an increasing number of external pressures since the Dearing Report (1997). As Bloxham (2004) indicates, these various imperatives have been reflected in:

> a plethora of policies such as Progress Files, Benchmarking statements, the Framework for Higher Education Qualifications (FHEQ) and programme specifications with a focus on 'outcome-based curricula' and specifically identifying generic or transferable skills.

It is clear that a number of institutions providing sports-related programmes are taking on board the need to embed skills and employability within the curriculum framework. UWIC is one of these.

Context

UWIC's School of Sport has approximately 1,300 students undertaking undergraduate and postgraduate sport-related programmes. In recent years, the school has initiated a policy of developing sport-specific academies. The directors of the Academies are members of the school's academic staff and part of their remit is to lead these academies and to pursue the elements of the school's strategic plan that relate directly

to their activities. The current designated academies are in athletics, basketball, football, gymnastics, netball, rugby and squash.

The school has adopted a 'from the playground to the podium' philosophy to encompass the activities of the academies. Currently this involves children from the local community, between the ages of eight to 16, attending the Junior Academy of Athletics and being coached by students from UWIC Athletics Club who, in turn, form part of the Senior Academy of Athletics. Extended elements of this Senior Academy include the senior coaches who are appointed by the Athletic Union through the Academy Director to coach the student athletes. Also associated with the Senior Academy is the UK Athletics' High Performance Centre for Wales, which is managed by the UKA Wales High Performance Coach who has responsibility for the World Class and Elite Cymru athletes including Olympic medallists who train at the same facility. Some of these elite athletes are also students from UWIC Athletics Club, a few of whom also operate as coaches in the Junior Academy.

The school has recently undertaken the process of reviewing and restructuring its undergraduate scheme. In the process has taken on board the need to embed student employability more effectively into its courses, particularly degrees in Sports Development and Sports Coaching.

Description

Part of the UWIC School of Sport's Strategic Plan addresses the development of its sport-specific academies. It indicates that one of the aims of the academies will be to:

> utilise, structure and operate academies in a manner that attracts high quality students from a variety of communities, supports their sporting and career aspirations, and enhance the sporting excellence profile of UWIC.

In 2000, through a combination of Lottery and UWIC funding, the National Indoor Athletics Centre (NIAC) was opened at UWIC. In 2002, the UWIC Academy of Athletics was instituted and became based in NIAC. The Athletics Academy is used as an exemplar of the UWIC academies of sport for the purposes of this case study, and will be referred to as the Academy.

Extracts from the Academy's Mission (UWIC, 2002)

include the following:

❑ To provide students with the optimum conditions to support training, competition and career aspirations.

❑ To create and develop initiatives with local, national and international groups covering the areas of education and training, research, strategy and student employment.

Sponsorship was acquired and as a consequence a Lottery Sports Match grant was also successfully obtained. This helped the Academy provide an athletics experience for children from schools in the more disadvantaged areas of the local community. Using the Sports Match grant, student coaches from the athletics club were given the task of ordering, organising and operating student union minibuses to collect children and their teachers from selected local primary and secondary schools so that they could experience the athletics courses in the same way as the other clientele. The responsibility for managing this process was given to the Junior Academy Head Coach (also a student), and with the guidance of the Academy Director, they undertook all the communicating and liaising between the various parties.

While there are a number of athletics award schemes and programmes available, the Academy Director established the Junior Academy of Athletics Proficiency Awards (JAAPA) based on his perception of a need to pursue a more specific programme of athletics skills for children. These were developed based on the work of a colleague whose research work is centred on motivation and pedagogy and, more specifically, motivation in athletics lessons. As a consequence, the JAAPA course was based on the content of his book, *Athletics Challenges: A Resource Pack for Teaching Athletics* (Morgan, 2002).

All prospective student coaches have to achieve at least the UK Athletics level-one coaching award, and attend a two-day course delivered by the author of *Athletics Challenges*. The Sports Facilities division of the School of Sport is responsible for the operational aspects of all of UWIC's sports facilities, and in conjunction with the local authority and Welsh Athletics, they also mount a number of coach education courses in a whole variety of sports for the benefit of the local community, as well as those for our students. Through

this process, the Junior Academy coaches were able to pursue UKA level one athletics coaching awards and beyond. As part of the Academy's coach development plan, these coaches are provided with financial support with their fees. All coaches are students who are in either year two of their degree programmes or above.

The JAAPA course operates across five levels of progression:

Level 1	(Year 4	age 8–9)
Level 2	(Years 5 & 6	age 9–11)
Level 3	(Years 7 & 8	age 11–13)
Level 4	(Year 9	age 13–14)
Level 5	(Years 10 & 11+	age 14–16+).

It operates each term in ten-week blocks. The Academy promotes week-long athletics camps for primary and secondary school children during the Christmas, Easter and summer holiday periods. These are also organised and managed on a daily basis by student coaches, and include the running of a mini-Olympics on the final day. Tasks for the children prior to the mini-Olympics include choosing a theme and designing a uniform for their particular teams. The day involves team march-pasts to music, competitions, invitations sent to parents to support their children, and award-giving ceremonies using our contacts between the student coaches and real Olympic competitors and medallists who train in NIAC. It takes careful planning and organisation by the students to

they have the advantage of being able to report on their own experience of applying theoretical and practical concepts to a real workplace situation

ensure that the whole week goes smoothly, and this is enjoyed greatly by the children The experience is directly applicable to the students' academic and performance module experiences.

In September 2004, approximately 1,600 children per week were involved in various sports activities at UWIC. While these activities did not all involve the academies, a considerable proportion of them did, and all the children were coached by students from within the school. Clearly, this involves large numbers of students. Given that the organisation and opportunities within other academies are similar to those that exist within the Academy of Athletics, then the potential for workplace experiences that enhance student employability is significant. This, coupled with the opportunity within their academic and performance modules for the students to give feedback on their work-based experiences, acts as an invaluable source for reflecting on the application of practice within the context of more theoretical concepts.

Throughout its history, UWIC's School of Sport has ensured that performance modules have been central to its degree programme curriculum. This greatly enhances the experience of the student working in the various sports academies. The back-up theoretical elements of both performance and academic modules allow students the opportunity to make connections far more effectively. For example, when student academy coaches are asked to conduct a knowledge experience and skills audit of themselves in one of their

| Coaches have the opportunity to cover coaching and training for specific events ... This enhances their ability to offer potential employers evidence of more advanced coaching skills

core modules, they have the advantage of being able to report on their own experience of applying theoretical and practical concepts to a real workplace situation. In another module, students are able to use this experience to help them produce an action plan for the future based on such an audit.

All student coaches within the Academy are mentored by the Academy Director, and this process includes keying into the student academic experience. Therefore, when the Academy Director talks to the coaches about theoretical concepts (such as the reflective coach, coaching goals, planning, management and organisation, communication, personal coaching evaluation) or the practical application and outcomes of these concepts in relation to their own coaching, they are able to relate them to their academic experience from within the theoretical and performance modules of their degree programmes. They will also have had experience of coaching, observing, analysing and providing feedback in either their sports performance or sports technology modules. Naturally, this is a complementary process, in that their Academy experiences inform the theoretical concepts within their taught modules.

Beyond this level of mentoring, there is also the mentoring that occurs at the Head Coach level. The Head Coach is also a student and has to take on a number of management, administrative and organisational roles, particularly when the camps occur during the school holidays. As part of this workplace role, the Head Coach liaises with the Junior Academy coaches on a day-to-day basis, ensuring that all sessions are fully covered, and conducts meetings with them from time to time in order to pursue any issues that arise as a result of feedback from the Academy Director or from the coaches themselves. The Head Coach is also responsible for ensuring that all coaches complete their weekly returns for payment and liaises with the Sports Facilities section of the school over coach-related matters. Again, all this involves the practical application of modules within areas such as Sports Management, Sport Administration and Sport Development.

In 2004, the School of Sport received the Investors in People (IIP) award and this included the Sports Facilities section in which the Junior Academy Coaches and Head Coach are located. The staff development and mentoring processes that are applied to these coaches within the Academy of Athletics were examined and found to be very effective.

The Sports Facilities process reflects the type of monitoring and mentoring that occurs within the industry. Consequently, as with all Head Coaches within the UWIC Junior Academies, the Junior Academy of Athletics Head Coach is charged with maintaining a personal-development file. To some extent, this pre-empts the proposed personal development planning files and includes specific sections on:

❑ Academy Director's aims, objective and action plan
❑ personal information – job description, person specification, CV
❑ induction, probation, progress checks
❑ mentoring, coaching
❑ reflective-learning logs – daily, weekly, monthly
❑ reflective-learning logs – course approval and course evaluation
❑ training records

□ records of certificates, achievements
□ evidence of the above.

The Head Coach and the Academy Director meet on a regular basis, normally several times during the week, in order to discuss operational matters and feedback from meetings with the coaches. This reflects the types of middle management meetings, mentoring and monitoring processes that occur within the industry and are referred to within degree courses.

Organisational and administrative activities are integral to the coach's role within the Academy. Coaches become involved with these, as well as the coaching process itself, when they have gone through the various aspects of athletics coaching courses and qualifications, the mentoring process and experience of role-play in the relevant theoretical and performance based modules within their courses.

The Academy works on a ratio of around 10–12 children to one coach. There is a syllabus based on the five levels of the JAAPA award derived from the materials supplied from the *Athletics Challenges* resource pack. As the children get older, they may wish to concentrate on their skills in specific events. Coaches have the opportunity to cover coaching and training for specific events as well as more general athletics skills. This enhances their ability to offer potential employers evidence of more advanced coaching skills.

Currently, a child's progression involves moving either between levels from one year to the next (the norm is that the children tend to stay within the Academy from year to year) or, if their age precludes them from moving to the next JAAPA level, they become involved in more advanced activities for their particular level.

At the end of each term or block, every coach is given the responsibility of completing a report card for each of their athletes that addresses areas such as effort, attainment, improvement and attitude, together with an indication of key areas for improvement as well as the coach's general comments on the young athlete. Each child also receives a customised certificate relating to the JAAPA level attained within a particular block of activity.

The plan for the near future is that children who reach the age where more specialisation is appropriate,

and who clearly have more advanced abilities within a particular event grouping, will be invited to become part of a fast-track group. These children have the option of attending extra sessions during the week, with a view to competing within athletics development meetings for children that are held in conjunction with the Athletics Association of Wales (AAW) during the winter period in the NIAC facility. The development of this group and the current level-four and level-five JAAPA groups will allow the coaches to use more advanced elements of knowledge gained from athletics-performance modules and their personal-performance experiences, in order to enhance and record experience of specific event coaching. The intention would be to then try to encourage these children from the fast-track group to join a local athletics club to promote an active career within the sport.

The athletics-development meetings referred to

> …young coaches have shown that they are very able to undertake the responsibilities involved in the planning, administration and coaching performance associated with working with athletes at this level

tend to be very relaxed and informal affairs and any child from within JAAPA is able to participate and is encouraged to do so. Academy coaches are encouraged to help and support the AAW in the organisation and running of these athletics meetings, thus improving their knowledge of event organisation and officiating. There is a direct link here for those students undertaking level-three athletics modules in which they are required to organise all aspects of a sports day using the whole of the first year student cohort as part of their assessment process.

As the Junior Academy coaches progress over their time at UWIC they are encouraged to pursue higher level coaching qualifications. The Academy supports them by contributing to the payment of the fees for these awards. These more advanced qualifications, along with the experience gained from their degree programme level-two and level-three theory and performance modules, allow the Junior Academy coaches to practise their coaching skills with the more advanced groups and at the same time to develop their own event specialisms.

Over the last two years, the Academy Director has been a member of the Cardiff Athletics Development Working Group. This group also includes representatives from UWIC's Sports Facilities Unit, Cardiff County Council, Sports Council for Wales, the Amateur Athletics Association of Wales, and Cardiff Amateur Athletics Club. The purpose of this group is to develop a structure within Cardiff whereby children will experience the sport of athletics in a constructive and enjoyable manner both inside and outside the school curriculum. As a result of this experience it is hoped that they will wish to join their local club and participate in the sport of their choice on a long-term basis.

The group has promoted various initiatives with local primary and secondary schools, the local authority, the local athletics club and the AAW development meetings. It is hoped that these initiatives, along with the JAAPA courses in UWIC, will mean that a considerable number of interested and motivated young-

postgraduates or recent graduates) who have gained level-three and level-four UKA coaching awards are now working within the Senior Academy. They are coaching and developing groups of student athletes who operate at quite an advanced level, some of whom are international athletes in their own right. These young coaches have shown that they are now very able to undertake the responsibilities involved in the planning, administration and coaching performance associated with working with athletes at this level, all areas that they have experienced – within the curriculum and the Junior Academy. Many people have commented that the nature of the operational ethos that the Academy Director has created within NIAC means that the whole process is far more co-operative than normal. It is almost a team-coaching approach, in which expertise from various coaches is called upon to support a number of athletes. Indeed, the Academy Director has called upon the expertise of one of the former Junior Academy coaches to monitor certain elements of his own athletes' training programmes and, in turn, the Academy Director continues to mentor that coach. The author believes that the young coaches who have gone through this whole academic, professional and experiential process should be the ones who form

> This coach not only achieved a 2:1 in her Sports Development degree but, as a successful athlete, was selected to compete internationally for Great Britain in the under-23 team during the same year

sters will wish to join their local club. However, this is where the problem begins, as there are rarely enough qualified coaches available to deal with such an influx, even for major clubs like Cardiff AC.

It has been proposed by the Academy Director that the various parties (particularly the local club) could utilise the many student coaches who have specific event expertise, through liaison with the Director and promotion of the coach development programme by the UWIC Academy of Athletics. These student,s who are gaining further coaching awards and coaching experience by their final year through the Academy and their level three modules, could perhaps be involved in taking on these older, interested children on behalf of the local club. This would certainly link very effectively with the Junior Academy's proposal to provide a fast-track group for the older and more able children and give the student coaches additional vital experience and enhanced employability.

One or two more mature student coaches (usually

the basis of the next generation of UK Athletics' high performance coaches and, indeed, the professional elite coaches who will ensure success with our elite athletes in the major athletics championships of the future.

As an example of the progression of some of these Junior Academy coaches, it may be appropriate to note the experience of one of them. The coach concerned had been involved in coaching in the Junior Academy during her second and third years at UWIC and she gained the UKA level-three coaching qualification. During this period she also coached on the UWIC Christmas, Easter and summer athletics camps and used this experience to apply for and successfully become involved with various local authority junior athletics coaching schemes in the South Wales area during term time and vacation periods. This coach not only achieved a 2:1 in her Sports Development degree but, as a successful athlete, was selected to compete internationally for Great Britain in the under-23 team during the same year. She was then successful in her application to become a full-time Community Sports Coach, a position she continues to hold. The Academy Director has provided a reference for her, and for an increasing number of Junior Academy coaches over the last two years.

Evaluation

It is hoped that all that has been described thus far underlines the fact that there is a well-structured Athletics Academy operating at a variety of levels, including the areas of student coach education and development. There is a direct link with the content of the students' course experiences, thus enhancing their employability. Indeed, the success of this student experience can be measured by the fact that in 2003 UWIC Junior Academy of Athletics was one of the four Junior Academies that formed UWIC's winning submission in Sportsmatch Wales' 2003 Local Sports Programme of the Year Award category. This success was repeated in the 2005 UK Athletics Clubs Future Awards. UWIC Academy of Athletics was the recipient of the Club Innovation award for the Wales region. This is largely due to the work described in this case study.

However, as yet, the Academy link with the student's academic experience has not been integrated within the curriculum in a manner that could allow it to be described as formally embedding employability within the curriculum.

Discussion

Recently, the school has reviewed and restructured its undergraduate sports studies scheme (UGSSS). As part of this process, Student Progress Files have been introduced to form part of Personal Development Planning (PDP). Students working within the Academy will be required not only to record their activities, but also to reflect on these activities in terms of their personal development.

Students will have the opportunity in the near future to access their progress files through work in the Academy of Athletics. Their Academy experience will allow them to provide concrete evidence of the ability to build and reflect in their PDP. There is a strong link between PDP and employability (Higher

Education Academy, 2005).

At level three in the restructured Sports Development and Sports Coaching degrees (the latter also takes into account the demands of the UK Coaching Certificate), will be a 30-credit Work Experience module. This will, for example, allow the activities of a student within the Academy of Athletics to be recognised in a more formal manner. The module aims to:

allow students to benefit from interacting with employers from organisations directly related to their programme of study and engage in reflective critical analysis of their experience and the organisation they have been placed with.

In terms of their work experience within the Academy, students should be able to:

- Develop and enhance the theoretical knowledge and skills acquired within their degree programme.
- Develop core transferable skills within the confines of a monitored Academy working environment.
- Experience and perform within the Academy to the standards required of an employer within the sports development and coaching industry.
- Understand and critically review the range of management processes used within the various elements within the Academy and the allied Sports Facilities Unit.
- As a result of the Academy experience, develop a critical understanding of the issues related to the sports development and coaching industry.

Students undertaking this module and working within the Academy of Athletics will be required to produce a 6,000-word portfolio incorporating evidence of these outcomes as part of their assessment.

These informal structures, which are highly effective in producing employable graduates by involving students in both Academy and course experience, will in future be greatly enhanced through the restructuring of these two degrees.

It is anticipated that the future will also involve at least one Academy Athletics Development Officer placement becoming available for a student undertaking the Sports Development degree. This would certainly key into some of the proposed developments described earlier regarding the Cardiff Athletics Development Working Group. Also being considered for the future within the Senior Academy is the implementation of posts for students from the Sport and Exercise Science degree specifically for the purpose of supporting the student-athlete performers. Such work placement experiences would undoubtedly enhance the employability prospects of these students.

This case study has attempted to describe the structure, activities and practices that permeate the Academy of Athletics, how they link informally with the academic experience of the students on courses and how this experience enhances student employability. What it has also attempted to show is that, with the school's link to the Academy of Athletics (and other academies) now formally written into the restructured courses, particularly through the PDP and Work Experience modules, it is anticipated that student employment prospects will be greatly enhanced. The outcome will be a more effective response to embedding the concept of employability within the overall experience of sports students at UWIC.

References and URLs

Bloxham, S. 2004. Embedding skills and employability in higher education: an institutional curriculum framework approach. Higher Education Academy: http://www.heacademy.ac.uk/

Context Case Studies http://www.geog.leeds.ac.uk/courses/other/casestudies/

Department for Culture, Media and Sport, 2002. *The Coaching Task Force: Final Report*. London: DCMS.

ENSSEE, 2003. BSDSS: Social dialogue between sport employees and employers [on-line]. http://www.cosmos.asso.fr/

ENSSEE, 2002. EOSE: European Observatory of Sport Employment [on-line]. http://www.eose.org/home.htm

ENSSEE, 2002. European Network of Sport Science, Education and Employment: Mission [on-line] http://www.ensshe.lu/

ENSSEE, 2005. EUROSEEN: European Observatory for Sport Education and Employer Network [on-line]. http://www.euroseen.net

ENSSEE, 2004. VOCASPORT: The relationship between vocational training and employment in sports in Europe [on-line]. http://www.eose.org/

Higher Education Academy, 2005. What is ESECT? [on-line]. http://www.heacademy.ac.uk/

Higher Education Academy, 2005. Employability [on-line]. http://www.heacademy.ac.uk/

Higher Education Academy, 2005. Personal development planning [on-line]. http://www.heacademy.ac.uk/

Higher Education Academy, 2005. Context case materials [on-line]. http://www.heacademy.ac.uk/

Morgan, K. 2002. *Athletics Challenges: A Resource Pack for Teaching Athletics*. Cardiff: UWIC Press.

National Committee of Inquiry into Higher Education Dearing Committee, 1997. *Higher Education in the Learning Society – Report of the National Committee of Inquiry into Higher Education*. London, Stationery Office.

UWIC 2002. UWIC Academy of Athletics: Mission Statement [on-line]. http://www.uwic.ac.uk/

SEAN POWER has worked in HE for more than 30 years, having started his career as a primary and secondary school teacher. This included a period as a teacher educator and a number of years as Discipline Director for Sport Psychology. He has been Head of School, Associate Dean Faculty of Education and Sport, Head of a Research and Enterprise Unit, and for six years UK universities' representative on the Co-ordinating Group of the European Network of Sport Science, Education and Employment. He is a UK Athletics Level 4 Coach, coaches a number of international level athletes, and is currently Director of the UWIC Academy of Athletics.

Glossary

ABS — Aston Business School
ABTA — Association of British Travel Agents
APEL — Accredited Prior Experiential Learning
ARPM — Annual Report on Programme Monitoring
ASET — Association for Sandwich Education and Training

BABM — BA (Hons) Business Management (In-Company) degree (Nottingham Business School)
BAIBL — BA (Hons) International Business with Languages (Sheffield Hallam University)
BPS — British Psychological Society
BSDSS — Building the Social Dialogue in the Sports Sector
BSR — Bachelor of Sport and Recreation (Auckland University of Technology)

CEIG — Career Education, Information and Guidance
CETL — Centre for Excellence in Teaching and Learning
CIEH — Chartered Institute of Environmental Health
CIPD — Chartered Institute of Personnel and Development
CTT — Curriculum Think Tank (Bournemouth University)
CV — curriculum vitae

DfES — Department for Education and Science
DIS — Diploma in Industrial Studies (University of Ulster)

ENSSHE — European Network of Sport Science in Higher Education
ENSSEE — European Network of Sport Science, Education and Employment
EOSE — European Observatoire of Sports Employment
ERASMUS — European Community Action Scheme for the Mobility of University Students
ERZ — Employability Resource Zone
ESECT — Enhancing Student Employability Co-ordination Team
EUROSEEN — European Observatory for Sport Education and Employer Network

HEFCE — Higher Education Funding Council for England
HEA — HE Academy, also HE Authority (N Ireland)
HEI — Higher Education Institution

ICP — International Consultancy Project (Sheffield Hallam University)
ILAM — Institute of Leisure and Amenity Management
ISRM — Institute of Sport and Recreation Management

JAAPA — Junior Academy of Athletics Proficiency Awards

LSC — Learning and Skills Council

NASD — National Association for Sports Development
NBS — Nottingham Business School
NCWE — National Council for Work Experience

PDP — Personal Development Planning
PPAD — Personal Professional and Academic Development in Tourism (University of Befordshire)

QAA — HE Quality Assurance Agency

RAE — Research Assessment Exercise
RDA — Regional Development Agency

SEDA — Staff and Educational Development Association
SIS — Students Industrial Society
SME — Small and Medium-sized Enterprise

T, D & As — Teaching, Development and Assessments

UGSSS — undergraduate sports studies scheme (UWIC)
UKA — UK Athletics
ULS — University Language Scheme
USEM — Understanding of subject matter, Skilful practices, Efficacy beliefs and Meta-cognition. *cf.* Knight and Yorke (2001)

VLE — virtual learning environment

Index